THE MODERN SURVIVAL MANUAL:

SURVIVING THE ECONOMIC COLLAPSE

Based on Personal First Hand Experience

of the

2001 Economic Collapse in Argentina, and the Aftermath

Fernando "FerFAL" Aguirre

First Edition

Copyright © 2009 by Fernando Aguirre

Text © 2009 Fernando Aguirre

Cover photo and design © 2009 Fernando Aguirre

Published by Fernando Aguirre

ISBN: 978-987-05-6345-7

This book is dedicated to my family, to my wife and kids who have been so patient. I love you all so much. Thanks for your unconditional support.

And to the rest of my family that was always there for me: My parents, brother, sister and grandparents.

It's especially dedicated to my grandfather, who taught me so much. I only wish that you were still around, so I could hear more of your stories. No matter how many years go by you are still missed like the first day after you passed away.

His saying, "If we don't do this, what are we going to tell our grandkids?" became my motto for many years. I owe that to you.

It's dedicated to those great people I haven't had a chance to meet face to face yet, but with whom I've spent so much time learning from online. Thank you.

It's also dedicated to those who had different opinions on certain issues, and with whom I spent maybe too much time debating and arguing.

Last, but certainly not least, it's dedicated to you, the reader, who took that first step by buying this book, and who will now understand better how life changes when things don't turn out as you were told they would.

To you, my friend, thanks for buying my book. I hope you enjoy it, and that it provides you with some useful knowledge in the coming years.

Fernando "FerFAL" Aguirre

Buenos Aires, 2009

For more articles by Fernando Aguirre visit:

www.ferfal.blogspot.com

This book is for educational and entertainment purposes only.

The author and publisher do not in any way condone illegal activities of any kind.

All of the advice in this book is for entertainment and educational purposes only, and the author cannot be held responsible for the use of the information provided in each particular legal context.

Check your local, state, and federal laws regarding everything related in this book and obey the laws which apply to you.

INDEX

YOUR SELF DEFENSE SKILLS

INTRODUCTION

A LITTLE ABOUT THE AUTHOR

I'm thirty years old, and I've been happily married to my beautiful wife for seven years now. We have two wonderful boys. I know how lucky I am to have such a great family.

We got married just when the crisis in Argentina started, so things were "interesting" to say the least. These have been difficult times, but a loving family makes all the difference.

I've worked doing a number of jobs, mostly related to architecture and real estate, which is a bit of a family business. I also enjoyed teaching Architecture Representation (Sketching and Drawing) at the University of Buenos Aires.

My parents are typical of the Argentine middle class, but living in the USA for three years a long time ago gave us all a much broader world perspective. Then they managed to move to Spain soon after the economic crisis began. This saved them from going through the worst of it.

My grandparents all came to Argentina from northern Spain in the 1930s. They were farmers in the old country, and worked mostly as carpenters once they left their homeland. They fled from Spain to escape hunger and civil war.

I learned defensive shooting when I was fifteen years old. I was lucky enough to come across an army major in Cordoba who, along with another friend of his, had set up a nice indoor shooting range.

They gave me one-on-one classes two or three times a week for a couple of months, and I learned to handle a variety of revolvers and autos in various calibers.

Most importantly of all, I learned the most valuable lesson a defensive shooter should know: Identify your target!

After that, I took other courses, but the major taught me some of the most important things I have ever learned about self defense shooting.

Every now and then my brother (who also took classes with him) and I impersonate him and have a good laugh. Either one of us will say:

"Here's the situation: A known rapist and serial killer is escaping with your sister. You have until he reaches the 25 yard line. If you don't shoot him in the head by then, you'll never see your sister again. GO!"

In those days I enjoyed shooting guns a lot, but I thought that carrying one on you all day wasn't necessary… A lot has changed in fifteen years.

After that I tried Taekwondo ITF for a few months, but ended up doing boxing afterwards. Traditional boxing was hard at first but very gratifying once I learned the basics, and I did that for a few years.

When I realized that boxing alone left a lot of empty holes in my hand-to-hand fighting toolbox, I practiced Thai boxing and ground fighting with an instructor that fights in Vale Tudo. Vale Tudo combines several martial arts into one combat sport with very few rules.

Camping and backpacking are also activities I've enjoyed and learned from.

There's still much to learn, and it always seems that there's not enough time…

Awareness? Mindset? An understanding of how important survival and preparedness are, regarding all aspects of life? How criminals operate and how to avoid them, and how to prepare myself and my home to defend against them? Those mental skills I acquired out of necessity.

WHAT HAPPENED IN ARGENTINA

The situation in Argentina reached the point of no return in December of 2001.

The International Monetary Fund, in spite of no signs of the Argentine government's willingness to pay them back, had been lending money to Argentina and postponing its payment schedules, to keep a fictional "convertibility" at a one-to-one rate of our Peso currency with the US Dollar.

It was obvious that the Argentine authorities had no intention of ever paying back the billions that were owed, but for some reason the IMF kept lending. I suppose they are very naïve and trusting people…

I wouldn't want to think that they were just as corrupt as the local authorities who stole those billions of dollars, and who ended up enslaving the population to a lifetime of outrageously high taxes to pay it all back later, with interest.

After years of corrupt government officials (both local and from foreign international institutions) accumulating foreign debt and putting this future repayment burden on the people, the situation exploded in a series of violent protests and general looting all over the country.

During the riots of December 20th 2001, over thirty people were murdered across the country. Martial law was later declared, bank accounts were frozen and economic activity stopped completely.

That same day, President Fernando de la Rúa resigned. Argentina would see four different presidents during the following week. None of them seemed to be able to control the situation. On January 2nd 2002, Eduardo Duhalde was appointed president by the Legislative Assembly.

The country had been systematically ravaged by both foreign and local institutions. Argentina is a food producing country, but children were starving to death every day, because their parents couldn't afford the price of food, since the unemployment rate had exceeded 25%, and inflation was making our currency less valuable by the hour.

Taking advantage of the government's hypocrisy and the artificial currency peg, some people would buy large amounts of USD at official institutions and later sell them on the street for a profit. Forces were built up between the Peso and the Dollar like between two massive tectonic plates that shift and build stresses before an earthquake. These stresses eventually forced the authorities to accept the actual lower value of the Peso.

Previously artificially pegged to the US Dollar at a one-to-one rate, the government announced a devaluation and soon the Peso reached a three-to-one rate with the Dollar. On the street, the difference during those days was even greater, usually four-to-one.

Those were chaotic days indeed. While the situation was somewhat controlled after a week in the Capital Federal District, and in the downtown areas of the other capital cities, anarchy reigned for over a month in the suburbs and the more far away locations.

To this day, it's common knowledge that large portions of Buenos Aires are "Zona Liberada," almost like a no man's land where police do what little they can to keep even an illusion of security.

Sometimes there's not even that, and there are many areas where even the police don't dare enter unless they have armored vehicles as backup and go in by the hundreds.

When banks first closed their doors the situation turned ugly. Shops didn't accept plastic money and cash was hard to come by.

Cash is definitely king during the first stages of an economic collapse, when the banks, ATMs and credit cards are not functioning.

To a greater or lesser degree, depending on whose opinion you ask and what particular part of the country you refer to, this generalized madness lasted during most of 2002. Order was restored in the capital cities and downtown areas first, and then spread to the more affluent surrounding suburbs.

With bank accounts frozen, the infamous "corralito" was created in a desperate attempt to stop bank runs. A 250 Peso per week withdrawal limit was enforced.

Finding an ATM machine with money became the equivalent of going out hunting for food. Finding a machine with money inside took you several hours, and many times you came back empty handed.

Those were the lucky ones. With a 25% unemployment rate and 75% of the population poor or below the poverty line, having even 250 Pesos a week was a luxury. At a one-to-four exchange rate 250 Argentine pesos were worth 62.5 USD. This wasn't much to get by in a country where a bottle of Coke costs 1.50 USD and a McDonald's happy meal goes for four. The average worker's income at that time was 250 USD per month. The year before, it had been 841 USD average. The Argentine worker went from being the best paid to being the worst paid worker in Latin America in just a couple months.

When the banks reopened, they had to enforce important security measures, with new barricades and lots of extra security personnel. Those people who had been robbed of their USD accounts would show up on daily basis and bash the bank buildings with pots, pipes and hammers. "Gives us back our money, you thieves!" was the most common chant.

Since an ATM with money became as rare a as a four-leaf clover, when banks reopened, the lines to withdraw the meager 250 bucks a week were huge.

Meanwhile, the elites would leave the country with suitcases full of money. They had contacts within the government and within the banks so they had that "privilege." The top "big fish" had left the country just before their accounts were frozen. They had inside information and knew what was about to happen.

Some were caught with hidden cameras and it was very frustrating to see these people, many responsible for years of economic looting of this country, leave in their private jets with several pieces of luggage, some big enough to fit a man into, all stuffed full of US Dollars. I suppose they had some fiscal paradise to go to.

I remember that I escaped the "corralito" just by a day or two. I went to the bank with my mother and sister to close our accounts. My parents are accountants and could see something was going down. They had been hearing rumors and decided to do the safe thing and at least take some of their money out.

"Sorry," said the lady at the bank. "We don't have that kind of money available right now. Would you like to try tomorrow?"

"Wait a minute," my mother told her "You're telling me you don't have 1,000 US Dollars in the entire bank?!"

Apparently they didn't, or they didn't want to give it to us.

That same day we went downtown to their central bank and closed all our accounts.

Folks, when you are in doubt, try that, just for an experiment.

Drop by your bank and tell them you want to close your account. Look at their face. Worried expressions and sweaty foreheads aren't good.

If the person says "ok" and tells you to wait a minute, then tell them that you just decided to leave it there if you don't actually want to close your account.

But if the employee starts trembling and coming up with excuses…that is NOT good. Move fast and get as much money out as you can.

After that, USD "Dollar accounts" were converted to Argentine Pesos.

Was it legal? No, but with an emergency decree, they did it anyway.

This is the same thing that happened with the bailout in the USA. They just say that there's no other way out, there is no alternative. In that way, with the stroke of a pen, they stole 66% of the people's hard earned money.

A small number of people actually benefited from this. Those who had just received a loan in USD now only owed Pesos, so their debt went down 66%. Still, overall the situation was bad for everyone. With a frozen economy and no work there's not much you can do.

Our world was suddenly transformed. The rest of humanity still lived by B.C. and A.C years. Argentines measure history by before and after "one-to-one," or before and after "the crisis."

"Nice car, nice jacket, are they new?"

"Are you kidding? I couldn't afford these today. No way; I bought them before one-to-one."

For example, here is a lunch break chat I had once with people from work:

"Paris is very nice, but I liked London better."

"Dude, you've just been to Europe?"

"No way man, I went before the crisis."

"Oh."

It turns out that everyone at the table had traveled around a lot. But we all did it before the crisis. Only the elites can afford international travel these days.

This was just the beginning. I don't think anyone expected things to turn out the way they did, or how the economic crisis transformed everyone's lives. The crime, inflation, corruption, generalized degradation of our cultural standards and way of life. The crumbling of infrastructure and how public education became something we're ashamed of, when it was once the best in Latin America.

It changed all of our lives forever. My intention with this book is that you'll at least be ready for those changes, if and when they occur in your country.

WHY I WROTE THIS BOOK

I've been writing about survival and preparedness for seven years now.

Most of the time I just write short essays--posting them in a number of survival and preparedness-related forums, as well as on my blog, **www.ferfal.blogspot.com**--doing what I can to reach out to as many people as I can.

What finally convinced me that I had something important to say was the huge, massive amount of misinformation within the survivalist and preparedness community, in particular regarding how to prepare for an economic collapse.

Unfortunately, many people take for granted concepts and ideas from movies or works of fiction that have little to do with reality, or they get ideas from religious fanatics with delusions about the world being engulfed in flames by the wrath of God.

Many self-proclaimed "authorities on everything survival" claim this or that "will be worth its weight in gold." This theory is based on what, exactly? Many times it's based on absolutely nothing.

There are also some good and intelligent people out there. Book authors and normal folks who finally "saw the light," shall we say, regarding the importance of taking the responsibility for their well-being and that of their families onto themselves.

These people come from all walks of life. The one thing they have in common is that they see how fragile our society is, and they understand the importance of not waiting for others to come rescue them or save them from whatever problematic situation they are in.

These people are out there looking to learn, and unfortunately most books on the market today were not written by someone with hands-on knowledge of what *really* happens when there is an economic and social collapse.

Something I learned during this process is that publishers are usually more interested in selling books, and the quality or practical application of the content comes in at a very distant second place, if they consider it at all.

A book with a good looking cover and a catchy title usually sells, and the content may or may not be good. Though content does matter, it's more important to sell books, they think.

While doing research for my own book, I learned that marketing people know that the decision to buy a book or not is made by the potential customer in five seconds on average. The cover design and title mostly decides if the customer takes the book home or not.

Regarding such a serious issue as survival and preparing for the economic crisis that is already well established in most countries around the globe, I think that it's irresponsible to sell people "feel good" books, or "Kumbaya" advice that is downright dangerous to put into practice.

Why write this book? Because there's no other book out there of its kind!

I know because I've searched and I only came up with resurrected survivalist concepts from the Cold War that have very little application to the problems people will be facing.

I found lots of wilderness survival experts trying to apply their knowledge to the kind of survival skills you need during and after an economic collapse and social unrest, and the kind of advice they were selling was just AWFUL!

Some of the advice I've read in a few of these "bestsellers" could get you killed in my country. You see, Y2K got a lot of people interested in survival and preparedness again, and 9/11 was a huge wakeup call concerning what could happen to them. This economic crisis is something that affects each and everyone but in a different way.

Military tactics and wilderness survival have very little application regarding modern survival. I'd say military experience is definitely more useful than wilderness survival experience. It was downright funny to read some of the wilderness survival guys trying to apply their knowledge to urban survival.

Given that crime will no doubt be one of the most serious problems you'll be facing, combat military training and experience will come in handy, but still, there are many essential differences.

It's one thing to be part of an enormous military machine, and it's another very different thing to be alone, or to be just you and your family.

My friends, some of you have already formed survival groups or are counting on extended family helping you to get through the crisis.

Stop reading right now and look around you…

That's right.

Unless you are in a barracks, you are on your own. Problems won't send you an e-mail so that you can get your gang together and gear up.

Most families can't go through Christmas or Thanksgiving dinner without fighting.

How long will you and your extended family last, all living together, with just one leader calling the shots when it counts, while the world goes through another Great Depression or worse?

How long until Uncle Jimmy comes and says, "You know what? I talked with some guys down in Denver and was offered a sweet job. This bugging-in deal and standing guard six hours a day was fun for a couple of weeks, but I can't let this opportunity pass. See ya'll later next year!"

You think there won't be any job offer for Uncle Jimmy in Denver, in spite of unemployment, because the world as we know it will end?... Please.

Of course there's a big market today for anything that has "Urban Survival," "Disaster" or "Emergency" on the cover.

People want to know how to get ready for it, and what life will be like, and they know that starting fires with a bow and a stick is a neat trick but that won't help them to solve the problems they see on the horizon.

Today, disaster preparedness sells. The problem is, there are just too few writers out there that have actually gone through a social and economic crisis, and even fewer that experienced it in a Western, capitalist country that was once one of the top five most powerful nations on the planet like I did. And even though we are now just a shadow of what we once were, anyone visiting Argentina is generally pleasantly surprised in terms of architecture, social life and the overall cultural level of the people with whom they come into contact.

There is still some of that Argentine middle-class left.

Because of this, there are many similarities between what we went through and the path the USA and other first world countries are taking.

I offer first-hand knowledge regarding these issues.

Other than some personal experience of my own, the incidents I'll describe or use as examples here are of course all real, and many are easy to find by doing a bit of searching on the internet.

You may hear, "I visited Buenos Aires last week and you are full of shit! It's the safest place in the world, the women are hot, and the food is great and cheap!"

Through the years, I did get maybe three or four comments or e-mails similar to that.

To those people I answer:

1) Visiting a country for a few days as a tourist does not give you much true experience. I can visit Cuba and have a great time in a luxurious hotel, but I'd be an idiot to think Cubans live like that. If you ever visited Buenos Aires, unless you walk around blindfolded, you can't avoid seeing or sometimes even bumping into the thousands of paper and junk scavengers that invade the city each night to live off the scrap made by more fortunate people such as yourself. Those aren't rats; those are men, women and children eating out of garbage bags. This is the result of the social collapse that turned most of the middle class in this country into poor, and turned most of the poor into desperate homeless creatures.

2) Buenos Aires is a dangerous place. Much of the crime is well documented and clearly shows that the government is "fixing up" the numbers, just like they do when they cook the books regarding the economy. Coming here and being one of the lucky tourists who doesn't get robbed or hurt while staying in one of the well-guarded luxury hotel areas doesn't change that.

3) What I write about is all very real, but what I do myself is not an accurate reflection of what other Argentines do. If it worked that way, there would be 44 million books relating personal experiences regarding life after the crisis, explaining how an average person adapted to the new reality, the economic problems, the crime and every other aspect of life influenced by the crisis. Yet this is the only book of its kind. People were forced to change, but very few of us took it a step further and tried to learn, adapt, mold ourselves into a more capable creature, and still be able to live happily, but more safely and with greater awareness than before. This is what many survivalists refer to as going from "sheep" to "sheepdog."

Again, if everyone in this country was like me, there would be 44 million books like mine out there. Then again, if everyone was like me, the people we now have in office would have never won, just like if every American thought like I do Dr. Ron Paul would have become president instead, and the future of America and the entire world would have changed a lot.

The crisis in general is well-documented; there are lots of good videos that describe the December 2001 events quite well on YouTube.

Many books have been written about the Argentine crisis, with lessons for economists and politicians (unfortunately most of them apparently didn't read them), but as far as I know there's not a first-hand account of how things changed and what can be done to adapt to those changes.

Many Argentines prefer not to talk about most of these things.

Many simply preferred to get over it as quickly as possible if they were robbed or scammed (sometimes by our own government), hoping that nothing worse would happen to them and just hoping things would eventually get better.

With a lot of hard work and a bit of denial, you can get through it…maybe.

You often hear on the news about how grateful a robbery victim should be. "Thank God they didn't hurt you," they'll say. Or they'll say how grateful a rape victim should feel. "Well honey, at least he didn't kill you!"

And when they do kill you in front of your family, the media comment will usually be, "How sad. See, people? This happens when you resist." The *victim* is the guilty one. And the victim is no longer there to tell how he was executed with a shot to the head like an animal, even after giving up everything he had.

Out of all the Argentines that saw the same things I do, why am I the only one writing this book?

Because I'm one of the proud few that will not go quietly into the dark and "accept" these things as normal. Just like I don't think its normal for kids to die of hunger in a country that produces food for 300 million people, when our population is 44 million, or to accept as normal the corrupt politicians that are filthy rich, when since 2001 we have a 50% poverty rate and 25% of the population lives BELOW the poverty line.

No man, that can't be normal. Not in a country with a disproportionate amount of natural resources and a rich cultural level, a country that just a few decades ago was one of the most prosperous nations on the planet.

I don't think those things are normal and I choose to do something about it.

What makes me different from most other Argentines that are going through the same thing, or worse? In my opinion, God always calls the shots in the end, but it's our responsibility to change the things that are within our means. You can't blame God or fate for personal laziness and lack of responsibility.

I'm one of the few that decided that there are things that can be done to prepare for these problems we face, and that's what I've been doing all these years.

In this book I'll share my experience with you. What has worked for me and what didn't, as we'll as numerous other observations that will help you prepare better for your particular situation.

WHAT TO EXPECT FROM THIS BOOK

If you didn't notice already, you soon will.

English is a second language for me. I know how to write and speak in English because I lived for a few years in Boston when I was little, and after that I went to bilingual schools in Buenos Aires.

There is nothing special about bilingual schools in Argentina, most middle class people can pay for one. Some are more expensive than others, but people here already accept that our public schools have no educational value. Many can be pretty dangerous, so private schools are very common and people usually make a bit of sacrifice to afford one.

Besides, I used to travel a lot to the USA back in the 1990s when our country was going through a period of "sweet money," as we used to call it.

This is similar to what people in the USA and in other first-world countries were accustomed to until the financial crisis. Our middle class was rather powerful. I remember well how many Americans looked surprised at the Argentine tourists; those were real shopping marathons.

It was common knowledge back then that the USA was "cheap" for us, and the only limit was the amount of stuff you could carry. The average middle-class

Argentine would probably travel to the USA, especially to Miami, once every few years. A week in Disney World and a week of shopping in Miami were pretty ordinary: Ordinary to the point that it became corny to do so among the higher middle class. Those guys shopped in Europe instead.

Besides living there when little, going to bilingual schools and traveling somewhat often to the USA, I've worked for one of the much-hated call-centers for some time, and I spent a good amount of time online on various forums, so I did pick up quite a bit of American slang.

Matthew Bracken, author of "Enemies Foreign and Domestic" and the "Enemies" trilogy, kindly edited this book and gave me invaluable suggestions and advice. Thanks to him, in spite of my limitations as a writer, the information in this book is easy to understand and most of the mistakes I made have been fixed. I am forever grateful because of it. I highly recommend "Enemies" since it shows the reader what could happen in the United States if the economy ever collapses like it did in Argentina.

Since it's printed on demand "The Modern Survival Manual" isn't a cheap book. I'm not trying to compete with the $11.99 books here. But as they say, you usually get what you pay for.

No, in this case you're not getting a good looking book. The book is self published and my literally skills are limited. If it's quality literature you want, this is not it.

But you are getting an honest first-hand account of something you'll soon go through and how to deal with it. That's pretty unique information. In my opinion, the lack of a commercial publisher means the information in this book isn't "filtered" to make it more politically correct.

The only company that showed any interest in publishing said that the book was too "aggressive" for their target readers.

A watered down version wasn't something I was willing to do.

This book would be the real thing: Sincere and reality-based, as violent as true life is in some cases, or it would be nothing at all.

Another company told me they already had the niche covered with a book they had released recently. I didn't bother to tell them that I had read the book they were referring to and found it to be 90% bullshit that doesn't cover most of the real problems people face in a city or suburbs when there's trouble.

This book will cover a number of issues I consider you MUST know during a crisis.

The USA for example, is right now going through the first stages of an economic breakdown. People are mostly scared about their jobs and financial issues. They still haven't reached the point where the economic crisis becomes a social one as well.

The greater poverty levels, combined with a lack of belief in a better future, creates a new level of apathy.

The plethora of problems that come out of the economic crisis will go from a significant increase in crime levels, medium scale epidemics due to lack of hygiene because of the general poverty, and lack of information and experience dealing with these issues, just to name a few.

I'll cover all of them, at least the most important ones. Going into every single detail would take hundreds of books, and that's not what I intend to do.

Tip: If you don't do it already, get used to washing your hands (well washed!) when you come back home. Diseases and illnesses will spread due to poverty and you can catch them at supermarkets or other public places. Use alcohol gel, even though soap is usually enough. At least as long as you have water

I intend this to be a manual for you, one that will help you navigate through the crisis much better and spare you some hard earned lessons.

People learn from their own mistakes, but smarter people learn from other people's mistakes.

Will you agree or even like everything you'll find in this book?

Hell, no. This isn't that type of feel-good self-help book.

Most probably you'll feel a bit naked and vulnerable after reading some of it.

But if I succeed at what I'm trying to do here, by the time you finish reading this book you'll view the whole world, the entire reality around you in a new way. "Fair" and "unfair" will mean nothing to you anymore. You'll realize life is mostly unfair, and you'll just have to man up and deal with it.

If you used to be one of the billions of sheep that pasture their entire lives, you'll feel the necessity to grow teeth and claws and be able to handle problems yourself.

You'll realize how stupid it is to simply rely on the system to keep you safe and alive, when the system is only designed to protect itself.

As you go on reading, you'll notice I'm adamant about certain issues.

It's not because I'm an arrogant bastard.

Ok, I am pretty arrogant, but that's not the point. What I mean is, when I'm particularly hard headed it's because I'm positive about it due to the number of times I saw it verified in real life, and therefore I want to get across to you how important it is for you to understand it as well.

This book is intended to be a manual for modern survival, particularly focused on the various aspects of living after a socio-economic collapse.

I came close to calling it "urban" instead of modern, but I didn't want people to think that what I write only applies to cities. No. It applies to modern life in general, unless you live under a chunk of ice in Antarctica. And it particularly applies to what life will be like after the economic crisis.

Maybe, many decades ago, one could still talk about the cities and the wild—the places where men live, and another separate place where untamed nature was found.

These days, it's mostly the other way around. Places where mankind doesn't have a firm grip are rare and would most likely disappear if great efforts weren't made to protect them.

Thank God there are still places where one can wander and spend months without finding a person if such is your intention. For those cases, a wilderness survival book is what you need.

Other than that, if there's a road or trail leading to it, it's part of civilization and you can't escape the need to bring mankind and civilization into the equation. My rule of thumb is, if you got there so can others, and if you got there with your car, you're as good as a sitting duck.

For these reasons, I felt modern was a word that describe the uses of this book best.

In order to use this book properly, you need to understand a few things.

What we experienced here in Argentina, even thought some choose to deny it, was the socio-economic collapse of a pretty much average Western society that was (apparently) doing well, economically speaking. That is, until the rot behind the facade revealed itself.

The rot I'm referring to was debt and corruption, helped by international groups with their own agendas.

But in spite of certain obvious cultural differences, this book will be useful to you no matter where you live.

You can say Argentina is an "Americanized" society. That much we admit ourselves. We are 98% white and Catholic, constantly consuming American TV, music and culture.

Yet when it comes to society breaking down, after corresponding with people in other Latin countries, in Africa and the Ukraine and other places, I saw how similar peoples' behavior is when confronting a crisis.

Also keep in mind, Argentina isn't what most people around the world picture as a primitive Latin American republic.

Buenos Aires is still sophisticated and has its own charisma. It's a large metropolis with subways, trains, lots of architecture and social life. It's a relatively rich country in both natural resources and culture. Argentina was the first country in the region to have nuclear power plants, something that many bordering countries still don't have.

A second important point you should keep in mind: try reading between lines.

I'm being 100% honest in this book, but, dear reader, please try to understand that certain things are better kept to ourselves. Some people may take offense, and in some places in the world offending the wrong kind of person can get you into a world of trouble.

I'm not going to put into writing anything that could cause my family and me trouble. So please, read between the lines, connect the dots, and draw your own conclusions on what's useful for you or not, and what may one day apply to your personal situation.

I'll say it yet again: unless you've been doing a lot of things right in terms of survival and preparedness, this book won't make you feel all warm and fuzzy about yourself, but it will trigger inside you a need for independence. A new thirst for knowledge with real world applications, which you'll understand are essential for you now.

Among the survival and preparedness community, there are two acronyms that are used frequently. People have different uses for them and what it means for one person does not apply to what another may have in mind.

"SHTF" means the "shit hit the fan." In broad terms it means something went very wrong.

Some people will use it to refer to an economic crisis, flooding, an earthquake, looting or civil unrest. Others may use it for small scale or more personal inconveniences or struggles such as having a serious car accident, losing a job or discovering that a family member has a serious illness.

In this book I'll use SHTF mostly to refer to the economic collapse that took place in Argentina in December 2001.

Since it affected and negatively changed every aspect of life for people here for decades, rather than "shit hitting the fan," it's more like a fully loaded septic truck fell into the turbine blades of a power plant, but SHTF will have to do.

TEOTWAWKI is also commonly used. It means, "The end of the world as we know it." Pretty drastic! Most people use this in reference to something that suddenly causes millions of deaths like a plague or a major meteor strike.

The idea here is that civilization as we know it no longer exists and the few survivors left live in a post-apocalyptic world. This of course has never happened, but it's mostly seen in movies such as "Mad Max," and "I am Legend" and such.

While the world has never ended I think there are enough real world cases of SHTF events, such as socio-economic collapses in various nations, civil wars, countries that become divided, and the falling of established empires.

These things happen with certain regularity in history, and I consider them more realistic examples to study than movies or fiction novels.

You'll find that there are a few blank pages at the end of this book. Use them. These just cost a couple of extra cents and will come in handy for you to make personal notes, attach articles or lists you print and want to carry around.

People have sometimes told me that they quickly make personal notes after reading what I write, mostly regarding parallels they find with their own personal situations in their own countries.

One last thing—I'll use some "unpleasant" language in this book, four letter words or whatever they are calling them these days.

I do this for two reasons.

1) Any person getting his panties twisted by something as harmless as language should start manning up or womanning up, depending on their gender. The cornerstone of modern survival and preparedness is to stop being a wimp. It's necessary to be strong physically and emotionally speaking, to deal with both physical dangers and emotional struggles.

It will be important to have the ability and mindset to kill without hesitation if your life is being threatened, or the lives of your loved ones. There's no place for sentimental bullshit about how precious life in general is. Life is nice but the life of a bastard trying to hurt you or your family isn't precious. You should be able to kill him without remorse. Besides, at the end of the day we all end up dying anyway.

A person who is willing to kill without hesitation in self defense should not be a crybaby regarding language.

2) It's a matter of principle.

As the great Argentine writer Roberto Fontanarrosa once said, "It's not the same thing to call someone silly or a dummy than to call him an asshole."

Our languages are rich and should be used to their full extent. So-called "bad words" fulfill a role when used appropriately. The important thing is using them when you really mean them and within the right context. Otherwise they lose their strength and you are just rude and impolite.

WHY PREPARE?

The first memory I have that could be related to survival and the importance of security was when I was nine years old. We were spending our summer at our beach house in Mar del Plata and having a great time.

Nothing fancy, just a small house that my father along with my grandfather (and a bit of help from my uncle) built mostly with their own hands. It was small but comfortable. The fireplace in the living room and a wood stove in the kitchen provided all the heat we needed.

The neighborhood wasn't as populated back then, and we were far enough from the downtown area, so that the houses were sporadically spread among the tall pine trees.

I remember the year because I had bought my first gun magazine, the Spanish gun rag called "Armas," and the Walther P-88 was on the cover, a novelty in the year 1988.

Also in this same magazine was a special report on how to build shelters in the wilderness if lost. It included several common tips and schematics on how to build several kinds of shelters, also tricks like taking advantage of fallen trees, looking for the empty space under the tree branches when there's snow, and using the empty backpack to keep your feet warm when sleeping.

My birthday being in January, I knew exactly what I wanted for Christmas: I wanted a survival knife, similar to the one discussed in the magazine article with a hollow grip.

The day came and my old man handed me the present. It was a rather long box… and heavy. Yes, a very good first impression for a birthday gift.

I can't put into words the joy I felt when I found just the knife I'd been dreaming about under the paper wrapping. It seemed like the eyes of every family member there would fall out of their sockets. The only ones smiling were my dad and yours truly.

There was a few words exchanged between my mother and father, but my old man won the little debate: I was declared responsible enough to have my own survival knife. Grandpa then came along and commented, "Nice knife, boy, I'll teach you how to sharpen it later."

The "Rambo" knife came with everything a boy needed in its hollow plastic grip: compass, wire saw, band aids, and matches. The blade had a "saw" on the back and a bottle opener, and a low quality sharpening stone could be found in a pouch attached to the fake leather sheath.

It was a cheap Chinese knockoff of course, but to me it was just the coolest thing in the world, and the gods of steel wanted it to endure the use and abuse my thirteen-year-old brother and I put it through.

We learned to build shelters with that knife, prepared traps, cut up wood for fires, and just do what kids that age do with a survival knife. The kids in the neighborhood soon became friends and at night we would build a fire and cook hotdogs or just share food we brought from home.

Those were good times, some of the happiest memories I have.

Still vacationing, one day my mother took my brother and younger sister and me to the bakery. My brother being the oldest one hopped out of the car and went to get some bread and pastry.

A few minutes later my brother came back empty handed and said he had been robbed.

"Come on, stop messing around," said my mother, and then he started crying. No, he was not messing around. Just after he went in a couple guys had followed. We didn't notice because we were distracted, talking about the day's activities. They both pulled guns, threatened everyone and took everyone's money, including my brother's.

So much for "Survival." If my brother didn't have a gun on him, all the shelters, fires, camping and hiking tips and tricks wouldn't matter.

Other than using the knife as a weapon, which was about the only application I could think of for my newly acquired survival skills.

It was one of those moments when you grow up a bit, and you understand things a little better.

Playing in the woods was fun, camping was a blast, and the skills being learned were real enough. But they had no use when it came to surviving in the world we live in, and that hasn't changed after all these years.

Rather the opposite, the need for other kinds of skills and mentality would become painfully obvious several years later.

During good times people can afford to be spoiled, lazy, and let others handle issues that they should solve themselves. Crime rates are low and "those things" just don't happen where you live. It doesn't happen to people like you, or those around you.

But one day that changes and it does happen. The guy next door, a friend or a family member gets hit and you see how vulnerable you are.

I'm not talking about crime alone. I'm talking about serious problems or disasters of all sorts. It can range from floods to hurricanes, social disorder or a family member getting sick and requiring medical attention. You didn't have the foresight to prepare for it financially and with proper medical coverage and insurance.

There's people out there that can't even change a tire, for crying out loud.

And maybe you can live like that for years without worrying about a thing, simply because the system is working better than usual.

But once you realize that our society is based on rather complex and fragile structures that can fail, or when you see how life just enjoys throwing you a hardball every now and then, then you see the wisdom in preparing.

If preparing and embracing a mentality where you take responsibility for the well being of yourself and your family is something that will make you paranoid, and you won't be able to sleep at night, then seriously…don't do it.

Being a depressing "doomer" or a petty fear-monger does no good. Rather the contrary, it will work against you during the hard times that everyone is going to face due to the world financial crisis.

As I told some guy once, "You have to be one peppy and cheerful son of a bitch, if you want to make it through a crisis." Being a negative person will only make you fall into the arms of drugs, alcohol and depression.

To those that think a crisis is an opportunity for a new start, and are looking forward to SHTF:

Guys, you don't know what you are talking about. Like the Chinese say, "beware of what you wish for." Everything is harder, more difficult and more complicated after the SHTF, and it's definitely not FAIR.

Just having guns, food and gear won't make you king of the hill, ok? Those are fantasies that kids that live in mom's basement have.

Inflation? Crime? 25+% unemployment?

If you're a loser now, you'll end up hanging yourself in the bathroom after that!

No. Real survival is about being extremely positive and resourceful, even if it requires you to remove the rose-colored glasses and see reality as it is.

I prepare because it makes me sleep much better at night. Because it gives me a sense of fulfillment to know I'm doing everything in my power to protect myself and my family from whatever life may throw in our direction.

It gives me great satisfaction to know I can handle a number of problems when they arise, and it also allows me to enjoy life more.

If survival and preparedness are making you part ways with those you love, converting you into a bitter and lonely person, you are doing things wrong and you'll go nuts.

TYPES OF SURVIVALISTS

Once you get started and talk to other like-minded people, you'll find that survivalists and preppers come in all shapes and forms.

You'll find people that are fixated with the Cold War and still seem to be expecting the Russians or Chinese to invade.

Others are supposedly preparing to survive the wrath of God, who according to them will cover the world in flames in some way.

Most of these folks usually prefer to live as far away from other as possible.

Unfortunately for them, they seem to think that living in apparent isolation will spare them from serious crime problems. This works fine as long as there's no serious crime problem to worry about in the first place.

It's like having a bear-repellent rock in South America… it will work great because there are no bears in the southern part of the continent, and not because the rock has any power.

They should learn about the farmers in Rhodesia (now Zimbabwe) and how criminals used to raid them and kill them by the thousands. Even people that live in the country here in Argentina were forced to arm themselves and organize, since they realize how vulnerable they are to violent home invasions where help simply won't arrive, and how in spite of their efforts they still get hit pretty hard.

You also have more modern versions of survivalists. Usually better off, make decent money and spend big bucks on lots of guns, knives and tactical gear, but when you ask them, you learn that they don't even have a week's worth of water stored in the house.

Their expensive gear looks brand new, and is rarely ever used.

The ones more "outdoorsy" put a bit of use on their blades and guns when camping, but you'd be surprised by how many of them can't even sharpen their own knives well, and will usually send them to a professional sharpener.

Some are better informed and spend lots of money stockpiling everything you can imagine, but to these guys it's more about buying stuff than putting into practice the survival philosophy. They'll have the money and gear, but the wife isn't on board with them, the kids are as spoiled as they could possibly be, and it's more like a hobby to them.

Others just concentrate a lot on shooting and military tactics. They'll shoot tons of ammo and know how to shoot well, but have poor levels of awareness when they leave the range. It's more like a sport to them, like action shooting.

They'll have little food stored, few practical skills, and they laugh at the idea of financial preparedness because they make 100,000 bucks a year. So they don't save or invest, they just suppose they'll always have a job (wrong assumption) and they suppose those 100,000 bucks will always allow them to purchase the same amount of stuff (wrong again).

Then yes, thankfully you have an entire generation of survivalists that embrace it as a way of life, still mange to function as part of society, worry about fighting for their rights, have the gear and most importantly, they have the mindset and training.

These are freedom loving, independent-minded people. Trade workers, cops, doctors, business owners, lawyers, teachers and students. They know what they need to survive various possible scenarios, they acquire the necessary goods and skills, they usually carry a handgun and received formal training in how to use it.

They have contingency plans, maybe a secondary location to go to. They work on building up savings and if possible investments as well. They network and have like-minded friends, as well as friends that aren't into any of this. They function in society; they don't try to escape from it.

This is in my opinion, the wisest, most sane approach. Instead of waiting for tragic events to occur, they go on with their lives as they prepare.

If nothing happens then just great, but if something does occur they are better prepared than 99% of the people.

THE "LITTLE HOUSE ON THE PRAIRIE" SYNDROME

Another group suffers from what I like to call "The Little House on the Prairie" syndrome.

This is a popular survivalism spin off. It concentrates mostly on 19th century skills, what you'd expect a frontier settler to know. Blacksmithing, trapping, barrel making, making carts, the idea of using draft animals for work in general, and overall going back to what people pictured in the series by Michael Landon.

These kinds of survivalists also think people will go back to those moral traditions as well—old notions of courting and dating, the daughters all of a sudden being very prudish and the boys respectful of girls and elders.

It all sounds very charming and appealing in a world that, at least morally speaking, is mostly freefalling into a pit of promiscuity and lack of family values. As much as I enjoyed the Ingalls family as a kid, those days are gone, guys.

Knowing how to work in general, carpentry and general repairs, it's all useful but we are not going back to the past. It's not a good idea to think that certain dated trades are ways of making good money after the SHTF, and things certainly won't get better in terms of morals and family values.

Barrel and cart making or trapping won't make you a fortune after the SHTF; you'll need smart marketing and modern niche investigation for that.

In terms of moral values, expect them to crumble instead. You will see more gambling, more prostitution, more drug abuse, more single moms, and more multiple-dad families.

Expect real churches to close and reopen as "pastoral" churches, what people here call "evangelical churches," that mostly concentrate on taking away as much money as possible from people. The good "pastor" not only steals people's money, but often sleeps around with their daughters as well.

We even saw a huge increase in "Satanist" rites, witchcraft, divination and "black/white magic" along with "umbanda" rituals.

In a world where people are pretty much desperate, apparently easy solutions for health, work and love problems sell very well. It's become common for some criminals to visit their "pai umbanda" (umbanda pastor) for protection and blessings before they go out to commit crimes. In at least one case I read about, the pastor even rented firearms to the criminals as well. Another pai in Moreno forced his female followers to become prostitutes and give him the money.

RISK ASSESSMENT

This is your first step to seriously formulating an objective and down to earth preparedness plan. There are things in common for most scenarios and SHTF events that you can think of, but once you make an actual list you will start to see things better.

Do you have hurricanes in your area, or earthquakes?

Is crime becoming a growing threat in the region?

Is this your worst threat? The one that is most likely to affect you?

Think of floods, forest fires, or ice storms where the power may go down and you'll need to stay warm.

As of right now, the economic crisis is on everyone's mind, so that's something you want to look into as well.

How safe is your job? If they fire 30-40% of the employees, are you likely to be one of them? Do you have enough savings to make it until you find a new job?

After the SHTF in Argentina, some people spent six months looking for work.

If you work for yourself, how would you handle a 50% reduction of work? How would you deal with 100% inflation? Prices in some cases doubled in a matter of days here after the crisis.

I can't express the desperation you feel. You don't know what its like to walk into a supermarket, and to be AFRAID of the prices.

How's the government looking? A little too "overprotective," shall we say?

Grab a pencil and write down your list right now in the pages provided at the end of the book.

Write down in a column the top five threats, from most likely to most unlikely.

Right next to that column, write down the top five, but this time from most dangerous to less dangerous.

Tip: If health problems aren't included in your list, either you aren't human or you did your list wrong. Being fired or unemployed should also be there somewhere unless you are Bill Gates.

You should prepare for all, but work your way from top to bottom. If time and resources are scarce, start with the top of your two lists, the most likely threats and the most dangerous ones, and work your way down on both columns.

Brainstorm how you would react, how you would deal with each problem. The hardware and skills needed. What gear will you need for each and what training or family procedure will it require.

If you do this you'll have a much clearer picture of what you are dealing with. You'll be able to focus on the most probable and most dangerous scenarios.

Hopefully you'll eventually work your way down on both columns and cover most of your possible threats.

GETTING YOUR MIND AND BODY READY

An economic crisis, just like any other SHTF event or problem we face in life, can be dealt with better if we have both mind and body prepared for it.

1) Man up. Things will get tough, unfair and painful both physically and emotionally speaking. Guess what? You'll have to deal with it. And being a cry baby won't help.

One thing I noticed when I traveled to other countries, was the "sissy-fication" process (I think I just invented that) that is evident in most first-world countries.

There are a few exceptions, and if you had the good sense to read this book you are already ahead of those that would have dropped it as soon as they read the cover, but it's still noticeable how people get soft when things have been working well in a society for a long time.

Even in circles where you'd expect more tough people sometimes you are surprised. I remember a guy that showed up in the People & Art channel, the guy was a police shooting instructor.

The show was one of those where they film an American couple during their normal day, and each one tells the host of the show what they don't like about each other. One of the complaints the wife had was that the cop spent 500 dollars a month on beauty products for himself!

A shooting instructor that spends 500 American bucks a month on shampoo, fancy conditioner and facial creams! They filmed him shopping around the spa full of chicks, reading the sissy little bottles while looking all serious.

I could imagine his balls shrinking to the size of peanuts and falling out of his white trousers. Call me old fashioned, but my idea of male beauty care is showering every day, cutting my nails and getting a haircut once a month.

Seriously folks, there's no place for that in a violent and ruthless society. Those signs of weakness will be exploited. You have to be emotionally tough too, and that sure doesn't help.

Tip: I couldn't care less what people do in their bedrooms, but a homosexual guy is no doubt a favorite target around here. Looking "feminine" translates to "weak" in the language of social predators. If it applies to you, hide it as much as you can.

The way you dress, the colors you use and how you carry yourself overall should project an image of a self-assured person, who is strong and capable.

Anything at all that could be used as an excuse to unleash violence against you, no matter how unfair it is, will be risky for you after the SHTF. The society you live in will reach new levels of violence in general terms. Not only regarding robberies, but also due to the social tension and general frustration.

Race, religion, sexual orientation or just looking weak…any excuse will be valid for some predators.

The strong will that I'm talking about here will also apply to work.

Don't expect to get a desk job just because you have higher education.

When things get tough you may have to work at anything you are lucky enough to find. Be grateful you at least have a job and be ready to get your hands dirty.

2) Wash away the indoctrinated social behavior that has been drilled into your mind since the day you were born.

You have to re-program yourself to react violently when surprised or threatened in any way. It's all very psychological, unconscious social behavior you probably haven't noticed much until now.

For example when someone pushed you a little in a crowded area, the most common reaction is to move away. When someone looks at you and says something, you hear more carefully and get a bit closer, even if the person talking to you is a total stranger.

Change that.

When someone pushes you and catches you by surprise, in a train or some other crowded area, your reaction should be to push back rather aggressively and turn towards the person ready to fight.

Later you can say "sorry," but first you react.

If a stranger talks to you, get your hands in front of you ready to go up in a guard and move away from the stranger a bit.

Even in conversations, we are taught to be polite and to not confront. When in doubt, the average person will say "yes" rather than "no." This is based on a natural tendency to please others, something that is carved into our minds since we are kids.

Did you try saying "no" as a standard reply?

For years I've gotten used to saying "no" as my natural reply in most cases. It's surprising but this has become rather valuable to me. This has proven beneficial to me not only when talking to strangers, but in everyday conversation and business as well.

A quick, polite but firm "no" as your standard reply usually catches people off guard, but it creates a virtual distance, you make the other person a bit more uncomfortable and that's not necessarily bad.

In business a quick "no" has been great for me. You always have time to say "yes" later. But "no" as your first reply puts you in a slightly more powerful position. Try it and see the results.

"I was wondering if you would accept…"

"No."

Now the person is trying to convince you otherwise without even realizing you are already in a more commanding position.

3) Get your body ready.

SHTF or not, getting into shape is THE most important thing you should do for yourself.

A body covered in fat and with a huge gut hanging out simply isn't healthy.

There are "survivalists" out there who couldn't run after Scarlet Johanson if she was butt naked. Guys, it's of no use to shoot like a world champ and not be able to run 100 yards to escape from trouble.

Even more realistic, overweight and sedentary life will cause health problems that will be the end of you before your time, SHTF or not.

I'm not even going to bother looking up the probabilities of dying in a gunfight compared to the odds of dying due to heart attacks.

"Skinny guys get heart attacks too"

I know that, but if you have a weight problem you should do something about it because it sure increases your odds of having a heart attack.

You body is your most valuable physical tool. Your brain provides the software but the hardware should be able to perform.

I'm not saying you have to look like an underwear ad model, but you should be slim (mostly for your own health), you have to be able to do heavy work, fight, run, and if needed carry a backpack weighting ten to twenty percent of your body weight.

4) "Upgrade" your body as much as possible.

One of the most important things I did to my own body in terms of "preps" was getting LASIK eye microsurgery.

I used contacts before that. I didn't use glasses because they can get lost or broken in a fight, and most importantly because they makes you look weaker and more vulnerable.

You don't want to look weak in the southern suburbs of Buenos Aires.

With corrective eye surgery, I got rid of that problem, and I no longer spend a single buck on contact lenses, liquids or glasses. During an emergency or disaster they won't be falling off either.

There are some (minor) complication risks involved with LASIK, but I recommend it none the less due to the benefits it provides. The US Navy and Air Force give it to prospective fighter pilots to make their vision perfect.

Vaccines are something a lot of people don't trust much. Here most of them are mandatory, and the ones that aren't you better get them none the less. As I said before, expect lots of those supposedly extinct diseases to make a comeback with poverty and poor hygiene.

Yellow fever, for example, was something most of us laughed at a couple of years ago. No one was laughing when it started spreading in the northern province of Misiones on the Brazilian border. As a matter of fact, a lot of people rushed to get their shots, and waited long hours in lines to get them.

Find a doctor you trust, preferably one that is a good friend of the family, and tell him that you are concerned about the problems that a crisis may cause in terms of new diseases due to increased poverty.

Mostly ask him what you should be worrying about if your country goes a bit more "third-worldly."

5) Also, get your teeth fixed, and have any suspicious beauty marks or moles removed. The ones with a black center or the ones that have been growing as time goes by deserve particular attention.

Summarizing, do everything you'd do if you knew that next month there would be no doctors and dentist available.

If there's a disaster or other kind of emergency, finding a doctor and getting proper medical attention will be "complicated" to say the least. With an economic crisis you also have to worry about not being able to afford a doctor even if they are available.

Get yourself "upgraded" now!

YOUR SHELTER

YOUR HOME

Anyone into survival and preparedness has probably heard about the "Law of Three." The law of three applies to all survival situations since they are basically the conditions to remain alive:

You can't live three minutes without air

You can't live three hours without shelter in extreme weather conditions.

You can't live three days without water.

You can't live three weeks without food.

The estimations are pretty rough but it's mostly true.

When it comes to shelter, yes, wearing only jeans and a t-shirt, during extreme low temperatures can kill you in three hours.

But when it comes to modern survival, shelter includes a number of other things. It's not only the place where you are safe from the elements. It's the place where you are safe from the growing crime around you, where you keep your gear and the savings you no longer feel safe leaving in the bank. It's where you probably work too, and if not it's were you come back at the end of the day and feel safe enough to relax a bit.

The modern version of shelter is your home, and you should consider its location as well as the physical security measures and other upgrades you implement for when the SHTF.

When things are okay, you can live wherever you want, and then come up with the rationale for why it's a wise choice. When things get tough, when you have high crime rates, high unemployment, poor public services (including rotten education and worse medical care), things will change a lot.

CITY OR COUNTRY: WHERE TO LIVE?

If you've been into survivalism for some time you've probably heard it too.

"Don't you know? Cities will burn, burn to the ground I tell you! They'll become death traps, people will loot and burn everything, and the cops won't be able to do a thing!"

Unlike most of these fear mongers, I've been through enough riots and roadblocks and I've seen enough looting up to the point that it became a boring pain in the ass. "Honey, I'll be late for dinner. Those assholes are road-blocking the bridge again."

All this is in a country where police and emergency services are not nearly as effective as they are in first-world countries.

Being in a supermarket that was about to get looted only meant you wasted your time and had to go somewhere else, or come back in a couple days when they fixed things up and cleaned after the looters left.

You think I'm exaggerating or kidding? Look it up. A government doesn't declare martial law and curfews just because there's nothing to watch on HBO, they do it because they've lost control of things and need the green light to start busting caps and shooting looters.

During 2001 we had days of pure anarchy, and that lawlessness lasted for weeks in most places. Some places in the capital city were secured faster, but there are others where even today cops just try to keep a minimum illusion of security. This mostly happens in the suburbs, and not that much in the capital downtown district.

I can tell you this: cities and towns exist for a reason. And no, cities around the world won't go up in flames and everyone will not move to the countryside living as settlers. It won't happen, ok? It's just BS.

Of course there are advantages to living in the country. Who wouldn't like to live surrounded by nature?

But you know what? When the SHTF things change a lot, and if there's something you can learn from similar events around the world it's that people out of the cities in the countryside get hit *hard*.

Even during "good" times, many survivalists have accepted that their "off grid retreat" dreams left them bankrupt, and well known survivalist author Mel Tappan accepted that he could live on his ranch the way he did thanks only to his wife's family fortune.

Security? There's little or no police presence at all, what do you expect?

Street robberies are of course something that doesn't happen that much because of the low population, but the kind of home invasions people living in the country have suffered here in Argentina are the stuff of *nightmares*.

The same tranquility that people like so much works in the bad guys' favor.

You can scream all you want, but no one will hear you. They can spend days in your house raping and torturing, without worry if a neighbor saw them go in or detected some other suspicious movement.

"You're kidding! Life is much better in the country," a guy from work told me. "I come from a little farming town, everything is so quiet. Well...except for what happened to Mr. Gonzales. Somehow bad guys learned that he had sold a few acres, and they tortured him to death to make sure that he hadn't any more money buried somewhere."

People are like that. Everything is fine and dandy... except for that brutal little home invasion murder. I asked him if that happens often.

He said, "Of course not, it just happened once only one time, a few months ago, when a man also sold some property. Other than that, it's mostly people just stealing cattle or some crops."

So you see people, we go from a safe little farming community to two brutal murders and constant theft in less than a year. It doesn't sound so safe now.

My point is, life in the country sure can be great, but while it may be very safe when things are fine, it will be hit hard by crime when the SHTF.

For crying out loud people, use that thing between your ears called a brain and think like criminals for a second. If you are a ruthless robber, rapist or murderer, who do you attack? The house surrounded by other people, or that neat house full of stuff, probably with lots of food, gear and guns, located way out in the middle of nowhere?

Here is where the chest thumping starts. "I'll set up a guard with my buddies. We'll shoot first and ask questions later." No you won't. Unless you can afford to pay 24/7 security, your buddies will eventually get tired and go home. They'll lose interest or find better jobs than standing guard all day for food and shelter alone.

About shooting first and asking questions later, yes, that's a nice way to end up in jail. No one said when the SHTF life would be fair. The police won't be there to protect you, but they'll be there to put you behind bars! That's life. You don't like it? Sue God. (State Senator Ernest W. Chambers from Nebraska actually did it in 2007, sort of as a joke.)

In terms of security, do you want to know how farmers live in Argentina? They spend most of the day and some of the night firing a couple of warning shots when they see trespassers, and they accept the loss of a share of their crops as something unavoidable. Shoot the ten-year-old stealing from you? You'll end up in jail…and once they let you go a few years later you'll realize there are ten more starving kids ready to take his place. Stuff like that happens in a country with a 50% poverty rate and 25% living below the poverty line.

Of course none of this happens in the good old USA, because you still have a long way to go before you reach our calamity level, and hopefully you'll never get there.

I'm just setting the record straight. Reality vs. fantasy and wishful thinking. In terms of security, you'll be much safer in a good neighborhood than living alone with no neighbors.

If the experience I relate about Argentina isn't convincing enough, do some research on the Rhodesian farmers, and how over 4,000 of them were killed, even after increasing their security levels beyond most survivalists' expectations.

Being far less dramatic, also think about more mundane things. Why did people create and move into cities in the first place?

Wait a second, don't Google it up. I know because I've studied it in college as part of my urbanism studies. The first known cities found in the Middle East 10,000 years ago were created because of two reasons:

1) Security: Of course, being alone made you an easy victim, just like today. Raiders and wild animals were the greatest threat.

2) Trade and Work: One poor crop could cause a family to starve to death. The first paid jobs were something that appealed to many. It's pretty simple, but some people don't seem to understand why a normal job (like most people have today) is a good idea, and why after all it became the most common thing.

Jobs are the reason people started moving from the country to the city after the industrial revolution, and the reason why cities became overpopulated. They preferred to live crowded into pestilent quarters in the city than living in the country. Why? Because they were all so stupid and lazy, and the guy on the internet I read about the other night is right, he's an anonymous freaking genius? I don't think so.

What do you think will happen when there's 25% unemployment? Even more people will move into the cities looking for work, NOT the other way around!

We saw it here in Argentina, and every other country that went through the same thing saw it as well. I do not recommend living in a large city though. Many of the city problems after the SHTF are real enough, and there are better alternatives.

I recommend basically what I later learned Mel Tappan recommended as well: Live in a small town or community. This community or subdivision should be close enough to a moderately-sized city with enough job opportunities, education and entertainment.

People need to have a social and cultural life. You need job opportunities in case you can no longer make a living doing what you do now. You need jobs for your wife and eventually for your children as well.

Home schooling is something deeply rooted in the survivalist community. Sorry to burst your bubbles, but you can do that today only because the S hasn't HTF yet and you are still living the good life, and not the post-collapse survivor life. Most people won't be able to afford that any more. Mommy will have to go out and find a job, or make enough profit working on the farm or running a home business. She won't have time to educate the kids properly. Those kids will grow up with fewer tools than kids who had a better education.

If you somehow managed to make things work differently, then that's just great. I'm just stating what will happen to the great majority of people, based on what happened here with stay-home moms and moms that worked at home. Again, other countries that went through the same things can tell a similar story. Both parents work, and either grandparents or a nanny of some sort watches over the kids if they can't go to school all day, like they do here with bilingual schools.

Bilingual schools are very popular in Argentina among the middle class because not only do they offer a second language and usually better education, they take care of kids from nine to five so both parents can work.

You could argue that a farm or house in the county can grow and produce much of its own food, and yes, that's true. But food is just part of the problem, not everything. You can also grow food in a house if you have a bit of land. Not much land is required for an orchard, some fruit trees and a few small animals. People have been doing this in the city forever.

I asked my dentist about this once, since she moved here from a small agricultural town. I was surprised to hear that food was actually one of the things she missed the most when she went there to visit.

"Are you kidding?" I asked her. "You must have lots of food there."

"No," she said. "Most of the towns concentrate on producing a few types of food. Some have cattle; other regions have vineyards, and so on. But with the fuel crisis and the crisis in general, transportation is suffering and the efforts are mostly placed in keeping the larger cities stocked where the most people live. One of the things I missed the most was the fruit I can easily buy here in Buenos Aries. It just doesn't reach my small town, and what little gets there is pretty expensive."

Another point I feel very strongly about is having good medical care nearby. My house should be around fifteen minutes away from a modern and well-sized hospital and proper medical attention.

Most people still die of diseases and illnesses, not zombies or looters. A fifteen minute drive to the hospital can save your life. One hour (or more) away from proper medical care sounds like poor planning to me.

If crime becomes a serious problem you'll also have neighbors to organize and work together. Not neighbors two miles away, but people close enough to provide some real help fast.

Eventually most neighborhoods here just decided to hire security guards and place posts or kiosks on the corners. A small town or subdivision has the resources to organize things much better than a guy living alone with his family.

Understand that a family doing guard shifts and shooting looters and gang members 200 yards away is just a fantasy. It will not happen.

Stay focused on reality, people. When you start thinking of possible scenarios, at least look it up and check if it ever happened before, in another time or another country.

If you can't find any you are probably just wasting your time.

Home security requires a book itself. Being an architect with particular interest in home design, make that half a dozen books, several of them just on the house design theory itself, before a single brick is laid.

In spite of that there are a few tips you can put into practice that will greatly increase your home security level:

1) Have a well designed house. Most often people just have the house they bought and try to upgrade it, but a house designed with security and disaster preparedness in mind will of course be much better.

If you are about to build, get professional help. Heck, look me up and hire me to design your home or at least take a look at the plans you have. Lots of things can be fixed from the design concept, including security and reducing the energy requirements for heat and lighting, just to mention the most common. You'll eventually save a lot of money and have a much safer home.

2) Get reinforced exterior doors. These are more expensive but will increase your security significantly. Most robbers just kick the door down or use a crowbar. Replace all hinge screws with at least three inch ones. Better yet, have a contractor replace the door frame with something more sturdy. No use in having a great door if the frame is weak.

3) Think like a burglar. How would you break in into your own house? Windows, a weak garage door, or climb to a tree nearby and get to a window on the top floor?

4) Place motion detector lights around the house. This is one of the cheapest and most effective ways to increase your home security. Burglars usually like to work in the shadows. You can also buy motion detector lights that run off of solar powered batteries, so they will still work during a power outage.

5) Have exterior motion sensitive cameras. These are usually used by hunters to see what kind of game they have running around. You can use these hidden in the surrounding trees to take a picture of the people that tried to break into your house. Cops will usually find the criminals soon enough if you provide a picture.

It's also one of the best ways to deal with petty criminals that steal stuff from around your home.

6) Have an alarm. It's a great deterrent too. Your alarm should be loud and call to your cell phone when it goes off. If you live in a small community and have good relationship with the sheriff, you can also set it up so it calls them too. Calling 911 with a message of "house being robbed at (address)" is also an alternative in some countries, but in others this is not allowed and you have to make the call yourself. The alarm should have a backup battery, and it can be set up for little money to use a hidden cell phone that is hooked to the backup battery in case they cut the hard-wire phone lines.

7) Install burglar/security bars on windows. They look ugly, I know, but they are the best way to secure windows and it's hard to find a home in Argentina or other third-world countries without them. In bedroom windows, make the extra effort and install releasable bars in case there's a fire.

8) Avoid materials that catch fire easily. Most American homes have wood frame structure so this can be more complicated. At least avoid carpets and having too much furniture in case there's a fire. A metal roof is also desirable.

9) Install security film on your windows. It's also called shatter proof film or safety coating. It's simply an adhesive plastic that makes your window hold together even if it breaks. This is a great upgrade you can do for very little money. A great weekend project!

The window won't shatter and fall apart if there's a storm or a burglar wants to break in. For those that are a bit more paranoid, it also keeps Molotov cocktails from getting thrown through the window into the house, or "commando" criminals" and cops gone bad from throwing flash-bang grenades inside to stun you before attacking…

10) Install good quality locks. These are expensive but well worth the money. You exterior doors should have at least two different locks. Buy quality name-brand deadbolt locks.

11) Secure your interior garage door. It should have at least two locks on both sides just like any other exterior door. The door that connects the garage to your house should be very sturdy as well, also with good locks. This door will be your family's last line of defense if criminals hurry into your garage when you come back home, so consider it an exterior door. It would be great if this door could be made bullet proof with the addition of steel plates or Kevlar panels.

12) Don't leave tools in the garden. A ladder in the back yard can be used to get to the roof and break into the house. If you have a shed, keep it well locked and secure any tools such as pry bars or hammers that can be used as weapons or to break in.

13) Don't provide concealment. Don't leave any overgrown bushes close to the house that criminals could use to hide behind and ambush you. Low walls and fences sometimes do more harm than good.

14) Place thorny plants under the windows. This will complicate things a bit more if someone tries to crawl inside. It doesn't sound like much, but every layer of security helps.

15) Install heavy curtains. Many criminals just walk by, looking around. Don't turn your windows into display cases for them. Place things such as expensive electronics out of sight and away from the windows.

16) Get two safes. Criminals mostly expect to find one, not two. The first one is mainly a decoy. There you have some cash, a few papers and envelopes that look important but are really junk, and some cheaper jewelry.

In the worst case scenario where they have you and your family at gunpoint, you surrender this visible or poorly hidden safe. You can rig it to send a silent alarm that calls the cops too.

A second smaller fireproof safe that is WELL hidden will be safer for keeping large amounts of cash, jewelry and precious metals in case you are lucky enough to have them.

17) Make your house much safer than the houses of your neighbors. It's sad, but it's a fact. The less secure home is the one that gets robbed. If the burglar has his eye on three homes, he'll go for the easiest one. Make sure your house is not it.

18) Have a perimeter fence. Or wall. An iron fence with spikes on top is just about prefect. Whatever you do, it must be at least seven feet high and go all around the house. This may not be an option for you, but know it's one of the best security measures you can implement. Chain link fencing is also great, and with the right plants covering it, it doesn't look bad.

19) Install security lights to go on automatically when there's no power. These emergency lights are easy to install and make life a lot easier if power goes down frequently.

YOUR SECURITY

Security is one of the things you'll have to worry about the most after SHTF.

As unemployment, crime and frustration gets worse, expect more and more violent criminal activity.

AT THE HOUSE

All the security measures taken in your home are of little use if your family doesn't incorporate security discipline as well.

*The exterior doors remain closed and locked at all times. Period!

*No one opens the door until 100% sure of who's on the other side. If it's the police or power company for example, they'll have no problem waiting outside until you look the number up and call the power company or police station to verify them.

*Install a peep hole and an intercom camera to clearly see who's outside.

*Don't give the key to strangers, like people that will be working in the house for any given reason. Copies can be made without your knowing it.

*When ventilating the house, open top floor windows or windows that have burglar bars. An open window is just as good as a wide-open door, people.

*Place china, cups or lamps next to the windows, so that if a burglar manages to break in, he'll drop it, making noise and alerting you.

*Going in and out of the house are, by FAR, your most vulnerable moments when criminals make their move. So do it fast, and before going out look through windows and the door's peephole to make sure no one is hiding.

*When on vacations, have someone pick up the mail, turn a few lights on inside, and take out the trash. You might want to leave "fake" trash bags ready for the friend or neighbor to take outside. These trash bags will have mostly paper, cardboard and plastic to throw away. The important thing is to have a bag of trash outside, to make your home appear to be occupied.

*Your garage door should be remote controlled. Before purchasing one, make sure to buy the one that opens and closes the garage door the fastest. Buy a quality keypad unit for the garage door that can't be pried off and "hot wired" to open the garage door.

*When answering the phone, don't give ANYONE your personal information. Don't tell them who you are with, if you are alone, or anything else. Just hang up if any of this is being asked. Cops don't call you to tell you that a relative had an accident (common trick used here), they show up at your door instead in those cases.

*Eventually a large number of people will start showing up at your door. Some beg for money, some for food, and others for whatever it is you can spare. My advice? Answer from a safe distance, and tell them you don't have anything to spare. If you want to do the "Christian" thing with all of them, you'll go poor yourself rather fast.

I only give a little food away and only to children. I don't give them money because they'll usually take it to their parents, who just end up buying drugs. If the same kids show up two days in a row or too often I tell them I can't spare any more.

DOGS

Dogs are great alarms. Roman emperors used to sleep surrounded by their guardian dogs since they didn't even trust their own guards when sleeping. The Gaucho Juan Moreira once said he only trusted his horse, his knife, and his dog when he slept under the stars.

Much better than one dog is having at least two dogs.

A friend of mine had all of his dogs killed with poison at his farm, so train your dogs so that they eat only from one same place and only when you feed them. They shouldn't just eat anything they find.

SMALL DOGS

Some of them are very good guardians and even proficient hunters.

I had a little Pekinese dog that was the smartest creature I ever knew. That dog understood everything I said, and could easily identify if the car getting close to the house was one of ours or not. It would bark if it didn't recognize the engine.

One of the greatest advantages small dogs have over bigger ones is that they eat less and need less water, therefore are more economic to have around, especially when supplies are running short.

The Jack Russell Terrier: This breed is the Swiss Army knife version of dogs. It's small, and can perform a number of tasks very well.

When my friend Paul and his family visited us in Buenos Aires he met "Jack" (my then five-year-old son picked the name) and told me the Jack Russell Terrier is also the favorite dog of John "Lofty" Wiseman, author of "The SAS Survival Handbook."

At the time I don't think I had many good things to say about the JRT.

I've had many dogs in my life, and the JRT is clearly the hardest one to work with, so it's not a dog for everyone.

As our vet once told us, it's like a big dog inside a little body. The little guy will attack much bigger dogs without hesitation. It's terribly hard headed and requires an owner with a firm hand, since the JRT will often test your "alpha dog position" if you give him a chance.

If you have the strong character the JRT requires, then it's a terrific dog.

It eats a bit more than most little dogs but it's still little compared to big breeds.

The JRT is a terrific hunter, easily catching birds and small game with very little training. This may be a great advantage if you need a dog that hunts game to add to the pot. I've been told that some people even used the JRT successfully to hunt big game when hunting in large enough numbers. The JRT is little, but stubborn, fast and with a well muscled body.

It has the world record for killing rats, its natural nemesis. This dog is like a little racing car, it just never gets tired, so kids love playing with him and it keeps them entertained and running around.

It's territorial, so it will bark loudly when it detects an intruder of any kind.

As I told my neighbor once, when he was bragging about how mean his Rottweiler was, "I just need my dog to let me know if there's someone in the backyard. I'll kill the guy myself if required."

For a person living in an apartment, take a good look at the JRT, the little dog that is like a compact version of a bigger one. You have to walk him everyday, but it's just another good excuse to exercise a bit.

BIG DOGS

When crime started to get even worse, a lot of people bought guardian dogs for security. I'm no dog expert, but I've owned several and also learned a lot from other people's experience.

While a big dog is more intimidating and powerful, it also demands greater responsibility, something few dog owners display.

Even worse than with guns, it seems that every guy with a "manhood" problem just goes out and buys a Rottweiler, a Pit-bull or other big mean-looking dog. The problem is that unlike a gun, no matter how much you love it, it's still an unpredictable animal.

You need to have certain experience with dogs before buying a guard dog. Know how to establish yourself as the alpha dog. Otherwise you just have a big furry time bomb, and it's potentially dangerous if you have kids in the house.

Rottweiler: This was the post crisis best-seller. It seemed as if everyone just went out and bought one. Many people, including children and babies, died because of irresponsible dog owners.

The dog is strong, big and looks mean so that's why many people bought it.

Me? I know a lot of people that just love them, but it's not my type of dog. If you have one or are about to get one, please, be a responsible dog owner.

German Shepherd: It's the Ford Model T of guard dogs, arguably one of the most popular working dogs world wide and for many good reasons.

It's one of the easiest dogs to train and educate. The German Shepherd is just a very smart creature that quickly accepts its place in "the family."

The German Shepherd is an excellent guard and attack dog. It barks and attacks when necessary, but unlike the Rottweiler, it's emotionally more stable in general. This is why most police forces around the globe have German Shepherd working dogs.

I owned a German Shepherd and ever since then it's been one of my favorite breeds. In America there is a genetic problem with the hips of many "over-bred" German Shepherds, so do your homework and don't buy one that will soon be crippled or require expensive medical treatment and surgery.

The Dogo Argentino: What to say about this magnificent animal? Only those that have the privilege of owning one really know what a Dogo Argentino is like. Someone once said that owning a Dogo Argentino is like owning a creature that is half dog, half lion. As terribly loyal as it may be, the Dogo Argentino will rarely run around submissively begging for attention. It's also a dog that will never get scared.

It's definitely not an animal for the novice, since the Dogo Argentino is reputably one of the fiercest dog breeds. When it attacks, it will only stop when it kills or gets killed. Before owning one, do a lot of research and know what you are getting yourself into.

Stopping a Dogo Argentino requires a lot of bullets since it feels no pain and it never retreats in fear. Consider that it won't let go even when a cougar cuts him up, the pain caused by gun-shot wounds won't have a better chance.

In at least two well known cases, a lot of shots were needed to stop this dog. In one of them, it required thirteen rounds of 9mm out of a High Power pistol and in the other seven rounds of .45 APC out of a Colt 1911. The burglar that shot the Dogo Argentino with the 1911 pistol (a prize-winning Dogo called "Caudillo") died later because the dog tore his throat out, saving his owner's life.

The Dogo Argentino is one of the most recent and therefore purest breeds to be found. The creator of the Dogo Argentino, Dr. Antonio Nores, wanted to make a big game hunter to chase cougar and boar.

He also wanted the dog to be of good character to play around the house with the children and be a good guardian as well. As ambitious as it sounds, anyone that knows a bit about the Dogo Argentino knows that the dog fulfilled Dr. Nores's expectations and even exceeded them.

One thing to keep in mind though, the Dogo Argentino is before anything else a hunter, and when it detects an intruder it won't bark like other guard dogs, but it will wait and attack, surprising the burglar.

One of the things I like about this dog is its great character and intelligence. Without training it will understand what his owner expects from him.

There have been lots of cases of Dogos Argentino attacking armed bad guys when the family was threatened. Due to their fierceness, strength and because of their lack of pain sensitivity, they keep attacking even after being shot, often killing the attacker or sending them away.

People that hunt boar with them have pushed their guts back inside the dog and stitched them up without the dog protesting. A formidable animal!

If the person has the right character and willingness to get to know the breed well, I'd recommend the Dogo Argentino as a great hunting and guardian dog. Give the Dogo Argentino special consideration if you want a dog that is capable of defending the family against other animals such as bears, wild boar and cougars.

One of Nores's Dogos Argentino, a thirty kilogram female, single-handedly killed a full grown bull. This is all well recorded information in Argentina.

Because of their fierceness, some unscrupulous people use the Dogo Argentino for dog fighting. Stay away from these breeders. You don't need an animal brought up in such a way.

When buying any dog, especially a Dogo Argentino, stick to the recognized breed standards. A bigger than ordinary Dogo Argentino is not desired, it may look more intimidating but these were mixed with Great Danes and are far less courageous that the ones that stay within the standards.

These are the breeds I recommend the most. A Jack Russell Terrier if you need a small dog, and a German Shepherd or Dogo Argentino if you want a big one, and have the necessary space.

Don't train any of these dogs to attack, especially not the Dogo Argentino. Just look after it and spend enough time with it. The basic dog education training will do. It will guard its terrain and will attack when it feels its "family" is being threatened.

A very good idea and something many people do, is to get used to walking around the neighborhood with their big dog. Mostly when shopping for groceries nearby or just going for a walk. Some people will even take their dog with them in their car.

This is something I've seen lots of women do. A big dog next to you will certainly make a criminal think twice before choosing you as a target. Remember to always use a short leash so as to not bother other pedestrians.

A dog isn't just for security. It's been proven that they help autistic kids and people going through depression.

ON FOOT

Crisis or not, no matter what happens you still have to go on with your life. People expect some radical change after the SHTF, but in most cases as soon as the minimum amount of order is restored you'll have to get back to work or school and do all the things you already do, only that you'll have to take some extra precautions to stay safe and avoid trouble.

As you go through your ordinary everyday life, there are a few things you should keep in mind. Try to implement them right now:

*Go unnoticed. Attracting little attention to yourself is generally referred to as "the gray man strategy." This definition works okay for me since I think it represents well the general attitude you should have. Be "gray," a blur in the crowd that no one notices.

*I pay particular attention to my clothing. No, I'm not Tommy Hilfiger, what I mean is that I try to look as neutral and as ordinary as I can. Most of the time I just wear jeans, and a t-shirt. I stick to black, blue, dark green or gray. The more "confusing" the color is, the better. A grayish green color can be confused for either one.

If I have to dress better because of whatever reason, again, I mostly wear darker colors with no logos or symbols that can be easily identified.

Look at how most people dress, and try to blend in as much as you can. People have been kidnapped in this country just because they looked rich. You can imagine it's not a good idea to show off "brand names." This advice especially goes to those women like my wife who like nice clothes a lot. You want to dress well but avoid looking wealthy.

*Everything I use will preferably do something else for me. The multiple task philosophy is a survival and preparedness classic.

If I buy shades, I get protective ones that will protect my eyes from debris as well as sun. Shatter proof safety shades aren't that expensive. Because of the protection they provide, I use them a lot.

Unlike regular prescription glasses, shades don't make you look weak in the eyes of social predators, rather the opposite.

*Avoid wearing jewelry since it often gets stolen. Here again, I'm referring mostly to women. It's been years since Argentine women gave up on using gold jewelry. It is still sold and worn, but only during special occasions with the necessary precautions.

For the usual work day, women here will avoid gold because of muggers and chain snatchers and will use either silver or steel jewelry instead.

Things are bad enough here in Argentina. My wife and I don't even wear our wedding rings any more. We plan on replacing them with silver bands instead.

The little gold cross and chain I usually wear I keep hidden under my t-shirt.

*Get good shoes. It's important because during an emergency what you are wearing may be all you have to get out of the area and walk back home over debris, trash or God knows what else--maybe for several miles.

Girls, some of those little fancy sandals may be very cool but they are junk. Try finding something else that doesn't look bad, but you can walk with them and they provide some feet protection. Maybe some good-looking leather boots or running shoes during summer.

Guys, some of the "trekking" stuff sold in the stores is junk as well. No matter the brand, if it doesn't work, get rid of it. I threw away brand new Nikes because they were poorly designed and I always tripped when using them. After

I tripped for the tenth time and almost hurt my ankle, I threw them away, deciding my health and being able to run if needed was more important.

The best shoes I've found so far are steel-toed working shoes. They have great stability, a thick rubber sole, they are made or leather and are still light enough to use all day long. The steel toe offers a lot of protection in very crowded places where people step on your feet, and in a fight a kick with it does more damage. They don't look bad either. What's not to like? At first the steel toe protection bothered me a lot. After a few weeks the leather softens and you don't notice it any more, just like a regular shoe.

*I'll never get tired of repeating it: Be aware of your surroundings, and don't be afraid of looking like fool. Turn around 180 degrees and walk or run away if you see something suspicious.

*Since the typical home invasion occurs when leaving and entering the house, keep your keys handy. You don't want to spend precious minutes diving in your purse or bag looking for them at the door. Keep them attached to something where they are easy to retrieve at all times and have the exact door key ready when you approach the door!

*Also with your car, have your keys ready before walking into the parking lot. Keep your car parked close and next to the exit, facing forward to drive away fast if you need to do so.

*Carry yourself around confidently. Don't look like a "sheep" but like a "sheepdog." Criminals are experts at reading people. Sometimes it doesn't even count if you are big or a bit small. What they try to read is if you can handle yourself or not.

IDENTIFYING THREATS

Knowing what to look for when looking for threats isn't as easy as most people believe.

Again, Hollywood is to blame, at least partially. Most people suppose that the "bad guys" will look as such, with shabby clothes, lots of tattoos and piercings, and a generally menacing look.

While such a person may indeed be looking for trouble, you have more serious social predators to worry about. Granted, the rag-dressed junkie may as well stick a knife or shoot you for a couple of bucks, so you must watch out for him too, but professional robbers, carjackers or kidnapers will not look like the image that pops into your mind when you think of one.

Most of them look just like regular people. "Well dressed" is often what the victims say, and I've heard more than enough people say "they were better dressed than I was."

Look for young men but also adults wearing clothes that would allow running and fast movements if necessary. Jeans, shirts, polo shirts, some even wear suits if that's the "camo" the situation requires, such as in the case of people that operate in or around banks or other institutions frequented by "suits."

Women are no exception either. There's been an important increase of women robbing, either alone or along with male accomplices. Some of these women are very young and good looking, the kind most men would gladly stop and have a word with, so that they tend to let their guards down.

During a recent robbery perpetrated nearby, I learned that the one shouting "shoot her, shoot her!" to her male crime partner was a women. Thankfully, the robber didn't shoot the poor clerk.

In another robbery perpetrated by a couple, the woman shot and killed a cop in cold blood. They later captured them because they accidentally dropped their house key chain that had a small picture of their little kids. Police asked around various kindergartens and finally found them.

It's common knowledge that kids are capable of robbing too, some as young as ten or younger have been known to commit armed robbery.

Even though a bit on the rare side, older people do commit robberies and crimes as well. I saw one man well into his sixties "picked-pocket" another man on the bus, only to run away when the bus stopped when the victim saw what was happening. And there was an older woman who robbed shops along with her middle-aged son.

Criminals can be well dressed, clean-cut and a great variety of ages and both genders. That description fits 90% of the population, so what do I look for?

That's the point. You shouldn't be looking for action movie stereotypes. You are looking for people that are out of place or people that look a bit too nervous. Is it noon and those two men walking towards you are empty handed with no bags, suitcases or backpacks? Shouldn't they be at work? Shouldn't they be carrying something?

People standing in the same place doing nothing, or a motorcycle slowly approaching you—50% of the robberies committed in Argentina's Capital Federal in 2006 involved a motorcycle. They allow quick escapes, so keep an eye on them too.

MOST COMMON TYPES OF CRIMES

Most crimes here are the common types of crime found everywhere in the world. It's just that they are usually more violent.

Purse snatchers are pretty common, same as gold chain snatchers. Cell phones get snatched pretty often and people try to be careful. Armed robbery on the streets has become something ordinary, unfortunately.

Kidnapping has become a characteristic post-SHTF crime. We didn't have any kidnappings until then. Argentina was not like Mexico or Colombia, so it took us by surprise.

The most common form of kidnap is called "express" kidnapping. They just pick you based on your looks, or the car you are driving. Usually they keep driving you around and let you go once your family comes up with a not-so-large amount of money or jewelry.

A common crime is simply driving you around the ATMs and withdrawing the maximum amount allowed at each one. Going to the ATM has become something you try doing alone without the kids since it can be dangerous.

Common kidnappings involve more logistics, more people, and the victim is well investigated before hand. It's usually based on a recent sale where they know the family has the money.

Famous and rich people now aren't kidnapped as often because they drive around with heavy security in armored cars.

"Virtual kidnappings" occur frequently too. If they know a family member has lost communication with the rest for some reason (he is traveling, or he forgot his cell phone), they call the other family member and say it's an express kidnapping. The family pays, only to later realize that the other family member forgot his cell phone, or it was stolen from him that same morning.

For this reason and many others, it's important that family members always carry cell phones and stay in touch with each other, so that everyone knows where the rest of them will be.

Violent home invasions are more common each day. A new method being used these days is to break in and take control of one house, set up a base of operations there, and then spend the rest of the night robbing the other houses on the block. This also occurs in apartment buildings.

Rape is getting more common, and I suppose it's linked with the overall feeling of "do what ever you want, you won't get caught anyway." Rapist and thieves just climb into apartments through the windows, a type of crime that is called "the spider-man."

Scams and fraud are still very common, but people here have adapted and it's not that easy to do unless the criminals have a very clever fraud planned. Most of the time more trusting older people are the victims.

It's important not to give away any kind of information on the phone.

Even the internet has become pretty dangerous, with criminals choosing their victims sometimes after profiling them on Facebook or other websites.

"Commando" robberies and home invasions also occur. These are very well organized assaults against known targets, either homes of the rich or other places where information has leaked about someone's wealth.

Road-related crime is also common. Carjackings occur when you have to stop at a traffic light. Trucks that carry merchandize are hijacked by so-called "asphalt pirates." This is now a common crime in Argentina. They take control of the truck driver, steal the merchandize and sell it in one of the many black markets.

These "asphalt pirates" also assault families on the highways during the vacation season. Again, their isolation sometimes translates into very violent crimes. Last summer many girls were raped as well during these robberies. Some people were murdered.

During those seasons criminals move to the known tourist locations and rob the tourists or break into their hotel rooms or rented homes, looking for cash and electronics.

Of course the criminals that stay behind keep an eye opened for any house that looks empty, and later check if the family has gone away on holidays.

These are some of the most common type of crimes.

What worries people the most are not just the crimes, but the violence and pure evil with which they are carried out, with criminals torturing, raping and killing their victims for no good reason.

YOUR VEHICLE

CHOOSING A VEHICLE

Without getting into specific models or brands, there are some guidelines that will help you pick a vehicle that that will work for you during troubled times, not only providing transportation and protection, but also doing so without burning a hole in your pocket.

MOTORCYCLES, QUADS AND BICYCLES

Anyone remember being a teenager and wanting a chopper to impress girls? And mom crying about it, saying it's too dangerous and that she'll burn in hell before having to pick up pieces of your brain from the pavement?

Yes, mom was right. Statistically speaking, your chance of surviving a traffic accident while riding a motorcycle is reduced significantly compared to a car, which offers more physical protection.

When the SHTF, everything starts slowly eroding and degrading. That includes street signs and the way people drive as well.

Streets aren't in good condition, some have true craters, there's little signaling and you often find traffic lights that don't work. And I'm not even getting into the fact that sometimes you simply do not stop at traffic lights because the risk of getting carjacked is just too great. Authorities eventually admitted this fact and many of the traffic lights were set at permanent yellow at night in some locations.

As everything suffers, so do other people's driving skills.

You get used to aggressive drivers, and people that don't bother using their lights when turning or switching lanes. It's an overall chaotic traffic situation that respects few rules. Maybe that's why this country is among the top three countries in car accident deaths.

I know a certain guy from Scotland that married an Argentinean girl and moved to Buenos Aires. He tried to drive here just once, and found he simply couldn't manage the stress of the chaotic traffic. I believe they eventually moved back to Scotland.

During social unrest or times when crime increases drastically, there's something else to take into account, and that's the risk of getting carjacked.

Even before the crisis, many of the "cool kids" in school got rid of their motorbikes in favor of cars. Most of them had been stolen, some several times and it just wasn't "cool" anymore.

A normal car isn't bulletproof, but you are not nearly as exposed as on a bike, where anyone can just grab you, pull you down and hold you at gunpoint, or simply hit you over the head with a brick or pipe and knock you off.

There are certainly some advantages to motorcycles, such as their small size and their ability to maneuver around roadblocks and travel off the road, and their lower gas consumption just to name a couple.

In the city, the security risk due to both accidents and robberies greatly surpasses the advantages mentioned. It's safe to say that most people in Buenos Aires that care enough to consider all of this would agree with me here.

A bicycle is priceless when you consider the awesome transportation method it represents with no fuel consumption, and its' rather fast for short distances. Still, the same disadvantages apply. Bicycles, motorcycles and quads are good options for rural locations or small towns, but in dangerous cities you are a big sitting duck with a bulls-eye on your back.

For all these reasons, an automobile is hands-down the best transportation you can think of. At least for as long as there are fuel and parts available.

A survivalist concentrating on TEOTWAWKI might make a serious but common mistake and simply go straight to a worst-case scenario and choose a vehicle such as a horse or bicycle, assuming that it makes him more self reliant.

No, actually that just makes him an easier, slower target. A person with such a mentality won't make it to see TEOTWAWKI, if such a thing ever even occurs. You need to survive the other more likely SHTF scenarios to get there, and an automobile is your best alternative.

Three-wheeled bikes have become increasingly popular here in Argentina. You see more and more people using them and you can tell how practical they are. They require less dexterity than a normal bicycle. Its greatest advantage: it has rather big baskets in the back and allows you to carry much more gear.

Gardeners use them a lot to carry machinery and tools, so do people picking up scrap metal and paper to sell. The disadvantage is that you are still pretty vulnerable just like with an ordinary bike, and it's somewhat limited to short and medium distances.

CARS

Here are a few tips and comments regarding what you should look for when choosing a car for when the SHTF.

1) Don't think fancy. Think common, inexpensive, and readily available.

This will ensure that more mechanics know the model and brand, so you have more alternatives to shop around for a mechanic that offers reasonable prices. Parts will also be cheaper and easier to find.

This is a terrific advantage. One of the worst mistakes I made was keeping the nicer car instead of the more popular and common one. Not a day goes by that I don't regret the decision.

It's also important to mention that while a popular car offers the advantages just mentioned, they are also the ones that get stolen the most since there's a greater market for used and stolen parts.

This is another example of guessing or supposing vs. verifying in the real world.

You'd think that a Suzuki worth four times as much as a beat up Renault 147 would be more likely to get stolen, but no. The 147 is far more common and thus of much greater interest to car thieves since there's a greater demand for the parts in the black market. When you look at the numbers of car thefts, the 147 is right there on the top, while much fancier cars are not even close.

Keep in mind, folks, that I'm talking about car theft. A guy in a very expensive car is still in danger not because of the car, but because bad guys may think he's rich and kidnap him.

2) If you can find one in good working order, choose a car that works with a carburetor, rather than the more modern fuel injection models. At least take it into consideration as a second car.

Carburetors are easier to repair and accept alternative fuel such as natural compressed gas (CNG) much better than the ones that work with fuel injection.

Diesel cars are even better. They can be modified to work with a wider number of alternative fuels. In my opinion a diesel is well worth the money. Eventually you can run them with biodiesel. Diesel also stores better than gasoline.

Tip: If you have a diesel vehicle you might want to keep this in mind during emergencies: Kerosene and heating oil can be used as well, as long as it's clean and well filtered so as to not erode the engine. It would be a good idea to add a good fuel filter between the gas tank and engine.

Kerosene being drier and working at higher temps, some people recommend mixing 1 liter of normal engine oil to 40 liters of kerosene.

Others use kerosene mixed with a bit of cooking oil to add viscosity and lubrication (80/20 or 90/10 ratio). On the other hand some say this is bad for more modern diesel engines. Just something to keep in mind and maybe look into a bit more before trying it in your particular vehicle.

One thing I learned though: older technology is usually tougher and less picky regarding fuels. My car runs with compressed natural gas (CNG) and gasoline. I really like the dual fuel advantage. I have the "Plan B" thing covered and I save a lot of money.

Diesel vehicles can be modified to run with cooking vegetable oil as well. My advice for someone that has a diesel car and wants to take advantage of vegetable oil: do your research, and get a properly installed two-tank system where the oil is pre-heated and you start up and shut down on diesel fuel or bio-diesel.

Tip: Add engine/injector cleaners to the fuel at least twice a year, and keep an eye on your fuel filter. Even in a normal gasoline car, gasoline is much dirtier after the SHTF.

3) Get a car with 4x4 capability. Even in a city, there's debris, tires, and other elements often used in roadblocks which you may need to drive over.

A 4x4 also allows you to go off road if you ever need to do so to evade attackers or roadblocks. They also have higher ground clearance for going up the curb onto the sidewalk, or over the median strips of boulevards.

4) Don't buy the biggest car or truck you can find. A medium or small vehicle is better. It uses less fuel and the smaller size allows you to squeeze through traffic jams or road blocking elements. A vehicle that is too large may be more difficult to maneuver when performing evasive driving moves.

5) If you get to pick the color, go for the one that is more "forgettable" and easier to confuse. Dark gray, dark blue or green, are much easier to confuse than say plain black, white or red. They also "camouflage" better in the urban environment.

White may be an exception depending on your location, since it disappears in a snowy surrounding, which would also be a disadvantage if you ever suffer an accident in such conditions.

6) Anti-shatter film, also known as safety film, is an important upgrade to perform. It costs very little and protects you better from the most common attacks such as throwing rocks at the windshield to force you to stop, or smashing the window to rob you, or the one on the passenger's side to steal your purse or bag. This is all very common in Buenos Aires, and it can certainly become common in other places as well after the SHTF. It even provides some protection against one of the smallest calibers, .22 Long Rifle (.22LR).

Tinted films are good to keep curious eyes away from what you are doing, making it harder to identify you and how many occupants are in the vehicle, as well as keeping the contents out of sight. In the USA and other countries, each state has its own rules regarding how dark the tint can be and still be legal. Keep that in mind and check your local codes.

7) If you can afford it, get an armored vehicle. Some look just like normal cars, trucks and SUVs, and sometimes they can be bought used from government agencies, diplomatic institutions, or security companies.

In real war zones, such as the one on the Israeli-Palestinian border, such a vehicle is priceless and a real life-saver.

Here in Argentina, it's becoming more and more popular and the number of people that save themselves thanks to their armored vehicle is increasing. This is of course expensive and not for everyone, but I'd do it if my budget allowed it.

A note on military armored vehicles: if you ever wondered and checked, you might have noticed how inexpensive one of theses real war machines can be. Heck, even a real live tank (with the cannon neutralized of course) can be bought for relatively little money in some countries.

An armored vehicle such as the English "Ferret" scout car not only looks like the coolest vehicle ever conceived by man to some people, it's also cheaper than your average soccer-mom minivan in some places.

But there's a reason why not everyone owns one of these. They are expensive to maintain, parts are hard to find and cost a fortune, and unless you are a military mechanic and can do your own work, mechanic bills will be the end of you. It's like owning a big boat burning a hole in your pocket 24/7.

If you just want to get one, try getting something with common mechanical components.

A very interesting alternative, at least in my opinion, would be a used CIT truck. Most cash-in-transit (CIT) armored trucks are built around common trucks, which make parts much easier to find. They are everywhere and shouldn't be hard to find used for a reasonable price.

They are usually too big (a disadvantage in most cases in my book) but it might make an interesting armored camper bug-out-vehicle (BOV) project if you enjoy working with machines.

8) I simply do not leave my car without the steering wheel lock. I'm serious, I've been using it for over a decade, and I use it every day. It's basic "car security 101" for most people here. One time they broke into my car but couldn't steal it, thanks to the steering wheel lock. Mine is also shaped like a small metal baseball bat and is a terrific blunt weapon. These are a bit harder to find but well worth it.

A working car alarm is also an important addition.

9) Get a second vehicle. It's important to have one, a must-have if you can afford it. Go for a common model for the reasons mentioned before. This car should run on a different fuel, in case one kind of fuel becomes hard to find. If your primary car runs on diesel, this second car should run on regular gasoline in case there's a diesel shortage.

The diesel car can be set to run on vegetable oil as well, just as the one that uses gasoline can be set up to run on compressed natural gas as an alternative. This way you cover four different types of fuel with two cars.

DEFENSIVE DRIVING: HOW TO DRIVE DURING TOUGH TIMES

Driving in high crime areas is VERY different from what you learn in driving school. Actually, in many cases it's the exact opposite. The stuff you learn at driving school is oriented to keeping pedestrians alive. Defensive driving is oriented to keeping YOU alive.

And yes, it's not like collecting Barbie dolls. This is dangerous and risky business. You have to care about innocent bystanders but you have to care about yourself even more. It's the only way, guys. No, I'm not just saying so, I know so, and I'm saying so even after hitting a poor guy with my car once.

It happened while turning a corner. I didn't see him; he didn't see me. It was an accident. The guy (thank God) went over my car and not under. There was saliva on my windshield as I hit the brakes. He had smashed his face against it.

I looked into the rear-view mirror and saw the guy there, lying on the street without moving. "I just killed the guy," I remember thinking.

I've mentioned it before that I have absolutely no remorse about killing if necessary for self defense, and it's true. I made up my mind about that long ago. But this was so very different. Killing a poor guy that meant me no harm, who was just trying to get back home after a long day at the office.

I got out of the car and ran to him.

This happened right in front of the Obelisco, the center of the Capital District. There were lots of people around. I must have done something right in another life because as I knelt next to him the guy just got up as if he just woke up.

I tried to convince him to get in my car and let me take him to the hospital. The bystanders told the guy to do what I said. He said something like, "No kid, I'm all right. Just be careful next time," and he walked away. I'll never forget that day.

And yet I tell you, defensive driving is about caring more about you than others.

Am I a selfish son of a bitch? Most likely. But this selfish son of a bitch is still alive and a hundred other nice guys are dead, and nice guys would have died in dozens of the situations I've been in. I shit you not, my dear friend.

I didn't take a defensive driving class. I read about a few basic defensive maneuvers, practiced them with my car until I got them right, and used them a number of times for real on the street when I needed them.

But the real change in my driving came out of survival necessity. It's all about mindset.

Looking back, it took me years to get to that point, and I can only hope to instill in your head some of the awareness and instincts I've gained.

Hopefully you'll understand what I say and it will impregnate your unconscious thought, and you'll react the way you need to react when the time comes.

Forget about the "right thing" to do. The "right thing" will get you killed.

The "politically-correct driver" in you will hit the brakes when a car cuts you off or when something hits your windshield. The "SHTF driver" inside of you will laugh and accelerate when someone stands in front of you to make you stop.

Take a deep breath, close your eyes, look for Mr. Politically-Correct-Driving Nice Guy and rip his damn head off. You hate that little bastard, because that little bastard will get you killed on the street when things get tough. Yes, I'm being funny so that you'll remember these words, but I'm sure as hell not kidding. I'm dead serious.

During these years, I've confirmed what I've been saying all along about SHTF driving and I've even found a few other like-minded folks that do many of the things I recommend:

1) When a guy tries to "dare" you to stop by standing in front of you, you just accelerate and aim straight for him. This has happened to me more times than I can remember: They always get out of your way.

If you foolishly stop, you will get shot or carjacked. Count on it.

2) Always leave at least ten yards between you and the car in front of you. Not only will you be preventing many common traffic accidents, but you'll have the distance to get on the sidewalk or shoulders to escape and maneuver. Remember this, its important. Don't pin yourself into a trap.

3) Car doors should be locked and seat belt should be on at all times. I've been told that soldiers in Iraq don't use seatbelts and they leave car doors unlocked so as to get out quickly in an ambush.

You're not a soldier, and if you are, this book is intended for life in your city when crime gets out of control. The chances of being in a very common, yet very deadly car accident are MUCH greater than the odds of not using your seatbelt saving your life.

The car doors must be locked because when you stop due to heavy traffic or traffic lights, the bad guys can get in and put a gun to your head. So car doors are LOCKED as soon as you get into the vehicle. Every time.

4) If you see someone trying to open your passenger-side car door (which of course you locked), don't wait until he smashes your window. Accelerate, and if you have a vehicle on that side slightly catch him between the two cars as you do so. Why? Because a lot of people here get shot as they speed away by pissed-off carjackers. Catching a guy between your car and the one next to you will scare him, squeeze him nicely, and as you move forward he'll roll like a burrito and fall, unable to take aim and shoot. The metal in the car is flexible enough (not that you should care about a few bumps) that you won't hurt him too badly.

Oh, this was told to me by a friend of a neighbor's uncle. I never did this myself. Just pretend I did it, it worked extremely well for me, and it worked exactly as I'm explaining; alright?

Guys, you do this under a serious threat that deserves taking the risk and probably using lethal force. Don't do it to a friend to impress your buddies, ok? You can break bones, crush guts and God knows what else. Only do it to bad guys when you have a right to defend yourself with deadly force.

5) Be ready for the unexpected. I've had a brick thrown at my windshield (thank God it held), a car in front of me threw foam and other things I never identified. It just hits you.

What you want to do is program yourself to keep driving no matter what. Usually they do these things to force you to stop. You want to be ready to keep driving, erase flinching from your brain. It's not acceptable to flinch. If it just hits you or even if it broke the windshield completely, just keep driving for a few miles and then stop at a gas station or look for the police. If you are going too fast, slow down just a bit but do not stop.

This also may happen when you blow a tire. Sometimes they put traps like rocks or spikes or bent nails on the road to blow your tires and make you stop. Your life is worth more than a tire. Reduce speed and keep driving.

A common tactic to steal women's purses and bags is to drive alongside with a bike (two guys on the bike, or sometimes just one), smash the passenger's window with a rock or other hard object, snatch the purse or bag and take off.

This happens a LOT, so keep your bag down where the feet go, where it's not easily seen or reached. Be careful about people on motorcycles in general. It's THE vehicle of choice for criminals, since it allows easy maneuvering to escape if necessary.

6) Don't drive too fast. Not only because of traps, but also animals that may be on the road, and of course potential traffic accidents. You need to move fast but still within a speed that will allow you to stop if there's a big rock on the road, or an animal. For me that speed is abut 100 km/h (60 MPH) on highways, about 50-80 km/h (30-50 mph) in the city.

It will depend on your eyesight and your reflexes, and if there's cover in your surroundings from where people may throw things at your car. Be alert and detect suspicious movements.

7) Traffic lights are still respected in this country during the day in most parts. But at night and in some of the more "complicated" parts of the country, people just don't stop at them any more. As a matter of fact, outside of the capital district and away from other downtown areas, you'd better not stop during the day as well.

This has become so common that in certain avenues after ten p.m. they just leave the traffic lights on yellow. This is because people don't stop at them at night and there were lots of accidents. You just can't stop in some parts, it's too dangerous.

Of course this represents a problem because it causes lot of accidents. You learn to reduce speed a bit and watch both ways, even if you have a green light.

8) You may have to push obstacles or cars aside with your vehicle. Here's where a small car is at a disadvantage. A mid-size SUV or smaller 4x4 truck would be okay, preferably with protective steel tube bumpers. This is an addition a lot of people buy and it's a good idea in my opinion.

Don't just go crashing into vehicles that are blocking your way. You need to reduce speed as much as the circumstances permit. You don't want to damage your engine.

Since cars are much lighter in the trunk, it's easier to make them rotate if you push there, on the back wheel axis. Put the bumper against it and accelerate. The car will rotate and you can escape.

9) Keep your gun handy at all times. During an ambush you might lower the window and put a few shots in their general direction to keep their heads down and buy you some time. Even inside a car, pointing a gun at someone will make them think better about standing there to get shot.

10) Having said all this, when there's trouble, just hit reverse and LEAVE. This should always be your number one plan as long as it's an option.

11) Know also that most serious kidnapers spend months studying their target. Change your route sporadically and avoid patterns. Drive home by at least three different routes, and if possible, don't always go at the same time of the day. This will make an ambush much more difficult to plan. If you think a car is following you, do not continue on your route home. Turn right four times, so you end up in the same place. If after this the car is still behind you then no doubt it's following you.

12) Wear glasses with shatter-proof lenses when driving. That way if something breaks your windshield your eyes are protected. Same if you have to start shooting from inside your car and you have no time to lower a window.

13) Fake police checkpoints are something that has become pretty common, unfortunately. If this is becoming a common crime, when you see a post like these just get close to the car in front of you and pass it just as you approach the post, so as to avoid eye contact with the road blockers. Looking toward the other side and playing dumb helps too. The point is not to take the risk. If they are real cops, they'll radio more patrol cars and pull you over if they want to have a word with you that much.

14) Watch out for fake car accidents, cyclists, baby carriages, or people waving their hands and asking for help. In Argentina people will rarely stop and there's a reason for that. There are lots of criminals using these tricks to rob you.

If someone needs help just pick up your cell phone and notify the police, but know that it's not a good idea to stop and get out of the car. It may be a ruse.

EVASIVE DRIVING TECHNIQUES

Here are some Evasive Driving Techniques. Know that you need to have 4x4 disengaged for most of these to work.

U-TURN, FORWARD 180° TURN

Maintaining a speed of 30 mph, disengage your clutch or put it in neutral.

Engage the emergency brake simultaneously while with the left hand you turn the wheel from 12 o'clock position to 6 o'clock. (Left if preferred unless you are in the UK or other places where they drive on the left) Return to the 12 o'clock position and disengage the parking brake once the front end reaches 90 degrees. Wet pavement or dirt roads make this happen faster, and it may be more difficult to control. Shift into first, re-engage clutch and accelerate away.

This will be a favorite move when you see the trouble ahead of time and still have some distance in front. It's fast, but you need room to move forward.

J-TURN, REVERSE 180° TURN

Stop the vehicle as soon as you detect trouble. Reverse at full speed, then disengage the clutch and engage emergency brake as using your left hand, you turn the steering wheel from the 12 o'clock position to 6 o'clock (clockwise for a left j-turn) When at 90 degrees, return the steering position to 12 o'clock and release the parking brake.

Now shift into first, engage the clutch upon reaching full 180° and accelerate away from the problem. For automatic transmissions, use neutral and drive.

This is what you use when you came across trouble suddenly, or have people closing in. I have used it on a couple of occasions. Better practice this one a lot. You need good backward speed for it to work well.

S DRIVING

This one I learned while watching cops opening space for a limo with the flag of China. I was going to work early in the morning and came across these Chinese diplomats, with lots of patrol cars guarding them.

What you do is draw S's with you car as you move forward. Going from 12 o'clock to 11 o'clock and then to 1 o'clock. The car will make "S" turns and the drivers next to you will instinctively try to avoid collision, maybe thinking your vehicle is out of control. As soon as you make an opening you go through it. Also, cars that are too close to you will put more distance between you and them, thinking something is wrong or that you are a drunk driver. This has worked for me very well in the past.

OFFENSIVE MOVES AGAINST VEHICLES

First, wait until there's a turn or bend in the road.

If the car in front of you is turning left, ram into the back right corner. If it's moving right, ram into the left back corner. This will make the car in front of you spin 180°.

PARALLEL ATTACKS

Here you want to get the timing right, and hit the car as soon as it moves away from you, so as to take advantage of the momentum.

If someone hits you sideways with the car, its done with a left to right or right to left movement, back and forth. If you get the timing right, you'll slam him as he retreats, the force of your car adding to his own movement.

Wait until he attacks and pulls back, then shove in the same direction along with him with your own car as he moves away to strike again. Timing should be perfect. This will throw him off the road.

You can also attempt to hit his back wheels with your front bumper. Hopefully you'll have steel tube bumpers.

YOUR GEAR AND SUPPLIES

YOUR GEAR

I was just back from my trip to Ushuaia, where all I had with me was a backpack. Not those huge ones, but a smaller forty liter one with the tent strapped to one side. On my first backpacking trips I carried much more stuff. The more experience I had, the more gear I ended up leaving home, and that made these travels more enjoyable.

Living from your backpack for a while changes the way you view things. I suppose the more you do it the longer it takes for that feeling to go away once you come back home. I remember thinking how silly it seemed to use a glass of water, so fragile and heavy, when you could just drink out of the bottle.

Of course in a house full of people that will eventually have consequences in terms of hygiene. Still, that thought crossed my mind as I poured cold (cold!) water from the fridge.

The person that is just getting started in the world of survivalism and preparedness will soon wonder how others do it without going broke. The amount of stuff you apparently "absolutely need!" to survive is endless.

There are two good reasons for this.

1) Survivalists and preppers like gadgets and gear.

It may sound silly, but for many guys buying "survival" stuff is the equivalent of buying shoes and purses for women. They never seem to have enough, and there's always one more thing they just *have* to get.

2) Survivalism, preparedness, emergency and adventure gear is a very appealing market. Many men are just fascinated by the latest gear and gadgets. They want to own the official Navy SEAL knife, the official Navy SEAL underwear and the pants used by the star of their favorite TV survival show. When you include guns, flashlights, generators, emergency rations, bug out vehicles and God knows what else, you are talking about several thousand dollars being spent by these guys, in less than a year.

With the latest world events, people are scared and they want to feel safe. If buying the gun used by the Special Forces makes them feel safer, they'll buy it.

The more unscrupulous dealers will often feed this fear frenzy just to sell more, while the more responsible ones will preach to stay calm and be conservative regarding buying stuff.

Survivalism, at least in the way I view it, is mostly about attitude and skills, not shopping and stockpiling tons of products.

Having said that, neither attitude nor skill will materialize a gun when you need it, or create water when there's none to be found.

I have a little stuff myself, so I'll go through some of the basics you should plan on acquiring as your finances allow.

HOME GEAR

These are the things you keep handy at home.

If you live in an apartment and own a hunting cabin 100 miles away, your home is still your little apartment, understood?

*Food and Water

I'd like to think I made it abundantly clear by now the importance of these too. SHTF or not, you'll always need these.

Remember, food must be nutritious, easy to cook or not require cooking at all. You must keep it in a dry, cool, dark place away from rodents and insects.

Storing larger amounts in five gallon food-grade buckets is an alternative.

The disadvantage is that if something happens to it, you lose the entire bucket. Inspect each bucket on regular basis, at least once a month, to make sure they are alright. Rats will chew through plastic and just ruin everything you have stored if you don't keep an eye on things.

Tip: Don't underestimate this advice. Even in a perfectly clean house a single rat that sneaks in can cause a huge mess and ruin your food storage. Besides, rats usually move around in pairs or trios. Leave your food storage unattended and you'll one day find an entire family of rats eating it up.

Six to twelve months of food should be your objective. Of course, buying six months worth of military Meals Ready to Eat (MREs) costs a small fortune.

But if you buy bulk at supermarkets and take advantage of discounts and sales, you'll see how easy it is to get to six months worth of food with little money.

People, food is still VERY cheap in the USA and other first-world countries. Take advantage of that and don't settle for twelve months, buy two years worth of food. Canned food will usually last several years. Rice (white), wheat, flour, and beans will last decades if stored well. Putting these inside a Mylar bag with two or three oxygen absorbers in a 5 gallon food-grade bucket and sealing the bag will store it for ten years and beyond.

Archeologists have found wheat that was over 2,000 years old in ceramic pots, and it was still edible.

Once the Mylar bag is opened, you want to divide your stash into smaller airtight containers. Five gallons worth of rice lasts a long time and your average family won't eat it up fast. The objective isn't buying a few buckets worth of food and throwing them away. You have to make the food you store part of your everyday diet. If you don't, it will just sit there only to be thrown away a few years later. Either that or rats will eat it.

We love lentils and rice, and they are part of our regular diet.

If you buy certain regular store food and keep it in its original package, it will store for many years if kept in a box in a safe, dry and dark place. It's simply a matter of knowing what kind of food stores well.

I've kept white rice, lentils, flour, dehydrated smashed potato flakes and dry pasta stored this way and it was perfectly okay two years later. As long as bugs, rodents and humidity don't get to it, it will be good for many years, but try to rotate and use up the supplies that you have.

Sugar, salt and honey will store indefinitely in a dry, dark place.

Canned food will usually store way beyond the expiration date. Cans over 100 years old have been found in the steamboat "Bertrand." The boat sank in the Missouri River in 1865. The cans were opened and analyzed by scientists. In spite of the poor texture and smell, peaches, oysters, plum tomatoes, honey, and mixed vegetables were still edible.

As long as the can isn't swollen or leaking and it smells okay, even if the food loses some texture and taste it will still be edible. Avoid cans with bumps and dents, since they can lose their storage properties more quickly.

Having said this, don't push it. Try to stick to expiration dates, something that's not so hard to do if you rotate the stock and use up what you store.

Remember to have a manual can opener! Or several of them.

*Firearms

You need the means to defend yourself. Ideally this should mean firearms, and if they are not available then get large knives and short machetes.

*Flashlights

Since the crisis in Argentina blackouts have occurred very often, especially during the summer when the demand for electricity is the highest. I've spent a lot of time working around the house and trying to get things done using flashlights.

If anyone has tried to cook while holding a flashlight, you know what I mean. An LED headlamp will leave you with both hands available to work. Hands down, the best lights to have are LED headlamps.

Light Emitting Diodes revolutionized the world of flashlights. They can be as bright as regular bulbs, and they last for several hours or even days on batteries.

Stick to LEDs, and try to standardize around AA and AAA batteries.

As goofy as they look, LED headlamps are so cheap and so practical that it's a mistake not to have enough of them. Buy at least one set per family member.

For general purpose use, I like to have around the house one-watt LED flashlights that use a single AA battery. These are the most economic alternative for your lighting needs.

I've used everything: Candles of all kinds, oil lamps, propane lamps and light sticks. If it emits light, I've used it for extended periods of time.

Give me some AAA LED headlamps, AA LED flashlights and a few packs of batteries any day.

The brighter the light, the faster it will eat up the batteries. You don't need much brightness for your everyday needs.

For security, yes, have at least one ninety Lumen or higher "tactical" flashlight.

Surefire is one of the best known brands. 4Sevens makes good products and they are gaining popularity. Brinkmann makes a cheap one that is good too.

*Batteries

Try to standardize around AA. They are cheap and it helps keep things simple. Keep at least fifty alkaline batteries in stock, of both AA and AAA.

With today's LED technology you can also find very bright "tactical" lights that uses them as well. Fenix flashlights are a good brand.

The lightweight and most practical LED headlamps made by Energizer use AAA batteries, but I think there are some AA models as well.

Sometimes you go to the store and don't find the batteries you want. In a long term emergency you may have to settle for whatever you find, so even if you standardize around AA, have a couple AAA and 123 flashlights as well.

Regular Duracell batteries are good enough for flashlights and last for many years. For your emergency car kit or bug-out bag (BOB) you may want to get lithium batteries that have a shelf life of 15 years.

*Battery Chargers and Rechargeable Batteries

When power goes out often, you'll find yourself spending a lot of money on batteries. LEDs help, but you want to have a few sets of AA and AAA rechargeable batteries and a good charger.

There are also gadgets that combine a solar charger, a hand crank charger, a radio and an LED flashlight in one single gadget. These would be ideal for extended emergencies. You can also find solar-powered battery chargers.

*Alcohol Gel

This is very practical and you should keep several bottles of this in your house. During "normal" times people don't appreciate it, but when there's no water this is just perfect to keep hands clean and avoid spreading diseases.

*Matches

Strike anywhere matches are harder to come by these days, but these make more sense for emergency kits. For the house, just buy several boxes of regular wood matches. Also add several Bic lighters. They are cheap and can be priceless during emergencies.

*Alternative Means of Cooking

Camping stoves, BBQ grills, electric ovens, microwaves and propane gas. The more alternatives you have for cooking, the better.

*Warm Clothes and Blankets.

A house without power and gas becomes very cold in winter. I've been there a number of times and it's not pretty. In the northern USA, this can be deadly.

When this happened we would all sleep in the same bedroom bunched together and well covered with blankets.

Tip: Make sure there's a small opening to allow some air flow. Do NOT use any kind of oil or propane burner to generate heat in a room where you sleep. Thousands of people have died of asphyxiation this way, while trying to stay warm.

Tip: If you are just too cold, put some hot water (not too hot!) in a canteen or two liter plastic bottle and place it between your legs. (Make sure it's shut tight!) The warm water will heat the blood that goes through your femoral arteries. Cover yourself with lots of blankets for better insulation.

Have several blankets and spare winter clothes. Polar blankets are softer, but for emergencies having wool blankets and clothing is better because they keep your body warm--even when wet.

*Mosquito Repellent

As Dengue fever starts infecting people in Buenos Aires, insect repellent becomes something people are hurrying to buy. I already have a few months worth of repellent tablets and three cans of repellent. Insect repellent is cheap, pick some extra next time you go to the supermarket.

This is something people in Florida and other Southern states might want to look into since Dengue cases in Mexico have increased more than 600% since 2001. Dengue has reached epidemic levels in Central America and could be a problem in the United States, specially the southern States.

If there's Dengue in your area, watch out for black mosquitoes with white stripes on their body and legs (Aedes Aegypti).

Also, keep the lawn mowed around the house. High grass attracts mosquitoes.

Don't leave cans, buckets or old tires that may collect water unattended. Turn them upside down. Mosquitoes will reproduce anywhere there is standing water.

Take lots of vitamin B and B1. It makes your sweat smell bad to mosquitoes and you get bitten less often. Humans don't detect this smell.

*Disposable Cups and Dishes.

As well as plastic forks, knives and spoons. These are cheap and practical during short term emergencies. This way, you don't have dirty dishes to wash (you save water) and in case you have friends or extended family you are sheltering, there's no need to use more dishes.

*Digital Camera

Keep some spare Lithium batteries especially for the camera.

In case there's an accident or natural disaster you can take pictures for the police or insurance company.

*Radio/CB Radio

AM/FM battery-operated radios will help you gather news. A good TV antenna will be handy if cable service is interrupted.

CB radios allow you to talk to other people and know what's going on. My house used to have a huge radio antenna. My father was very interested in CB radio and he would spend hours on it every night until he lost interest. It was dad's "internet."

*Generator

It's important mostly to keep the fridge going for preserving food. Frankly I still don't have one since I learned to mostly store food that doesn't require a fridge. In the old days my grandmother simply had an "ice box". The ice man came by and you bought ice from him for your ice box where you kept your food.

Tip: What I do is keep lots of five-liter bottles of water in the freezer. When the power goes out I simply move a couple bottles into the fridge and use it like an old "ice box".

I've kept food from going bad this way for two days during summer (105 F). This is of course a very cheap alternative, but it's something everyone can implement for free.

I'd still like to get a powerful generator, but I would settle for a 2,500 KW one. Remember to have several gallons of fuel ready for it.

*Laptop Computer

It requires less power than a desktop computer and you can use it in your car with an inverter.

*Corded Phone

Corded phones ("land-lines") still work when power goes out but "portable cordless phones" do not. Have at least on of the old-fashioned kind that plugs directly from the phone to the wall!

*TV/Entertainment Center/Books

Due to costs and security concerns, people won't go out much after the economic collapse. Going out for dinner and a movie will become something you can't afford to do as much as you probably did, if you go out at all.

A good DVD collection will help your family have a good time and relax.

Videogames are something I like, and so do my kids, so we usually play together. Books are entertaining and also a valuable source of information.

*First Aid Kit

Stock up on the most common supplies. Don't underestimate the importance of antibiotics. I've used them a lot during all these years, so did my kids. When poverty causes diseases to spread more widely, you'll understand how important it is to have a good supply of antibiotics of a broad spectrum to treat infections, mostly Amoxicillin 250 and 500. You'll also need antibiotics for gun shot wounds and other serious injuries.

Have spare thermometers.

Have dressings for wounds, surgical tape, liquid stitches for cuts, Ibuprofen, aspirin, and any other medications you may need.

*Duct Tape

No explanation is needed here. Duct tape has so many uses. You should have a few rolls in storage. Gorilla brand seems to be the best, but any will do.

Also look into the uses of Self Soldering Rubber Tape. This is a well kept secret. It has almost as many uses as duct tape.

*Household Supplies

Toilet paper, soap, bleach, detergent, shampoo and everything you use around the house. Stock up little by little until you have a six to twelve month supply.

*Well-Equipped Tool Box

For general house repairs. You'll also need the skills to use them, of course.

IF YOU COULD GO BACK IN TIME...

I get asked this question every couple of weeks.

"If you could go back in time right before the crisis, what would you get?"

Every time I get asked this I come up with different things I can think of. A generator and more food are usually part of my standard answer. Really, what would I get if I went back to early 2001, before the crisis?

The first thing I can think of right now is knowledge, but that I acquired as time went by, through learning and from personal experience. You couldn't pick that from a shelf, before December of 2001.

I would like to think that studying this book will be as close as you can get to downloading the knowledge I gathered the hard way directly over to your brain.

As for other tangible goods, I have already mentioned the essentials. Some things I would have done differently and a few nice-to-have items would include:

*My Old Car

I would have kept my old car. My old Renault 9 (known as Renault Alliance in USA) was a great warrior for the roads we have here. The car was tough, it was a popular and proven design. It had simple mechanics and cheap spare parts produced locally. The ground clearance was pretty high, and overall it was a much better SHTF car than the more modern car I have now.

I'm talking about tough cars, of proven design, such as the Bronco, Chevrolet Blazer or sedans like the Toyota Corolla. As a matter of fact, the Corolla E70 looks pretty similar to the old Renault 9.

If I could just pick any vehicle, I would have loved to buy a Toyota Hilux 4x4. Again, it's a simple, proven design, and parts are plentiful and not that expensive. Learn from my mistake, and buy a practical "road warrior" now!

*Fuel Containers

I would have bought some extra fuel containers. Not just jerry cans, but one of those big metal trailers that hook up like small "u-hauls." I'm not sure about their capacity. Maybe they can hold 100 gallons of gas or so. I see them at construction sites, and they are not that expensive if bought used.

Tip: Some final advice. Try buying spares for the things you consider really necessary in yard sales or pawn shops. A spare generator, a spare water pump if you have a water well. A hand pump would be a great addition in that case. Don't go nuts; just keep an eye open in case you find good deals.

A spare fridge, spare microwave, spare clothes washing machine, even a spare car if you find one cheap enough that fits your requirements.

This may seem like a little too much, but trust me, I've already been there. When inflation hits you hard almost everything goes up in price, and stuff starts breaking just when there's little money around to purchase a badly needed replacement.

My BOB is not perfect, but it will work as a starting point for your own.

A lot depends on your location and climate, but most items will be useful for a variety of situations. Much of this is a matter of personal choice. This is a city kit, so it's missing much of what you'd have for a wilderness kit.

It's more of a Survival/Emergency kit than a BOB. It should work as a get-home bag, helping you survive for a while if something unexpected happens. It should help to get you out of some minor troubles as well.

It's divided into two parts. A small Samsonite backpack and an outdoors fanny pack with webbing to carry a ½ liter bottle of water. I carry the fanny pack with me at all times when traveling for any period of time. It has gone with me to many other countries as well.

For everyday use where I live, I carry my everyday carry bag (EDC) instead.

The backpack stays in the car at all times, but the fanny pack comes and goes depending on the situation. I find it easier that way, leaving the backpack there and having the more valuable items (gun, ammo, binoculars) in the smaller fanny pack, which is much easier to drop into the car or retrieve it.

There's also another bag in the car with more spare clothes, a blanket and sleeping bag as well as a big five-liter bottle of water. Those stay in the car at all times, along with the backpack.

My bags are pale green, the Samsonite back pack has some camel on the sides, but it all blends pretty well in the city and doesn't catch the eye as bright colors or distinguishable patterns would.

Okay, let's start with the Samsonite back pack.

It's really small, kind of flat. But it has excellent cushioning for the back and the shoulder straps fit nicely and are wide where they meet the shoulders, and they are cushioned and comfortable to wear.

Contents - Outside pocket:

Candy. Sugar, for fast energy.

Box-Cutter.

Surgical scalpel.

Folding knife with pocket clip. A sturdy one with aluminum handles. The blade is half serrated and half straight edged.

Floss. This can be used for a lot of things other than actually flossing.

Small Bic lighter.

Regular Bic Lighter.

"Super Glue"(cyanoacrylate). For fixing things, and also for closing wounds.

Epoxy adhesive tube.

Salt. Small fast food packets.

A five LED flashlight. I used it for a few months to test its durability. It works ok and it's sturdy enough to rely on it.

Small radio. Gather news and information during troubled times.

Roll of coins. Extra money for vending machines.

Survival tool with a compass, a match compartment, a flint and whistle.

Batteries. AA for the LED and a couple AAA for the radio.

Scotch tape.

Duct tape. Just a bit, with the core removed and the roll flattened.

50 feet of thin steel cable with plastic covering. I'm not sure how much weight it can tolerate, but it can easily handle my weight.

Note pad and pencil.

Effervescent hydration tablets (lemon taste). They are usually sold in tubes.

Two peanut health bars.

Roll of Toilet Paper. with the cardboard core removed, inside a Ziploc bag. TP absorbs moisture real fast. I've used damp TP before and I do not want to repeat the experience!

Three one-half-liter bottles of water. They can be refilled if another source of clean drinking water is found.

Emergency Space blanket (Mylar).

New Testament Bible, miniature.

Map of Buenos Aires.

Fifty feet of 300 kg rope. Enough to climb down from a 4th floor. Many other uses. It's always good to have rope handy.

First Aid:

Dressings and bandages.

Surgical tape.

Band-Aids. Different sizes.

Antibiotics.

Hand wipes.

Cauterization powder, similar to Quick-Clot.

Iodine.

Paper handkerchiefs.

12 energy chewing tablets sealed in aluminum foil.

Ibuprofen pills, sealed. Similar to Advil.

Spare clothes. One pair of socks, underwear and t-shirt. There are more clothes in another bag in the car. The t-shirt can be used as a towel if needed, or to grab a hot cup or other very hot item.

Metal Cup. For cooking, drinking, etc.

Candle with four wicks. Made it myself using wicks, paraffin and a tuna can. With the four wicks lit, it boils a cup of water in ten minutes. Not perfect but good enough to cook with in a pinch. Also good heat and light source.

One hour Epoxy. I chose it over the ten minute kind because you can work calmly and the final result is usually better.

Two tuna metal pouches. Tastes good, and lasts 3 or 4 years. The thick aluminum pouch is pretty sturdy. You can eat it without preparation and will keep you going for a while. Takes up very little space in the pack, you can combine it with some rice for a real tasty meal. Best emergency meal out there, at least from those available to me.

Can of corned beef. Heavy, but needs no cooking and lasts forever. If weight is a concern, it would be one of the first meals to eat.

Tang Orange-Drink powder.

Two soup mixes. Dry soup in pouches.

Two rice mixes. Cheese, and with dehydrated vegetables. Tastes good and provide enough calories.

Two soup bouillon cubes.

Old Gerber Multi Tool

1 Kg of dry pasta.

McDonald's salt, ketchup.

550 pound test "parachute cord" Type III. Must have at least seven core yarns.

Pencil. (Just ½ actually)

Hotel Sewing Kit. You know the kind. Needles, buttons, some threads, hook needle, etc. The cotton thread is too weak for serious repairs. I added one quality needle and some black nylon thread (unbreakable), the kind I use on my cordura nylon gear.

Tooth brush.

Small tooth paste. Tooth paste does little to keep your teeth clean. Brushing them is what really cleans them, so I'm not carrying a big tooth paste tube during an emergency. I may add a No. 10 tube, a small one. Small sample or "travel-size" toothpaste tubes are the ones to get.

Small metal saw.

Deodorant (1/2 way through to reduce weight), or a "sample-sized" deodorant.

Rubber bands and tire bands, also called Ranger bands.

Soap. I thought about including a small hotel soap, but I found out that soap is a valuable commodity and the small ones don't last that long. I'd like to take as many baths as possible, so I carry a real bar of soap.

Foam Plugs. Shooting, explosions, who knows?

Nivea body cream, free sample. Precious for the ladies, and also valuable for those who have changed a tire with their bare hands. Takes little space and weight, but it may be extremely valuable if you do need it.

Now the Fanny Pack:

Browning Hi Power 9mm. Nothing fancy but it works okay and it's the most popular pistol in my country. I polished the feeding ramp for added JHP reliability. No problems. Depending on the situation and where I'm traveling, it may get replaced by the Bersa 9mm or a Glock. But most of the time the Hi Power stays there, even if I'm carrying another weapon. It's part of the kit, and not readily available. It's inside an IWB holster, and inside a cotton bag as well. Sometimes when I travel I use the fanny pack to take money or documents and I end up opening it in front of strangers. The small cotton bag keeps the gun hidden even if I open the fanny pack.

Tuna Pouch.

Fire starter.

Lighter.

Thin, galvanized wire. 5 yards.

Lip balm.

Small pliers.

Aluminum foil.

Candle.

Small epoxy glue tube for fixing shoes.

Coghlan's Magnesium block fire starter.

Emergency blanket.

Epoxy band-aids for general repairs (Poxitas brand)

Small Tasco binoculars.

Small can of meat pate.

Flat metal pencil-box tin with 50 rounds of +P+ 9mm. Sealed with tape.

Inside the plastic bag:

Big Victorinox "Forester" Swiss Army knife.

Emergency poncho.

Candle.

Whistle

Compass

Duct Tape (removed cardboard core and flattened)

String.

Windproof Matches in waterproof container.

Signal mirror.

Epoxy band-aids (inside signal mirror envelope)

Bic lighter.

LED Keychain, similar to Photon brand.

Small, flexible wire saw.

Box of 10 match size firecrackers. (signaling, diversion)

Two charcoal fuel rods wrapped in plastic foil. These burn for four or five hours. They were made to be used in pocket warmers.

EVERY DAY CARRY (EDC)

This is what I carry with me at all times.

It seems like a lot, but my EDC bag is just half full so I can carry whatever else needs to be carried at the time.

Gold chain around the neck with cross, Sacred Heart image, and Virgin Mary image, and the key to where I keep my loaded guns.

Right front pocket: Coins for parking and vending machines. Paper money sometimes has a hard time in these, and locally most machines use coins, not paper money. Also handy to make a phone call when the cell network is down, just to mention a couple of times when you need coins badly and you wish you carried some.

Left front pocket:

Elsa's 4 leaf clover "Lucky Charm" Zippo. Both for luck and fire, besides, it's pretty darn cool.

"El Hombre" folding knife by Cold Steel. Strictly for defense, don't use it for anything else so the serrated edge is razor sharp.

Back left pocket:

Wallet. Money, cards, a few subway tickets in case I need them, band aids and paper matches also in there.

Keychain: This one is usually attached to my bag but occasionally goes in my right front pocket if I just go out the door to get something across the street.

It has a 1 watt LED flashlight, uses a single AA battery (most common battery) attached with a small quick release buckle.

Victorinox Midnight Minichamp. This little tool deserves a chapter of it's own. It has numerous tools. The blades are small and fragile but it includes many tools as well as a red LED and ballpoint pen. Very nice addition to the keychain.

Shades. These are Global vision "Neptune" security shades. Just sixteen bucks!

As with everything else, the idea is to have something that provides a bit of actual protection.

These shades are ANSI Z87.1 Safety Glasses, with shatterproof Polycarbonate lenses and they have UV400 level protection.

My shoes too, they look ordinary but they are steel toed for added protection.

The Everyday Carry Bag I use is a M1936 "Musette" bag, with a few customized things such as two zippered compartments, an attachment for keys, and a small pocket in the exterior compartment for my cell phone and OC pepper spray. All modifications were done by myself, with needle and thread.

The zippers are absolutely necessary because if traveling by bus, train or other crowded public transport, pickpocketers would likely try to slip a hand in. The zipper keeps important stuff safe, so that is where I put anything valuable I might be carrying.

Since both the LED light and the Victorinox knife have their own quick release attachments, I usually hook the entire key chain to the bag and if I need the LED or the Victorinox, I can remove them without removing the keys.

Inside one of the pockets:

First aid kit with large dressing, ibuprofen, iodine, alcohol patches, antibiotics, painkillers, cauterizing powder, band-aids, superglue for wounds and assorted smaller dressings.

There's also some soap.

The other Ziploc bag below contains my "Altoids Survival Kit", head lamp (with extra button batteries), space blanket, Tang stick and butane lighter.

I have several spares for knives, lighters and flashlights. Those are pretty important, so I apply the three is two, two is one, and one is none rule.

Tang, Starbursts, larger dressing roll, and a disposable diaper (I have a baby).

Pocket notebook, with Parker ball pen and black fountain pen. I usually have a pencil as well.

Gerber Multi-Tool, nothing fancy there. I have other multi-tools but this one is the one I carry the most because it works well, has enough tools, and isn't something I'd miss much if I lose it.

Bottle of water, always keep one. Drinking or cleaning, even cleaning a wound if I add some salt.

Hand sanitizer, used a lot to avoid contagious diseases due to the poverty of the general population. This is something you might want to add to your bag as conditions deteriorate in your area and people become sicker and less careful about hygiene.

"Elite" cleanex for the obvious, of course I use these often like anyone else does.

Nail file foam pad for when I do my nails… just kidding, it's for sharpening my knives and keeping the ones I use often razor sharp.

My trusty Victorinox Spartan knife. It's just the right size, with no silly stuff like orange peelers.

OC spray. Do carry one of these, even if you carry a gun. There are situations where a gun simply isn't the right tool for the job, even where legal to carry. If you can't own guns, DO get an OC pepper spray can. And (again where legal) carry a serious fighting knife.

Cell phone. Mine is pretty old. I simply don't like cell phones much. Not my thing. Weird because I do like gadgets and tools generally speaking, but I can't get to like phones much. I forced myself to take cell phones seriously because of security reasons. Every family member should carry one to keep in touch with one another.

During certain incidents cell phones may go down, but that's not good enough reason to ignore their advantages when they do work. A lot of "virtual kidnappings" could have been avoided with a cell phone call to check on the missing person, and at least one girl that made it to the news used a cell to escape from slavers (enslaved for prostitution; yes, that kind of thing happens here now).

Spare AA battery for the LED flashlight. Between all the flashlights I carry and the batteries I have, I have almost a week's worth of light.

A light is priceless when the subway breaks and you have to get out and walk through the tunnels. This happens more often than you'd think around here, probably because of poor maintenance. I can easily see how useful it would be during an accident, a terrorist attack, or a natural disaster, not to mention the much more common blackouts we frequently experience post-crisis.

Gun. And now we've reached the guns.

Where legal to do so, I'd advise you to carry an auto for concealed carry and the revolver or compact auto as a backup in the bag.

What I have handy around my house is a Glock 31 (it's .357 SIG caliber, with fifteen rounds in the magazine plus one in the chamber), and a Smith & Wesson .38 Special revolver with a two-inch barrel. This "snubby" carries six rounds.

Sometimes I carry the Bersa Thunder 9mm, which is basically a beefed up version of the Walther P-88.

I'd advise people to carry an extra loaded magazine in their bags.

THE SURVIVAL EMERGENCY KIT (SEK)

This is something many people have tried to make. Maybe as a kid when camping, or when first getting started into survival and preparedness.

The idea is to fit a number of small items you'd need to survive into the small container, so that you can always have it available during an emergency.

Many of these things I already carry one of everyday, (lighter, LED, knife, etc) on me or in my bag, but the idea of a small emergency kit is still valid, because you end up including other things you usually forget about.

There are other better metal containers, but the Altoids tin is what most people use for the SEK.

There's thousands of small kits like this one, some more location-oriented than others, but most have a few common items.

The SEK Contents:

Altoids tin to hold everything.

Home made mini-knife.

This is made using a piece of new steel saw. Made a drop point for this little knife, and left it razor sharp. It also has the original saw teeth left, so it can be used for sawing with a bit of patience. The handle is made with self-soldering rubber.

Small Bic lighter. Red so it doesn't get lost that easily if dropped in the grass.

Nothing to brag about, but it can be used for cooking small meals by boiling a bit of water, and the lid can be polished and used as a signal mirror.

Paper matches, for fire making redundancy.

Ziploc bag. Roughly one liter. Can be used to keep stuff dry. Get condensation out of living plants. Treat water in it using potable water pills.

Two Bobby Pins, useful for countless tasks including lock-picking.

Photon Micro LED light. Works for 12 hours.

Chinese Red Tiger and Dragon Balm tin. It's a muscle pain ointment with a strong, menthol scent. Popular in martial arts dojos.

Small red box with match firecrackers. These are for signaling, creating a distraction or blowing up small things.

4 Strong pain killers (ketorolac)

2 Ibuprofen 600mg tablets.

3 feet of thin, galvanized wire.

Folding box-cutter blade.

Small button compass. These are available at dealextreme.com.

Salt for treating dehydration, or making saline solution in the bag to clean wounds.

Four Band-Aids: two small, two medium size.

About five needles of different sizes.

One big button for fixing pants, bag and such.

One epoxy cloth Band-Aid (Poxita brand) Good for fixing everything from torn shoes to a hole in the tent.

One piece of fine grit sand paper. For sharpening the blades included in the kit.

Nine feet of unbreakable black nylon thread.

Nine feet of thread in OD green. Fixing gear and clothing.

Nine feet of waxed dental floss. Also have a big needle to use it to fix stuff if needed.

Four one-peso coins. For phone calls, vending machines, bus, subway.

(Four pesos will also buy you a hotdog in some of the cheap places, or a Coke or a bottle of water.)

Fifty USD. Some emergency money. Dollars are readily accepted most of the time, or someone will be willing to change it for local paper money.

Why not include local paper money? Because our peso is much more volatile than the USD (even with the world crisis).

If your pocket allows it, a small gold coin might not be a bad idea. This gives the maximum value for the minimum size, to pay an emergency bribe etc.

Water purification pills. Not enough space for a vial, but some can be added to the Ziploc bag.

Five large safety pins, hooked together. This is an easy way to hold a broken zipper together until better repairs can be made.

Today while eating dinner, I was thinking about this particular chapter I intended to write. I'm no farmer and I know as much about the technical aspects of food as the next guy that is into survival and preparedness. Hell, I've never eaten five-year-old rice: We eat food around here long before it gets that old.

We were having meat and potatoes, which isn't exactly my son's favorite food.

"I don't like meat!" he stated.

My wife counterattacked "Does it look as if I care? You have to eat it, like it or not!"

This little discussion carried on for a few more seconds, which is what most parents expect to be normal behavior from a six-year-old that does too much physical activity yet isn't fond of eating too much, therefore is healthy but as thin as a stick.

Yes, what most parents would expect. But I'm not most parents, just like my son isn't like most kids. If you ask my opinion, the average "anything" is pretty pathetic. I demand more of myself, and I demand more of my family, my wife and kids.

Egocentric and self-centered? You bet. "Pressure makes diamonds," said General George Patton, who won World War II with that attitude. My wife and I use General Patton's quote often. After all, if there's one thing Argentines in general are used to, is psychological pressure, and yes, sometimes it makes diamonds. Some other times, it simply crushes people.

My son really didn't want to eat it and he was just about to cry, something that he managed to control a bit given the other rule in my house: You are only allowed to cry if a significant portion of your body, such as limb, is hanging off and about to fall amputated, or if you are dead.

Since dead people don't cry, you are only allowed to cry if you lose a limb.

So instead of doing what my old man would have done, which would be a line such as, "eat or else I'll kick you ass," which by the way works like magic, I used a more "civilized" approach, and explained to my son WHY I would certainly kick his ass if he didn't eat his food.

"You don't like meat, so you don't want to eat?"

He shook his head, meaning no, he didn't want to eat.

"Okay, come with me."

I took him to my computer and sat him on my lap in front of the twenty-inch monitor. I looked up a video of "Barbarita," and played it for my son.

Barbarita was an eight-year-old girl that was interviewed in 2002, and shocked the entire country. I can't measure the impact those seconds of film had on our society.

No one in this country with an ounce of brains could ever forget that starving girl. It was a milestone, and an important factor that would trigger further social revolt and the realization of how poor we really were now, as a nation.

It was a plain and simple no BS fact to my son: kids are starving to death in YOUR country, and you just saw it on the eight o'clock news.

So, my son and I were in front of the screen. The clip started. The skinny little girl in her white school uniform smiles next to another boy of somewhat similar age as the woman reporter starts asking questions.

Reporter: What did you eat this morning? Right now, you were eating something?

Barbarita smiles. "A tortilla."

Reporter: "And yesterday for supper?"

(Barbarita's smile starts to disappear as she starts to cry.) Barbarita: "Nothing."

Reporter: "Now that you're going to school, do they give you food?"

Barbarita : "No." Barbarita starts wiping the tears from her eyes.

The shocked reporter asks a stupid question. "Are you sad?"

Barbarita: "Yes." She cries for a couple seconds.

Reporter: "What are you thinking? Tell me."

Barbarita: "We haven't eaten anything. We don't have any money."

The scene is cut and then continues. The camera is close and you see that Barbarita is not only thin: She's skin and bones and her skin is a grayish color. Her big eyes are set deep into her skull and you can see wrinkles around them.

Reporter: "How old are you?"

Barbrita: "Eight."

The reporter asks her last stupid question, and Barbarita's reply puts a significant nail in the coffin where the future of this country was buried.

Reporter: "What do you want to be when you grow up?"

*Barbarita: "**Nothing**."*

That was in 2002.

In 2003 Barbarita Flores was hospitalized again for malnutrition. She weighted 22 kilos (48 lbs), when her absolute minimum weight should have been 30 kilos (66 lbs) according to her height.

So as the 49 second clip ends I look into my son's eyes and tell him: "That little girl, she has a right to cry because she's starving to death. Do you have a right to cry like a little brat?"

"No, Daddy."

"Do you think I'm going to let you throw away your food, while that little girl starves, while a dozen kids die of starvation in our country every day?"

His head moves again, to say no.

"Go finish your dinner."

He went and ate up. I doubt I'll have to do that again any time soon.

That's what I do know about food, and that's going to be my contribution to the discussion.

After that came hyperinflation, the empty shelves at supermarkets that would give me the creeps, the farmers' crisis and tomatoes reaching the highest price ever registered, worldwide.

All this in a country of just 44 million inhabitants. All this in a country that still produces food for 300 million people. All this in a country that until not long ago was known as "The granary of the world."

Water is of greater importance from a wilderness survival point of view. After all, you'll die sooner if you don't have water, than if you don't have food. But when it comes to modern survival you can see that water, although scarce as it is, isn't that much of a problem when compared to food.

After a crisis food is even harder to come by, and it's far more expensive.

Even in the wilderness, finding a river or other relatively clean water source isn't that hard in most places, while food is much harder to come by. Think about it in terms of losing your job. Most likely you can still pay for water but keeping the pantry stocked will be much harder.

Even without electrical power or natural gas, you can survive in your home for a long time. Supposedly it takes three weeks for you to starve to death. Try going without eating for just a couple of days.

Three days is the maximum I've ever spent without eating, just drinking water. After that my reflexes weren't that good and I canceled my little experiment because I had to drive everyday.

There are three degrees of malnutrition.

Stage One: Deficient nutrition. You are missing certain minerals and vitamins. If this goes on for some time (a couple months or more) you may start having skin problems, wounds inside the mouth, and feeling more tired than usual.

Stage Two: 20% loss of weight. You eat little food and it has little nutritious value. You are mostly eating bread and some pasta. Pasta is the most common food among poor people, but it lacks the proteins, calcium and iron your body needs. From this stage, it's still relatively easy to heal the patient with an adequate diet.

Stage Three: In most cases the child in already malnourished before he's even born. This is due to the mother being poorly fed herself. There is a 40% weight loss, and if the child survives the first two years of life without being properly fed, the neurological damage is irreparable.

A child crying because of hunger and asking for food will turn parents frantic.

The famous soccer player Diego Maradona still remembers how his mother would say that she had a stomach ache when it was time for dinner, so she would not eat and she could leave more food for her children.

Pray that you'll never have to go through such a situation yourself.

Pray, and stock up on food now. The more the better.

WHAT FOOD TO STORE

The rule of thumb is to store what you eat. If you don't do it already, well, get started. Food is cheap and plentiful now, so don't wait until after a crisis.

You don't need MREs (Military Meals Ready to Eat) or other fancy stuff for your home food supply. The food found in supermarkets will do well enough. You just need to learn which products have longer shelf life and store them in a cool, dry, dark place away from rodents and insects. Check the basic food groups and make sure you've got them covered. You need to eat carbohydrates, proteins, lipids, fiber, minerals and vitamins.

Here are some of the things we store and eat:

Tang Orange Drink powder: Lots of vitamins, and at least it gives water some taste when having dinner. You can store it for a couple years, though I doubt many vitamins will be there. Just the sugar and orange flavor, I guess. Try to rotate this according to its expiration date to make sure the vitamins are there when you need them.

Tuna. Canned and in tin foil. We love this stuff. Especially in the tinfoil pouch which is also light, for keeping in your bug out bag. Get the tuna in oil since it has more calories and lipids. Tuna has lots of proteins, omega three, it tastes good, and you can mix it up with rice or lentils for a nice nutritious meal. Canned tuna will easily last three years without losing its flavor.

Rice: This grain keeps the Chinese nation fed, along with many other Oriental nations. It's estimated that 50% to 80% of the calories consumed by the Chinese comes from rice. A rice stew is easy to make using any leftovers that you may have handy. You can combine it with many other foods.

Brown rice has more fiber but it goes rancid somewhat quickly because of the fats in its outer layer. It's much healthier than white rice, but it doesn't store as well, so use it within its expiration date.

The only way in which you can solve this problem is if you store the brown rice in a Mylar bag inside a food grade bucket. Placing several oxygen absorbers within a well sealed bag, the fatty acids wouldn't have any oxygen to oxidize. This way it should store for years. The key here is not letting oxygen oxidize the fatty acids.

White rice has this outer layer removed. It's not as nutritious, but stores much better and is still a good overall source of energy. Kept dry and out of the reach of bugs, it will store for years.

Dehydrated mashed potatoes: I like this stuff a lot. It stores almost indefinitely as long as it's kept dry. The ancient Incas used to make something similar. "The Incas had an interesting way of dehydrating potatoes. Small potatoes were placed outside on the ground at high elevations to freeze during the night. The next morning the potatoes would be gathered into piles. The men and women would stomp on them which would cause the water to squirt out. When they wanted to use the dehydrated potatoes they would just add water." http://coe.fgcu.edu/STUDENTS/WEBB/MESO/incafood.htm

Potatoes are ones of the basic food staples around the world. A lightweight package that stores almost indefinitely and just needs water? Priceless!

Pizza mix: It stores well, it's cheap, looks like ordinary flour, and you just need to add water, tomato sauce and some cheese. Not as easy as frozen pizza but easy enough for me. The pizza tastes better than anything you buy from the store, and I don't need a freezer to keep it in. At least this particular brand I buy tastes better than the one I make myself with flour.

Lentils: If you can only eat two or three staples, make sure lentils is one of your top choices. It's one of the most nutritious foods in the planet, and it has lots of health benefits. Health magazine has selected lentils as one of the five healthiest foods. Protein, iron, calories, fiber, dietary fiber, vitamin B1, and minerals: lentils have them all, or at least most of them covered.

Dried Pasta: I suppose many poor countries are basically fed on one kind of dried pasta or another. A plate of dried pasta with tomato sauce will keep your belly full and your body going for another day.

Many children here have been living for years on dried pasta and little else. It's cheap too, and it's easy to find and store for long periods of time.

Tomato Sauce: This is one of those things you need mainly to give taste to most of the other staples you have. I use tomato sauce a lot. I use it on my pasta, pizza, lentil stew, tuna and veggie pie mix. It stores pretty well too, due to its acid content.

Tip: (85 yr old grandma tip.) If the tomato sauce tastes too acid, half a teaspoon of sugar will fix it.

Frozen meat: I keep canned meat and a lot of tuna, but fresh meat is important for your diet and you either have to freeze it or have your own critters in your backyard for when you need them.

I keep it in Ziploc bags, with three portions of meat in each. (Three family members eat meat). Organizing it this way makes things a lot easier. Most of my freezer is full of meat, frozen vegetables, and some bottles of frozen water.

Dulce de Leche: Sometimes called "milk caramel", this is probably something you never tried before but it can be considered a basic food item around here. People mostly eat it on bread or crackers for breakfast. It's simply boiled condensed milk with sugar added. Brown, with a thick texture. Most Americans that try it find it to be a bit too sweet, but it's a terrific source of fat, calcium, protein and carbs to boost your energy.

It can be bought at specialty stores or you can make your own by punching a hole into the top of a can of sweetened condensed milk, then leaving it in a pot with two or three inches of boiling water. Add water to the pot as needed so you don't burn the milk. This is known as "bain-marie" or water bath. Once the condensed milk turns brown, usually after two or three hours, you've made Dulce de Leche. Once it's done you can add a couple drops of vanilla extract, mix and let it cool before putting in the fridge.

Sweetened condensed milk: A great product, since it basically stores milk for many years. Contains a lot of calories, protein, fat and carbohydrates. It was used in the U.S. Civil War as a field ration.

Flour: Nothing you don't already know about flour can be added. Just have enough around. I used to buy a pack every time I went to the supermarket until I built up a nice supply, and then I rotated it.

Mate, and mate implements: I don't think many drink mate outside of South America, except for maybe Vigo Mortensen, who lived here most of his childhood and doesn't go anywhere without his mate. According to what he said in an interview, he usually tries to find another Argentine to drink mate with on the set during his films.

Some say mate has all the minerals your body needs to live. I don't know if that's true or not, but poor people drink a lot of mate, that's for sure.

It's also kind of therapeutic. You calm down a moment and sip some mate, alone or with friends, in which case you always share mate. Not sharing mate with your friends is pretty much an insult, and don't even think about mentioning spit and germs, you might as well say you are getting a sex change operation next week.

Remember to store enough salt, sugar, tea, coffee and chocolate.

Powdered milk and vegetable oil will need to be rotated more often. Low fat powdered milk stores a bit better.

Don't forget to add lots of canned and frozen vegetables.

HOW TO COOK AFTER THE SHTF

What we use most often here in Argentina for cooking is natural gas. Many people out of Buenos Aires city don't have an electrical power connection, so they already depend on bottled gas for cooking and heating.

This is pretty primitive but the good thing is that many people are already used to using this bottled gas and the logistics and distribution points are already in place.

The Argentine version of barbeque, called "asado", is a deeply rooted tradition so pretty much every man (and most women too) know how to prepare meat and vegetables cooking over an open fire, either wood or charcoal.

If you are an Argentine guy that can't start a fire and cook meat with it, and you have no problem admitting it, well then, you might as well get it over with and have a sex change operation done.

Tip: Argentines are rather resourceful people. One thing I've seen done on the street is improvising a grill using a shopping cart. The side that swings inside is removed and tied in place with wire to the inside of the cart as the grill. The burning wood goes inside below the "grill" and the ashes simply fall to the ground. You can even move the grill around thanks to the wheels, or use it to carry stuff around like homeless people do.

A guy I saw used this improvised grill to prepare sandwiches right there on the spot outside factories during lunch time. He sure wasn't making a fortune but apparently he earned enough to get by.

Boiling some water in a small pot or metal cup is no big deal.

I've done this a lot when camping; placing three rocks as supports separated by an inch or two and then starting a small fire in the center. This works well and requires very little wood to get water boiling. Most of the time I just used a few twigs and small branches to prepare dinner in my metal cup.

The more "confined" your fire is, the less wood it requires to get water boiling, and the more fuel efficient it is. Also the less smoke it emits, and therefore the less noticeable it is to strangers you might not want to meet.

It's a good idea to have several ways of cooking food at home. Remember that three is two, two is one and one is none. If you use natural gas in your kitchen, also have a microwave and an electric oven. Most people have microwaves but those little electric ovens are sometimes overlooked and it's yet another alternative.

For boiling water there are those little gadgets that have a heating element and a cord that uses normal household electric current. They are small, inexpensive and it's a smart idea to have a couple around. Remember to keep one in your car kit and maybe your Bug out Bag (B.O.B.), too.

A BBQ grill that uses charcoal or wood can be handy for flipping burgers on weekends, but also during emergencies when there's no power or natural gas.

Also get a camping stove, one that uses propane and another one that uses several types of fuel. These aren't that expensive, they can be used for camping and they also prove invaluable during emergencies. That's money well spent.

Something that I like a lot are iron wood-cooking stoves. Here they are called "Economic Kitchens," and they are mostly used in the country.

These iron cooking stoves can heat large rooms, cook food, some even have hot water reservoirs or can be hooked up to heat water for other uses. And it does it all using wood and an extremely simple technology.

I would seriously consider buying one of these for my home, though they turn out to be much more efficient when the entire house is designed around it and the many advantages it provides.

EDIBLE GAME FOUND IN THE CITY

For a while after the 2001 collapse some of the poorest people in the country ate just about anything they could get their hands on. In the city of Cordoba, people ate all the ducks that were to be found in the city's public park that were kept there as "decoration." In Buenos Aires, game was even harder to find and people just ate anything.

Cats: The meat of the crisis champions. All of a sudden all those street cats just started to disappear. The rumor spread: "Cat tastes almost like chicken," and soon cat became the other white meat among the poor. I never tried cat myself but it's supposed to taste okay. With some rice and tomato sauce, cat stew doesn't sound bad at all. Not when you're starving.

Doves and pigeons: The big fat ones found in parks are usually called "winged rats" because of the amount of diseases some of them have. The meat is tender and tastes good. This critter is plentiful in most cities and you can hunt it easily with an air rifle. Kids here kill them with slingshots too. The only problem with pigeons is that, especially in the cities, they can carry a number of contagious diseases, so they wouldn't be my first choice. Try hunting them outside of the city, and throw them away if the bird looks sick. Clean them very well and cook or better yet boil them for a long time. There should be NO red spots of blood when you cut the meat. This is important for all meats.

Dogs: People say the meat tastes rather bad, kind of hard. Not a number one choice, but if it's well cooked it's still meat. This kind of tougher meat is best suited for stews. Cut the meat into small cubes and boil it for a long time with rice, beans and tomato sauce. Then again, a guy interviewed on TV right after the crisis said he prepared a killer "dog asado."

Rats: Avoid rats. Unless you are FAR away from cities, avoid them like the plague. Maybe those little country mice are safer, but then again, if you are that far out into the country you should be able to find much better wild game than rats and mice.

City rats have a number of deadly diseases and the risk of catching one is too great in my opinion. Rats found in the train stations and subways of Buenos Aires are as big as cats. I've seen those ugly critters in broad daylight since there are so many of them. The ones in Buenos Aires are known to have Hantavirus, and we have a few cases of people getting sick with it every now and then.

Did people eat rats after the crisis? Yes, they did. They cleaned it EXTREMLY well, making sure not to contaminate cooking utensils, hands and clothes, and cooking it until there's no juice left. Do I recommend eating city rats? Hell no; unless you are starving to death, the risk you are taking is too big.

Squirrels, raccoons or any other animal you can catch and eat is fair game when you are starving. Cook them very well to be sure.

If things are that bad and you end up doing any of this "city hunting," get yourself a nice cat, or go looking for some healthy pigeons.

Be careful when gutting the critter you caught. You want to cut off the head and paws/wings, cut away the testicles. Cut an inverted "Y" in the lower torso, another "Y" for the upper extremities so you can skin the animal. Open the abdomen vertically being careful not to cut the intestines and other internal organs. Then cut the upper membrane and remove lungs, heart and windpipe. Remove everything and wash with lots of purified water, preferably water with some extra bleach on it. Certain animals such as cats and dogs have glands near the anus and you want to remove them or else the food will taste pretty bad.

When preparing a stew, it's better cut the meat into small cubes and leave the carcass behind. You can use the carcass for some soup if you are really hungry.

Whatever you catch, clean it well and make sure to wash your hands, clothes and cooking implements very well so as to avoid indirect contamination. Cook slowly for a long time.

YOUR WATER

You don't fully appreciate water until you need it and don't have it.

Even if it's a scarce commodity around the world, water is readily available to most people in first-world countries, so they don't understand how precious it is.

I remember once while biking through the Seven Lakes trail, on the Argentine Patagonia, I came across a couple of backpacker girls.

As ridiculous as it was (given the name of the trail) they were seriously dehydrated and could hardly go on. They were very inexperienced hikers and they had just brought a single liter of water for the two of them. Since it was summer, that wasn't much of a good idea, especially since it takes several kilometers of mountain trail to go from one lake to another.

They were very grateful for the liter of water I gave them, and I told them where to find water nearby. Hell, I don't think they even had a map or knew how to navigate. It looked as if they just followed the trail.

During an ordinary day in the city most people probably drink about 1/4 gallon or less, but in the summer and when working hard, especially if you're going to be under the sun a lot, expect to drink up to two or three times as much on average. Add to that the average water you need for some meals, and you need at least a gallon of water per day.

Now, in your home, you'll also need water to brush your teeth, prepare food, and wash your hands a couple times a day. You'll also need to flush toilets, wash the dishes, and take showers.

Laundry will require a lot of water, so you might want to put that on hold until either the service is restored of you find another source of clean water.

Expect water outages after a crisis. Plan for them. Water is too precious to waste on washing clothes until you have a steady supply of water available.

STORING WATER

The good news is that water stores rather well.

As long as it's kept in a clean, dry, dark place in a sealed container, water will be good for a year and beyond. You should consider replacing the water after a year or so because, even though okay for drinking, it will start tasting a bit like plastic. Besides, plastic is permeable to certain bacteria so it's better not to risk it. Renew your stored water every once in a while, when the service is on.

Since Y2K and 9/11 there's been a renewed interest in everything related to survival and preparedness, and that includes water purification and storage. There are a lot of gadgets out there. There are thousands of water containers of every possible size, even huge bladders the survivalist would supposedly fill up before he needs it.

The part I still don't understand is how would Mr. Huge Water Bladder know there's a crisis or SHTF event coming? Generally, there's no warning. You just turn the faucet and nothing comes out, or dirty water trickles out. That's how we learn we're out of water.

Of course I never had any of these things before our crisis struck.

There are some nice big barrels where you can store a lot of water, and they're a good idea if you have the space. Just keep in mind that a two-liter plastic bottle is much more practical for washing your teeth, hands, or cleaning the dishes.

Trying to do that with a five-gallon bladder or a barrel is simply impossible. You'll need a smaller, more practical container. Keep that in mind and don't learn it the hard way.

What I use is either two liter soda pop bottles, or five liter bottles. (One gallon =3.8 liters). In the USA, common sports drinks bottles like Gatorade bottles are perfect for water storage.

This is an inexpensive alternative and has worked well for me so far. I just rinse them very well with clean water and fill them up. Some people also add a couple of drops of ordinary household bleach (unscented, with no additives). This shouldn't be necessary if you are using potable tap water and you're leaving the container in a dark place.

The nice thing about the plastic soda or sports drink bottles is that you can store them in every little empty space you find around the house, as long as it's cool and dark. This is particularly important if you live in a small apartment where storage space is hard to find. Find sturdy cardboard boxes that fit them, and stack them up.

The soda pop or sports drinks bottles get used for drinking, washing hands, brushing teeth and washing the dishes. The larger five-liter bottles get used for preparing food and mostly refilling the smaller containers.

Using one of these square five-liter bottles, I improvised a showering device using a garden hose and sprinkler (twist on/off), some connectors and self-soldering rubber tape (one of the many uses for this tape).

I duct-taped string to the sides so as to hang it upside down from the shower, made a hole in the bottom to fill it up with warm water while I hold it upside down.

I had been without water for two days when I first tried it and man, my gadget worked great. It was barely enough to wash my hair, soap up and rinse, but being very careful, five liters is just enough. It also requires less fuel and time to heat up less water, so that's also an advantage if you have a limited fuel supply.

My wife has long hair and had to use a bit more water.

There are also vinyl solar showers sold in camping and boating supply stores. These have a clear side and a black side, and heat water by leaving them under the sun. They have a large hole for filling, and stand up to years of use. Even on cool days, they will warm the water after an hour or so of lying in the sun.

Eventually you'll need to use the toilet, and then you'll need to flush it.

I keep five-liter plastic bottles for water that will be used for flushing toilets.

Using half a bucket full of this water (or maybe a bit more, depending on how much toilet paper you use), you just pour it at a steady pace into the toilet. Water pressure does the rest, leaving it ready for using again.

But remember, you need to use the bucket for pouring. If you try to flush the toilet directly using the five-liter or one-gallon bottle, you'll find out that you can't pour enough water fast enough to flush.

You want to be careful with water and not flush it every time you go, only when solids are involved or when things start getting smelly.

For larger water containers, there are 55 gallon barrels. These should be set with a faucet for ease of use and the water inside should be replaced with fresh water once a year.

It's better if they are a few feet higher than floor level, sitting on a frame made from a couple of 2x4s, so they can be used by gravity.

Military-style five-gallon or twenty-liter GI plastic Jerry cans like the ones made by Scepter are very tough containers.

Just remember to keep smaller, more practical containers as well. Especially don't throw out those nice sport drink bottles. They are great after a crisis.

HOW MUCH WATER DO YOU NEED?

The average American uses fifty gallons of water a day, but this is mostly used in cleaning the house, watering the lawn, the washing machine and the bathroom. Keep in mind that each flush of a modern toilet in the USA uses 1.6 gallons of water, an amount that can be reduced significantly if you flush it yourself using a bucket of water.

The amount of drinking water a person needs will vary depending on age, weight, climate and the kind of activity you do. During an average day with little physical work, a person will require six to eight glasses of water, at eight ounces to a glass. Most people don't drink that much, but you also have to take into consideration that some foods have a lot of water already in them.

Also keep in mind that most people don't drink as much water as they should and spend their day slightly dehydrated. Dehydration reduces performance significantly. The military learned that the hard way and now closely monitors the amount of water their troops are drinking. Military water systems such as "camelbacks" have become standard.

Next time you feel headaches, are more tired than usual or have trouble staying focused and concentrating, try drinking more water instead of swallowing pills. It's very likely that all your need is more water.

If you are doing a lot of exercise or are walking and running all day long under the sun, expect to drink at least a gallon per day, and probably more. Again, this depends on many factors, such as age, gender, weight, and how much salt you already have in your body.

Salt prevents dehydration and it used to be a valuable commodity in desert regions. Entire caravan economies were based around salt transportation. If water is scarce, eating food with enough salt will help you retain more water.

How do you know you are dehydrated? Well, before more serious symptoms like headaches and nausea begin, you should take a look at your urine. The darker it is the more dehydrated you are.

Ideally, your urine should be as clear as the water you drink. During the morning it's common to see it a bit straw colored, this is because you just woke up and spent several hours without drinking. But, during the day urine should be as clear as water, and that's a sign of being well hydrated. If it's getting dark, take this as a serious warning.

Okay, so how much water should I store?

On average, make it a gallon per person per day for drinking, preparing food, cleaning the dishes and brushing your teeth. This gallon per day is your basic just "staying alive supply." Maybe you'll even afford a "sponge bath" if you are careful with it, but after a few days I wouldn't want to be your roommate, if you know what I mean.

You'll need to add another gallon for every shower and every flush you intend to make. Or else you'll only end up showering when it rains and going to the potty in a hole in the back yard, which is an alternative if things are that bad.

That will roughly put you in two gallons per person per day mode.

If right now you think you are poorly prepared in terms of water, allow me to be a total ass about it and tell you yes, you are. Everybody is, pre-crisis. Not having enough water stored ahead of time is one of the most common mistakes survivalists make. Unless you have a clean stream, river, or lake nearby, water will be your main concern if services are interrupted.

Having a water well should be a top priority for you, if it's possible where you live. And keep in mind that an electric pump will work only as long you have power or fuel for the generator, so that may be a weakness in your preparations.

There are wind and solar powered pumps, and they are a good idea, but try to have a backup for something as important as water. Technology usually lets you down when you need it the most, and that's a risk you shouldn't take with water.

Some wells can be fitted with old-style hand pumps, and it sure would look nice in the yard with proper decoration. They are simple and reliable.

During extended periods of time without water, a latrine or outhouse may be required since you won't be able to afford the luxury of wasting water flushing the toilet. If you have to improvise, remember to build a latrine far from the house, covering with earth and leaves after each use, or lime if you have it.

This would only be required in a rather unusual event, since even in third-world countries, the water infrastructure has frequent problems but it is usually restored sooner or later. Be smart, and prepare now for interruptions of water service.

A few days without water is something well within what you could go through, but be extra cautious and plan for at least two weeks of potable water, plus water for a few flushes and showers. If days go by and you see there's no evidence of the service coming back any time soon, you better have a source of water, or relocate to where one is available.

POTABLE WATER

A financial collapse sooner or later affects infrastructure, and that includes water treatment plants. Delivering clear, sparkling water to each house is no simple task. Not only do you have to treat the water, you have to make sure it arrives to each home in good conditions, and this involves complex and expensive maintenance.

"Complex" and "expensive" aren't words that go along well with SHTF.

The government, institutions and companies try to reduce costs as much as possible, sometimes beyond the possible, falling into the realm of "well, they're doing the best they can." Most of the time this just isn't good enough, so expect VERY bad services after the SHTF, IF there are any available at all.

In our case the water company came up with a typical post-2001 collapse solution. Why stop charging people for tap water just because we can't treat it well? Let's just dump lots of chlorine into it so that everyone doesn't drop dead because of bacteria and poisoning.

So that's the solution they came up with. The water has several times the maximum amount of chlorine any first world country would consider the maximum acceptable.

Besides, tap water is also contaminated with heavy metals and other chemicals. Our tap water bill in Buenos Aires has an absurd warning: "The water should not be drunk by pregnant women or children under 3 years of age."

Let's just say you won't feel like drinking a nice glass of tap water after reading that warning.

What I do, and what a lot of people do around here, is use water filters. Water filtering technology is constantly advancing and getting a good water filter should be a top priority for you.

I use one that is made by a reputable local manufacturer. It has silver impregnated ceramic filters that don't allow the growth of algae inside the filter, as well as using active carbon filtration.

This produces clean water, and removes most harmful chemicals, including the chlorine. Since the filter retains most of the chlorine and heavy metals, it has a limited life span.

My advice would be to buy a water filter that also has pre-filtering cups. You can have several of these, and if you replace them as required you'll make your main filter last longer. These cups catch most of the larger particles.

The ceramic filtering components (0.2 micron) are cleanable, but the active carbon gets used up and so does the silver impregnated into the ceramic. Even though they can be retrofitted for reverse flushing, there's no filter that will last indefinitely.

Do your research and look for the filter that fits your needs. Buy a spare one and a good amount of spare filtering cups, replacement cartridges and parts.

Buying a complete extra filter wouldn't be a bad idea. Heck, as long as it's kept new and in its original package, I'm sure a lot of people would pay nicely for your filter once the poor water quality becomes obvious and people start talking.

Camping filters like the ones made by Katadyn sometimes come with hand pumps and water bottles. These setups are practical for when you are on the move and have to scrounge for water. So you might want to keep one of these in your car emergency kit.

By the way, Katadyn is one of the best, most respectable brands. You might want to look into their products when doing research for an adequate water filter. Remember that it's not just for drinking. You should also use filtered water for cleaning and preparing food as well.

There are water sources you might be tempted to use that are rather dangerous and you should not use them.

*Car radiators. Most of these have poisonous anti-freeze and other chemicals. Stay away from it. You'll hardly ever find a car that has unpolluted water in its radiator.

*Water from the home heating system. With the amounts of mineral solids in it, and the anti-rust chemicals, you had better stay away from it.

*Water beds. They will have more chemicals than water in them. They have fungicides added to the water, and the chemicals in the vinyl may make the water unsafe. Use only as a last resort, after filtering as best you can.

*Water from the toilet. Water from the toilet bowl and flush tank isn't safe to drink either; the risk you are taking is too great. Better work at finding some other source.

TREATING WATER

There are a number of ways you can do it and while some are better than others, none are perfect. Before trying any of these methods try pre-filtering the water with coffee filters or several layers of clean cloth. Let's start with the most common method used in most third-world countries.

CHLORINATION

Chlorine is pretty cheap and has several uses, the most important one during emergencies being water treatment.

This is regular household liquid bleach. Look for one with 5.25 to 6.0 percent sodium hypochlorite, and stay away from the ones that are color safe, scented, or ones with added cleaners. Check the ingredients on the bottle; you don't want any added chemicals. Add eight to sixteen drops per gallon, or two to four drops per liter.

How much to use will depend on how polluted the water is and its temperature.

I've treated water this way while backpacking and found that four drops per liter was a bit too much for perfectly clean stream water. No matter how clean water looks, it should be treated because it can still contain e-coli and a number of other bugs that will ruin your day, or worse.

What you should do is add the minimum amount, eight drops per gallon or two drops per litter, stir, and let it rest for thirty minutes. It should have a slight bleach odor. If it doesn't, repeat and leave it for another thirty minutes.

Repeat until it does have just a slight bleach odor. If you repeat this procedure four times and the water still does not have a bit of bleach odor, discard it and find another source.

Bleach potency diminishes rapidly with time, so rotate your bleach storage at least once a year. Unlike other product expiration dates, bleach loses potency rather fast. Still, it's cheap enough and you can store several gallons of it, since it can also be used to clean and disinfect the house as well.

A bucket of water with a few squirts of bleach will help you keep diseases away from your home. This will be a mayor concern as the hygiene conditions in general decrease in the area.

BOILING

Boiling is a pretty good method since it only requires a metal container and a heat source. Still, you'll need fuel and, like chlorination, it does not remove harmful heavy metals or chemicals that may be in the water.

Use a lid to avoid losing water to evaporation. Bring the water to a rolling boil for one minute. Supposedly boiling alone will kill most harmful microbes, but keep doing it for a full minute as a safety measure. After you let it cool, stir and vigorously shake the water so it gets some oxygen back in again and doesn't taste "flat." This also works for water that has been stored for long periods of time.

You have to be cautious, not letting untreated water get in contact with the treated water in any way. This is a common mistake. People think that one method or another doesn't really work, but the problem is actually that they made a mistake themselves by either leaving a few drops of untreated water in a container and then using it to store the treated water, or using utensils with untreated water and then using those same utensils for cooking.

DISTILLATION

The methods describes so far will kill most microbes, but distillation removes the ones that are resistant, as well as removing heavy metals and most harmful chemicals.

The downside is that this method requires more time and a lot of fuel. This method requires using the lid upside down, with a cup or other smaller container tied to the handle so that it collects the condensed vapor.

The pot should only be half way full so the cup hanging inside is not dangling into the water. The water that drips into the cup is distilled and safe for drinking once it cools. For better results, you should combine methods, such as distillation and chlorination.

These are all methods that have been used for a while and they work rather well.

Chlorination in particular is used a lot in my country and has saved thousands of lives, since here we have cholera, e-coli and hepatitis, just to mention a couple of health threats. Many people can barely afford the bleach they use.

But is this something you want to do as a long term solution? No.

What many people do around here, including myself, is buy a good quality tabletop water filter. Accept that you'll need to replace it every once in a while (after three years or so) as a fact and get on with your life.

Some hardcore super survivalist may love chlorinated water. To me it tastes pretty bad, and even worse, it does not remove harmful chemicals and heavy metals which are a common problem in industrialized countries. By the time they are fifty these chlorine-iodine guys may have football-size tumors in their heads because of all of the chlorine they've been drinking. Chlorine is bad for your skin in case no one noticed it. The amount of chlorine suggested for water treatment will have effects on your body in the long run.

My friend, have several liters of bleach and rotate them, not only for water treatment but also for cleaning and disinfecting. But also spend the bucks, do your research, and get the best water filter you can afford. Buy several replacement cartridges for it.

Trust me when I tell you, it's worth every dime.

YOUR SELF DEFENSE SKILLS

HAND-TO-HAND FIGHTING

Just like most things in life, you'll have to train if you expect to be good at hand-to-hand fighting. With hand-to-hand fighting this is particularly true. Hand-to-hand combat is one of the things I know enough about to understand the difference between bullshit and reality.

During this chapter I'll do three things for you:

1) I'll help you gain the mental attitude you need to be a tough person in general terms, as a fighter and in all of life.

2) I'll tell you about some of the things I've done, where I invested time and money, and therefore save you time and money.

3) I'll give you a few pointers I learned to value, and that I'm sure will come in handy to you if you ever need to fight someone on the street.

THE RIGHT INSTINCTS

The local gun shop called "Gun Parts" is the place where most of the gun nuts in Buenos Aires can be found. People that choose to arm themselves for defense in Buenos Aires usually have interesting stories to tell.

Many of the guys you meet there have been shot at, have shot back in return, have killed people in self defense, and many have been wounded. And no, it's not Hollywood where the good guys always win. Some patrons lost their lives too, and at least one that I know of was sent to jail after killing home invaders, because he had the bad luck to come across a bad judge.

This guy I was talking to on this one occasion was pretty friendly. "Yes, I was carjacked on an exit off General Paz Highway. When I slowed down as I got off the highway, they pulled a blocking car across the ramp in front of me. Bastards shot me because I fought them."

My wife says I sometimes am as sensible as a brick; I guess that was one of those times. I looked at the empty space where the guy's right leg was supposed to be. "Dude, you only have one leg. Why the hell did you fight three armed guys?"

"Well, when they opened the door to drag me out I kicked one in the face with the only leg I've got. I kept fighting as they pulled me out. They threw me to the ground and shot me, pissed that a crippled man was giving them such a hard time"

He pulled his clothes down a bit and showed me a nasty wound right under the shoulder.

"One Legged Guy" should learn to choose his battles better, but you have to give him credit, he has guts. But guts must go along with brains. If three armed guys have the drop on you and you are unarmed, just give up the car and count your blessings.

The lesson here would be to always be armed, and never drop your guard. Start shooting as soon as a car forces you to stop. Better yet, not stopping at all would be better, but we'll cover that better in the driving chapter.

The point here was that this guy, in spite of being disabled had the will to fight, and that's the most important mental attitude a person interested in hand-to-hand combat should embrace.

The key is developing the drive to destroy your adversary. It doesn't matter if he's bigger, or stronger, those things matter but not as much as the heart.

It doesn't matter if you have a gun, a bat or your bare hands, you are going to damage that person's body as much as you can, as quickly as possible. I'm not saying you should enjoy killing these SOBs, but at least you could appreciate the fact that you may be saving an innocent person from being their victim in the future.

I often hear people going on and on about the emotional struggle and the moral dilemma of killing these scumbags…well get the hell over it NOW!

Don't you know what these people would do to you if they had the chance? Don't you know the number of innocent victims who have watched their loved ones being raped, tortured and killed while they were tied to a chair and helpless as babies?

Oh, I had a moral and emotional struggle all right. And I've settled that long ago by deciding that I'd give these bastards a quick death. And a quick death is more than what they deserve.

On the other end of the spectrum opposite from "One Leg Guy," we have what happened to some girls in their early twenties a few days ago in Belgrano, Buenos Aires. They were getting together Saturday night in the apartment of one of the girls. They planned on going out to dinner after that.

At 10:30 p.m., one of the girls went downstairs to open the outer door for her two other friends. When she opens the door, a big guy (well dressed with short hair) hurries and dashes in along with her two friends. When the girl who lives there asks him what apartment he was going to, he tells them that this is a robbery and that he has a gun. In spite of not having any visible weapon, the girls do as he says and he takes them all upstairs to her apartment.

One of the girls interviewed said that he was big and he looked intimidating.

Once inside, he ties two of the girls and leaves them locked in the bathroom. He takes the one he likes the most, the one that lives there, to the bedroom.

When she sees his intentions she asks him to at least use a condom, but Mr. Rapist prefers not to use one. He wraps a sheet over her head and rapes her.

The victim is terrified and completely under this scumbag's control, so much so that the rapist feels comfortable enough to go to the kitchen and eat some pie the girl had ready for her friends, and drinks most of the soda too.

All of a sudden the raped girl's boyfriend arrives. The rapist tells him to lie down on the floor of the bedroom and the boyfriend obeys. The rapist then rapes the girl again, touches her and humiliates the boyfriend some more.

Before leaving, he orders her to go to the bathroom and wash herself to eliminate any genetic material. She obeys him. Finally when he's satisfied, he takes all their money, cell phones, and the girl's skirt as a prize, and leaves the apartment with the girl's door key at five a.m.

Why didn't they defend themselves? Three girls against one unarmed guy in an apartment lobby sounds pretty even, especially in an apartment building full of other people. Why did the boyfriend do nothing, and let the rapist have his way with his girlfriend yet again? Why? Because these people lack the right mentality.

Belgrano is a fancy neighborhood of Buenos Aires. This is a place where people who have lots of money live. In general, you can tell they are "softer" than the people from the suburbs. They are less used to violence, and are more likely to act like sheep when threatened.

And remember: sheep get eaten by the wolves, people.

Regarding downtown areas and the suburbs, things work differently in Argentina. The downtown neighborhoods is where the police force is concentrated the most, where you find the most expensive houses and apartments and where they take better care of infrastructure in general. Other than a handful of exceptions, the suburbs are poorer in most cases, and much more dangerous. Like a living cell, they put all the effort and resources to keep the center alive and well, the heart going while the extremities are expendable.

YOUR TRAINING

There are few things that have as much BS thrown into them as martial arts, and unfortunately you'll notice how many times I use the initials BS in this chapter. Sorry; it's impossible not to with the amount of BS (there we go again) to be found in the world of martial arts and self defense "systems."

You find a healthy amount of BS in everything people do, but with martial arts it's a whole new level of BS. Right up there with fortune-telling and magic male enhancement pills.

It's not just Hollywood that's always feeding testosterone candy to the public, it's BS imported from the entire Eastern world. Jesus, the amount of Oriental bullshit sold to the Western world regarding martial arts is just too much. We should sue the bastards.

"Oh, I do Shaolin Kung Fu. I've been doing it for five years now and it's the best thing in the world. My master can break a ton of bricks with his pinky finger with his 'Pissed-Off-Hummingbird' technique. I'll learn it too one day, in twenty years."

"Ninjitsu is the shit! It's what ninjas did! My best friend's neighbor does that and he once beat an entire bar full of Marines. And after that be drank all the beer in the bar, ate the furniture and had a couple Green Berets for dessert."

You think I'm exaggerating? The saddest part is that I'm not. I'm trying to be funny but some of the things you hear people say are just THAT pitiful.

You should hear Kravmaga practitioners talk. They'll even say Kravmaga fighters get their butts kicked in every free style fight they participate in because their technique is just "too deadly for anything but the streets."

"Shhh... it's what Israeli commandos are taught," they'll say that in a low voice, so no one can hear this covert operations secret. They eat all of that bullshit up as if it was covered with chocolate syrup.

Thank God the Gracie family and their Brazilian Jiu-Jitsu reached international recognition in the 1990's and the Empire of Martial Arts BS started to decline. The Gracies had been practicing Jiu-Jitsu since the 1920's, but they had the courage to forge their martial art in Vale Tudo (Everything Goes) fights, where the BS factor is eliminated.

Plain and simple, for decades the Gracies fought in "everything goes" matches against boxers, wrestlers and karate experts. Everyone that had the nerve to go up against them was welcomed, and the great majority of them were quickly defeated.

What ended up differentiating Brazilian Jiu-Jitsu from the first versions of Jiu-Jitus and Judo was that since it was dedicated to fighting in Vale Tudo matches, it ended up specializing much more in ground fighting, since that's where most real fights usually end up. After that, "mixed martial arts" or MMA gained legitimacy and turned into a revolution, the fastest growing sport of the new century.

Of course, fans of BS martial art schools will try to deny its efficiency as real world hand-to-hand combat by saying, "It's just a sport." Well, to them I'd reply, "If you can't beat a guy in something as safe as the ring, what makes you thing you'll win when fighting for real for the first time (sport or not) on the street with your life on the line?"

Most people these days that are serious about hand-to-hand combat have accepted that cross-training and mixed martial arts are the way to go. There's really no one-fighting-school-fits-all scenario. You have to cover a few basics to be a good fighter.

If there's something we learned with "Vale Tudo" and the more civilized version of MMA, is that the better wrestler/grappler will generally win, but there's still the potential knock-out power of the striker, so punching, kicking, knee and elbow strikes are also important.

For grappling, you'll be hard pressed finding anything better than Brazilian Jiu-Jitsu and its great floor fighting. Boxers are hands down the best punchers, and Thai boxers bring kicks, elbows and knees into the game.

"Pankration" has been growing a lot lately and may well be the door through which MMA might end up in the Olympics one day. Pankration literally means "all powers" in ancient Greek, and it can be considered the first version of MMA since it combined boxing and wrestling.

If I'm giving the impression here that Brazilian Jiu Jitsu is the ultimate fighting system, that's not my intention. It might be great as a foundation for a MMA fighter, but not for hand-to-hand street combat.

My advice? First, learn to box. Boxing will give you quick hands, and you'll learn to punch well instead of relying on heel-of-the-hand or open palm attacks. While easy to perform, those aren't as good as the knockout potential you reach with boxing.

You've seen it several times on TV in boxing fights, MMA or even street fights: The guy's head just jerks, the brain bounces inside the skull, causing the brain to shutdown, and he falls like a sack of potatoes. Accelerate a guy's head as fast as you can. The head will move fast but unless you ripped the head off it will stop at some point. The brain inside that is mostly surrounded by liquid bumps against the walls.

The classic spot to try to hit in boxing, and the one boxers know well enough to keep covered, is the chin. Rattling someone's brain with a punch to the head requires a lot of strength, but a good punch to the jaw will level an opponent with less punching power being required.

There is a nerve in your jaw that runs through the lower part of the jaw known as the mandibular nerve. The nerves in your body are interconnected, so hitting one hard enough will cause a chain reaction.

Hit the jaw hard enough, and your opponent goes down. Go for the sweet spot, the chin. While chin grabs and other open hand techniques can be effective, few strikes are as effective as an uppercut or hook to the jaw.

"But I see boxers lose in UFC and other MMA fights."

That you do. But that's MMA, and I'm talking about hand-to-hand (H2H) street fighting. In street fighting you aren't trying to win a tournament, you are trying to stay alive.

Take for example street fights that occur during generalized civil unrest, like riots. A Brazilian Jiu-Jitsu fighter would take one guy to the ground…only to get kicked in the head by a buddy of the guy he was defeating. Or by many of his buddies.

A boxer that knows how to apply his H2H skills to the situation will set a very conservative guard, maybe take a few hits, throw a few punches, but mostly he can fight on his feet and "brawl" with a few attackers. Eventually he will buy some time and find an opening to escape from the generalized battle.

Thai boxing and Brazilian Jiu-Jitsu complete your striking and grappling arsenal.

Remember to keep it simple, and stick to a few well known strikes you use when full-contact sparring.

SOME BASIC POINTS ON HAND-TO-HAND FIGHTING

1) React violently.

MMA fights and other sporting events last several minutes. Street fights in most cases last only seconds. React fast and with the greatest level of violence. But don't go wild, losing focus on what you are doing. You still have to be 100% in control of yourself. Channel that violence into destructive power.

2) Keep you guard up.

Even world champions of all disciplines sometimes make that mistake. You'll see tough UFC fighters lowering their guard in a "come get some!" attitude... only to be knocked out with a punch or kick to the head, that even an amateur would have prevented just by keeping the hands up.

Even babies with only minutes in this world will throw their hands in front of their faces, instinctively covering it when startled. Stand well balanced, with your hands up, and that alone will protect you from the most common striking attacks and will make grappling harder.

3) Have a plan

This you need to practice endlessly against a heavy bag and in the gym when sparring. Your attacker has a plan. Maybe not a very smart plan, but it's much better than your plan, since in a surprise attack only one party knows what will happen in the next few seconds.

If your awareness level is high, you simply do not let people get too close without acknowledging them. If the place is crowded or if someone is getting too close, you already make a mental note of it and bring your hands up to your chest bone level. You are relaxed, but you are ready and the hands are close to a guard stance.

4) Expect the attack.

About 99% of the time it won't occur. But if it does you are ready, and that's something your attacker wasn't expecting. He still thinks you're a sucker.

You moved away or brought your hands up and stopped him. Now what?

Again, be fast and brutal. Punches, low kicks, elbow to the face, crush his windpipe, drop him with a Thai low kick. You need to practice a combination that will come to you naturally.

Stick to simple combinations with two or three attacks. Maybe a jab that pulls his guard in the direction you want, creating an opening, followed by a cross or elbow strike (if he's too close) and a kick to his legs to drop him to the ground. Work with what you know best. Practice your best combinations.

5) Stick to simple moves and strikes.

The "Drunk Monkey" may be a very deadly technique, but I prefer to keep it simple and effective. Jabs, cross, hooks and uppercuts, learn to throw them all. For closer range you need to be a good wrestler and grappler, but you can still strike with your elbow, knees, head-butt the attacker's nose, or slip in an uppercut that will bust his jaw.

A knee to the groin is effective if you can do it, if he leaves himself open.

When it comes to kicks, stick to waist high kicks and lower. Even if you are well trained and can throw high kicks, avoid kicks to the head or other kicks that take too much time to perform, or that may leave you too vulnerable. You often see people falling in street fights after kicking. Even in the ring or octagon it happens often enough. Your stability is more important, so don't risk falling to the ground. If you go to the ground, you are in very grave danger.

*At contact range if you are strong enough you can go for a Thai clinch, pulling his head down with your hands behind his head, and hit his face with your knee.

*If you only have one arm around his neck, use your torso's strength, bring him down and wrap that arm around the neck, bringing the back of his neck under your armpit in a guillotine move. There you can punch the face and attack the eyes. It's not pretty but it's effective.

*An effective attack, especially for weaker persons being frontally choked, is to simultaneously "clap" the ears of your attacker with the palms of both hands. Keep the fingers pressed together and slightly cup your palm. You are looking for an air tight clap. You will only get one effective try, so make it a strong clap!

This will burst your attacker's ear drums, causing pain and instability.

I first saw this done by a bouncer in a club when I was still in school. The bouncer just clapped the guy's head with great force. At first I didn't understand why the guy collapsed like a dead fly, but later I learned about this attack.

*Women that have longer nails can clench the fist and sink the thumb nail into the eyes or neck. A car key or pen would be even better, of course.

*Low kicks can be very effective on the street because the attacker will generally fall on a hard surface. Then you can follow up by kicking his head.

*Kicking with the outer edge of the shoe or heel to the side of the knee can cause a lot of damage or even break the knee. Unable to stand, your attacker will fall.

*Avoid using any kind of flying kick. Keep your feet on the ground. Preferably, both of them. You must not risk going to the ground.

6) There must be continuity in your attack.

Just like when shooting, you shouldn't shoot once and stop to see the results. Same goes for hand-to-hand fighting. You have to be fast and keep attacking like a whirlwind. You can (maybe) stop attacking when he's on the ground in the fetal position. Then again, depending on how dangerous the attacker is you might want to finish him with a soccer kick to the head. Especially if he is not alone.

7) Spar, work out, then spar some more.

The golden rule to developing good hand-to-hand skills is sparring. There is NO substitute. If someone tells your their system is "too deadly" for sparring, RUN from that place. You're just wasting your time and money.

Those people will want to make you believe that they can't win a fight in a gym, but by some miracle they'll do well when fighting for real on the street. Bullshit.

Just like with firearms training, even if it's not real combat you have to practice as realistically as you can. For hand-to-hand that means sparring with a mouth piece and gloves. You can't poke eyes, kick testicles or break fingers when sparring, but those are simple enough to do when needed.

You need to work out to build up your endurance. A strong body helps a lot in hand-to-hand combat.

Using the opponent's strength against him? That sounds beautiful but I'd rather be the one that can break the opponent's neck, thank you very much.

Mostly concentrate on upper body strength. You want strong arms, forearms, hands, neck and shoulders, both for doing damage and tolerating attacks and chokes. Believe me, a strong neck helps a LOT, and being able to crush the guy's windpipe with just one hand can come in handy in hand-to-hand.

8) Be tough enough to withstand a few punches.

You need to be able to take a punch or two. That only is achieved by sparring a lot. You may put your arms up to take a punch or two, just to take advantage of an opening, or grab an arm and go for an arm bar.

9) When grappling, go for the neck.

Yes, that thing that connects the head to the body. Break it, and your attacker is finished.

A rear naked choke is the most effective move since it cuts the blood flow to the brain. You get yourself on your attacker's back, and put your arm tightly around his neck. The crook of the elbow should be right in his windpipe. This arm's hand grabs the other arm's biceps. Your other hand is placed on the back of your attacker's head, the palm pushing forward. Bring elbows together tightly applying pressure to the sides of the neck, stopping the flow of blood through the carotid to the brain. Your attacker will go unconscious in about ten seconds or so. If you don't let go when he's unconscious you'll kill him, so practice this with extreme care.

When training, let go as soon as your partner taps out. Don't wait until he's unconscious. Let go right away.

I used this choke once very effectively against my sister-in-law's boyfriend. She was showing up with mysterious bruises and the guy was outspokenly proud of having beaten up an ex-girlfriend of his.

The guy didn't like me much and I sure didn't like him. When the fight started I quickly got him in a rear naked choke. I only let go of him when he started to pass out, after thinking of the legal consequences of breaking his neck. He sure wasn't worth going to jail for.

Sometimes you end up fighting in the last place you would have thought of. It's better to always be ready.

In a life or death fight you may want to speed things up by jerking violently and applying leverage between your arm and the attacker's shoulder, so as to separate the neck's vertebras. It requires certain physical strength but it's pretty darn effective. Do NOT do this while sparring or you'll actually break your partner's neck. Only do this when you must quickly turn to another attacker.

After the neck, your best bets are arm bars and Jiu-Jitsu wrist locks.

The Hammerlock is a pain compliance shoulder lock typically used by cops for handcuffing. The attacker's arm is held bent against his back, and his hand forced upwards towards the neck causing a lot of pain. That's why the suspect will willingly give up the other hand to get handcuffed. It's pretty effective and can be used standing or on the ground, and combined with choke moves.

SELF DEFENSE FOR WOMEN

Often guys are the most interested in weapons and self defense, and most women consider it a "guy" thing. There are numerous exceptions but this is the most common situation. In fighting sports, self defense classes and shooting courses the majority are clearly men.

I find this peculiar since women are a favorite target chosen by criminals. Muggers will usually go for women, then older people, children and finally weak looking men, in that order of preference.

Many of the self defense tactics that apply to men don't work for women. Most women are physically weaker than most men, and that means the problem must be attacked from a different angle, mostly relying on speed and the use of edged weapons.

You'll need to find a self defense instructor that specializes in self defense for women. Again, remember the golden rule: You need to spar a lot against non cooperative partners, especially men.

Tip: If after sparring for the first time you are not flat on the ground, you didn't do it right. Either your partner was a very weak man, or both of you didn't take your training seriously.

On the streets, if you lose you get raped or killed. In the gym, only your ego is hurt. You can live with that. Spar hard!

The most natural thing to happen in your first fight is to LOSE. And that's just perfect, that's what you need to get good at it. After losing a couple of dozen times you'll start doing better, and that's the edge you'll have when you go against a real attacker on the street without protective gear. You'll already know what it's like to lose and you'll have a good idea of what you need to do to win. An attacker will not expect to hit or grab a woman, and have her fight back!

The "Tigresa" Acuña, an Argentine lady that is the current feminine boxing World Champion, owes her long-lasting success to an outspoken little secret of hers: She fights male boxers in sparring practice.

She will fight against half a dozen men, one after another. Of course, after that, and she said this herself during an interview, fighting women boxers is very easy for her.

Even when you become good at self defense and you spar often, it would be wise to add weapons to your self defense tool set.

My wife, for example, was never much into self defense. But things have changed a lot and the humans' most powerful survival tool is their ability to adapt. Now my wife carries OC pepper spray and a Cold Steel folding knife all the time, and she has a great level of situational awareness that has gotten her out of many potentially dangerous situations.

A firearm is of course one of the best weapons you can carry.

If that's not an option, a knife and OC pepper spray are far better than just relying on your hand-to-hand skills alone.

RAPE

This is one of the most cruel of all crimes, and unfortunately it was a common one both before and after the SHTF in Argentina. Due to the overall feeling of lawlessness, the number of predators will grow significantly after the SHTF. Depend on this to happen.

Many crimes, including rape and murder, are perpetrated by someone that knew the victim well.

We had a serial rapist in the city of Cordoba that raped 93 women, before committing suicide when cops finally tracked him down to his home.

On one occasion I walked into my friendly gun shop looking for some more OC pepper spray and they told me they didn't had any left: It had all been shipped out and sold in Cordoba because of the serial rapist.

This year a series of rapes in the fancy neighborhood of Recoleta had many woman carrying regular serrated steak/table knives in their trendy purses for defense. While a small, sharp, serrated table knife is far better than nothing, a more adequate weapon is preferable.

There are a number of things you can do to avoid being raped, or to defend yourself better from this horrendous type of crime.

A twenty-year-old college student who was a rape victim herself has some advice for women. The rapist had already attacked thirty other girls on the same campus. This is the serial rapist I talked about before. She was one of the victims and wrote this before he was caught.

She sent her advice through email so that other women would be prepared. I'm literally translating most of her advice:

*Don't walk around alone, and don't ever let your guard down. The guy is loose and he knows how to handle himself, and how to talk to you.

*You have to be ready. If someone talks to you from behind or puts a hand on your shoulder, you have to scream. Run and hug someone nearby. Run into a shop or just run away.

*The rapist grabs his victims in public places, where if you react quickly, not only can you escape, but there's a good chance they can catch him as well.

*In case you can't scream, frozen by fear like when it happened to me, carry a whistle. Your vocal cords don't seem to work but you can still blow a whistle.

*Don't walk around at night. Better spend the money and get a cab.

* I took a bath, dressed up and walked towards my friend's house. There were a lot of people on the street that night. It was a nice part of town too. I realized there was a guy walking a few steps behind me. He told me something and when I tried to turn around he tells me not to look at him because he's going to cut me up.

*He put his arm around me, told me not to be scared, that he only needed me to pretend I was his girlfriend just to escape the cops that were looking for him.

*He took me to an abandoned place, there he told me not to scream because no one would hear. He put my blouse around my head, and touched me... It was denigrating, horrible, the most denigrating, terrible and humiliating thing that ever happened to me.

*Don't walk around alone, don't be trustful, always be aware. I suppose you are thinking, why didn't I run? At the time I couldn't react.

This girl has some great advice. I'd like to add some more:

1) Try to avoid wearing skirts. It's no guarantee but every bit helps, and pants are a bit more complicated than skirts. Rapists take this into account.

2) Rapists also like long hair for some reason. Probably because it makes it easier to take hold of the victim's head, to control her. If you have long hair, try wearing it in some hairstyle where it can't be so easily grabbed.

3) As the girl said, react. Preferably react violently. Rapists count on psychological submission. When the victim starts screaming, insulting him, pushing him away, in most cases they just run away surprised. Hopefully you'll have a weapon as well.

4) Even better than whistles, there are personal alarm and flashlight combo gadgets that sound off a high-pitched siren and flash when you push a button. This is even easier to use than a whistle, and you can have it in the pocket ready at all time as you walk around. If none of these are available there are small handheld marine boat horns that can do the trick. Some are no bigger than a deodorant spray and can be carried in the purse. These are some of the gadgets you should buy right away, along with OC pepper spray and a folding knife.

SELF DEFENSE FOR SMALL CHILDREN

Much of the advice mentioned above works also for small children and against the social predators that go after them. Unfortunately kids are often the victims of robbers and kidnappers too. Children are also much more likely to be helped by bystanders than grownups.

For them, the best strategy is to scream like crazy, kick, punch the genitals, cry out for help, and scream that "this is not my dad/mom!" The child must know to run away when the attacker is surprised by the reaction, and get help. The child must understand that it's okay to scream and cry under those circumstances, and not to be shy about it.

A personal alarm is a good idea if the child is old enough to assume the responsibility.

Not many of us ever suffered a gunshot wound, and if we are lucky, few of us ever will. But knives, we've all had accidents with them at one time or other. Everyone has been cut to a greater or lesser degree and can relate to the type of wound.

The itchy, metallic pain associated with knife wounds is something we are all familiar with and it comes to mind quickly when someone brings out a blade and turns it aggressively towards us. Simply put, people don't want to get cut.

It doesn't matter if it's a Swiss Army Knife, a broken piece of bottle or a fancy 200 USD folder, the fear of getting cut is the same.

It's also important to mention that, other than firearms, a knife is one of the most deadly tools a person can carry. This weekend for example, two men got killed with edged weapons during robberies in my neighborhood, Lomas de Zamora.

In one case a knife was used. The other poor fellow was stabbed with a screwdriver. This proves you can't simply ban weapons, because objects that can be used as lethal weapons are readily available or easily made.

Another factor to take into consideration: unlike firearms, knives are everywhere, and even in the most obtuse countries with the worst draconian gun laws, knives are easy to come by.

Any knife is better than no knife, even a kitchen knife if that's all you can get. The larger the better.

Women in the fancy neighborhood of Recoleta turned to carrying ordinary serrated steak knives in their purses and bags for protection against a couple serial rapists that stalked the area during December 2008. Some managed to acquire OC pepper spray but a serrated steak knife is more readily available and better than nothing, and I sure wouldn't want to get stabbed with it.

In Spain, as soon as I got to my parents' place, one of the first things I did was to go out and buy a good folding knife.

Knives will never run out of ammo, require no paperwork (at least in most civilized places), and used properly, you can defend yourself from several unarmed people.

If you also take into account the everyday use knives have, I simply can't understand how some people manage to not carry one at all times. Don't be afraid to buy a knife and carry it on daily basis if it's legal to do so in your area.

In spite of public opinion in some countries, it does not make you a criminal in any way, just a smart person who has the vision to carry one of the most useful tools man has ever known for defending against an attacker.

A good fixed blade or folding knife may be used for work and for defense, but I prefer to have a dedicated fighting knife on me at all times. This knife will only be used for self-defense, and since it won't be used for anything else its edge will be razor sharp when needed.

For everyday cutting tasks, I use my Victorinox "Spartan" Swiss Army Knife that also goes with me wherever I go. This saves the edge of my fighting knife.

For training you should use a knife similar to your fighting knife, preferably an exact same copy. This you'll use to slash and stab at a practice target. A board, pole or rags all tied up. Gauchos used to test their knives against hay bales. Be careful not to let your fingers run over the edge when stabbing!

For sparring you'll use chalked-up training knives to see where you "cut." For easy and fun training anytime, you can use old shirts and felt-tip "magic markers."

One could argue that using just one knife for all tasks including self defense would mean that if the time ever comes to use it for defense, you'll already be more used to handling it. That is indeed an advantage.

But I also found out that a knife used for everyday tasks will not be at its best during an emergency. More than likely, it will be sharp, but not that hair-shaving razor sharp you get from brand new knives made by quality knife manufacturers, or after a long dedicated sharpening session.

Personally, for a fight, I prefer the sharpest blade I can possibly get my hands on, one that will cut through clothing, fat, muscle and tendon like butter.

I've been carrying my Cold Steel "El Hombre" serrated folder (discontinued) in my front left pocket for twelve years now. I've been doing so on daily basis. As long as I have pants on, that knife is with me.

I have brought it out a couple times when threatened. On one occasion I was outnumbered two to one in a train car, but I suppose they didn't want to risk getting hurt, so they left and looked for a more defenseless victim.

CHOOSING A KNIFE FOR SELF DEFENSE

It's easy to get lost in today's nearly infinite variety of knives. The market is saturated with "tactical" and "combat" knives.

Some of these "tactical" knives cost several hundred dollars but aren't worth that amount of money. Some aren't even practical or they don't follow proven knife patterns and shapes. They just look neat. Of course they will cut. Any blade made of carbon steel and sharpened will cut well.

Just don't fall for looks and dear God, don't spend the equivalent of a quality handgun on a knife. Unless it's made of gold, it's not worth it.

There are thousands of books out there, and thousands of people get on line several hours a day on various internet discussion boards just to talk about knives, believe it or not.

I'll do my best to keep it simple, and as with everything else mentioned in this book, please, this is just the starting point. Do continue your research and investigate further so you can come up with your own conclusions and find what works best for you, in your location and your situation.

I'll give you some pointers though, so as to flatten your learning curve a bit and spare you some time based on my personal experience. This will save you from making some of the mistakes I did, even save you from simply wasting money on things that are not worth it.

1) Stick to quality brands.

It gets to a point where a blade enthusiast can tell to some degree the quality of the steel he's holding. He can tell if it's cheap stainless or quality carbon steel. He can tell if it's easy to sharpen and how brittle the material is when inspecting the edge carefully after use.

They can even tell to some degree the carbon content in the steel based on the amount of bright yellow sparks that fly when a grinder is applied to it or determining the hardness just by using a file and watching if it "bites" the steel or not.

I'm not talking about years of experience, I'm talking about decades. There's a reason why some blacksmiths spend they entire lives learning their craft and still keep learning at old age.

This probably surpasses the personal interest you may have on the subject. The best solution is buying recognized brands that have been in the knife business for years, such as Cold Steel, Ka-Bar, Spyderco, Gerber and Benchmade, just to name some of the most popular ones. These brands I just mentioned are top quality. Not exactly cheap, but still affordable.

There are many other brands that pretend to be "elite" and cost a small fortune.

Don't fall for this. Unless it's made of Kryptonite or has the soul of a reincarnated Samurai warrior trapped in its steel, you'll be paying too much money for something that is not worth it.

There's no magical super steel out there. Some of the best custom made knives that cost several thousand dollars are made out of a piece of steel that costs less than fifty bucks. You see, even some of the best quality steel is not worth a fortune.

So you should know that if someone is charging you several hundred dollars or even thousands, the steel itself is probably the same one used in a good eighty USD knife.

In some cases it's the guy's equivalent of buying a Bulgari handbag and spending thousands on it when you could have bought something much more serviceable and durable for just a fraction of that price, without the name tag.

What do I buy and use the most?

I like Cold Steel products a lot. They aren't too expensive, the steel is good, folders lock tight, the designs are generally well made and there's a nice variety to choose from. There are some exotic models I sincerely don't find much use for, but most of them are pretty good.

As of today, Cold Steel also produces a series of short machetes that are actually just large knives.

These come in several formats such as spear point, sax (saxon type, scramasax knife), Kukri and Bowie and cost less than thirty USD.

These are terrific knives at a very reasonable cost. Better than most of the "tacticool" knives out there that cost several hundred dollars.

Even if you can't find these short machetes, it is pretty easy to make one yourself. Just buy a carbon steel machete and cut it to a shorter length. Draw and cut the kind of shape you prefer. Since machete blades aren't too thick, they are easy to cut with a saw or with a hand grinder. I made myself a very nice one using a "Tramontina" brand machete. I shortened it a few inches and made a clip point. If you do this, be careful not to overheat the blade. Cut it slowly, with time for cooling, or you may destroy the temper of the steel. I did it with a bucket full of water next to me, dipping the blade in it to cool it often.

The clip point is much better for stabbing than the original Latin shape. This blade is now a very handy big knife that can be used for several tasks, including self defense at close range. There are of course poorly crafted cheapo copies that cost only a few bucks and don't look that bad, but keep in mind you are buying a tool that you may one day use to fight for your life.

As always, let's assume a nearly worst case scenario.

You end up fighting and wrestling with a big bad guy, who maybe has fifty pounds of advantage or more on you. You two end up fighting on the ground, and his buddies are closing in. These guys will kick and beat you to death in no time unless you do something.

You manage to bring out your folder, open it, and desperately stick it into the guy's rib cage. Do you want a cheapo blade that may snap under the guy's weight? Do you want a poor quality lock that breaks when you stab, folding shut and cutting your own fingers?

It's better to stick to quality tools, especially for those tools your life may depend on one day.

2) Get an effective fighting blade design.

The variety of models is mind blowing. Fixed blade or folder?

How long should the blade be? Curved or not? Plain edge, serrated, or a combination? Do I want a narrow dagger or something that reassembles a Tanto Japanese knife, or maybe one with a proven Bowie-style clip point? It's easy to get lost here.

There's probably a perfect knife for each individual, but since I've been collecting and using knives for as long as I can remember I'll express my personal experience and conclusion here.

Sticking to concealable defense knives, what should a knife be able to do, in my opinion?

I want something that, even though large enough, I want to be able to carry it at all times. This means I'll go for a folding knife I'll keep clipped in my pocket.

I want my knife to be able to both stab and slash.

This alone already excludes the models with certain curved or hooked blades that make stabbing very difficult or impossible, such as certain "claws", "corvo" and a few "karambit" models.

Don't get me wrong, some of these models are simply the best "slashers" you can get.

The knife fighter that first started teaching modern knife fighting in the Chilean military in the sixties, an inmate from the San Bernardo penitentiary, used his "corvo" to kill seven men during various fights, sometimes outnumbered.

The "claw" blade geometry ensures an important portion of flesh will effectively get caught. Such fantastic slashing ability sometimes comes at the cost of losing the ability to stab, and that's one side of knife fighting I'm not willing to give up, since you need stabbing penetration to reach many organs.

Relying just on slashing you will depend mostly on blood loss, which can occur rapidly if an artery is cut, but getting to the lungs and other internal organs becomes harder.

There are some blade designs that have a bit of a belly, a slight "S" edge profile.

In my experience, this "belly" noticeably increases the slashing power of a knife, digging into the material you slash, almost like a claw. The bigger the belly, the greater the claw effect you get when slashing. This is one of the reasons why the famous Ghurka "Kukri" knife is so effective.

After running some tests I came to the conclusion that this extra slashing power is significant enough to make a difference. No, I didn't try it on slaves or prisoners, but I did slash an old boxing bag full of rags just before getting rid of it. I used many of the knives in my collection and found out that of course, heavy knives would cut deeper, but when comparing similar size folders, the one with a belly, the "s" shaped blade would cut much deeper that the straight ones. You could feel the blade "dig in" instead of slipping along the surface.

The knife I used for this little experiment was a Cold Steel El Hombre folder, now discontinued but similar to the "Vaquero" line.

3) Go for a serrated edge.

As a utility knife, a straight edge is much more practical. It's easier to sharpen and it is more "predictable" when working with wood or other material. But for fighting the serrated blade is better in my opinion.

There's no significant difference when stabbing, but when slashing the straight edge may slip a bit more, while the serrated blade will "catch" onto the slashed surface much better, taking full advantage of the applied force.

FIXED BLADES

Fixed blades are of course harder to conceal but they do offer more reach, leverage for slashing and striking, and they look more intimidating as well. You might want to consider concealing a fixed blade if a firearm is not an option for you and your knife will be your only weapon.

I like the Tanto tipped blade better because they "punch" holes into the tissue, rather than separating it. When the blade is removed the sides don't just close in, but there's a hole left instead, one that will continue to bleed nicely.

If you can't keep a gun at home either, a short machete or a large bayonet will be the best next thing. Keep it sharp and learn how to use it. Machetes are still used as terrible weapons in many places of the world. It doesn't take a Samurai to hack someone in the head with it, both cutting and breaking bone.

KNIFE FIGHTING

The guy was barely moving at all, and that was astonishing, considering the amount of blood he had lost.

I remember thinking "So that's what five liters of blood looks like"

The pool of blood the guy was lying in was huge. The guy was full of small holes, with some wounds in his arms, and he had bled out pretty fast.

Of course no one worried much about the dying man. He was a prisoner after all, and maybe in a fancy first-world country there would be nurses or guards hurrying to help him, but in the San Martin Penitentiary in the Province of Cordoba, Argentina, no one gave a damn.

Maybe later when someone felt like getting his hands dirty, or got tired of having that mess on the floor, maybe then they would drag him to the infirmary. If he lived, good for him, if not, well no one really cared.

During more than two years I visited penitentiaries once a month, and got to learn a few things about how brutal people can be, and how people take for granted something as precious as freedom.

Knife fighting is brutal as nothing else is. A sharp object applied with rage against something as soft as flesh quickly puts things into perspective.

Gun shot wounds are much more "civilized" in comparison. Unless you are talking about head shots, and high powered rounds such as rifle rounds, most people can't even tell if they hit someone or not. Heck, sometimes the person that gets shot doesn't realize he's been shot for a while.

I've never met (or heard of for that matter) anyone that said, "Oh, look, that lunatic cut me up like a tomato. I just didn't notice it!" While shooting someone in self defense is much "cleaner," defending yourself with a knife is messy business.

There's going to be lots of blood. Forget about the movies where people get stabbed and just drop dead as if paralyzed or something. Unless you crush the skull with a heavy blade or somehow cut into the spine or brain, the person will keep fighting and screaming for some time.

The most common thing that makes a person drop in a knife fight is blood loss. Stabbing with a larger blade and compromising internal organs, causing tremendous pain and puncturing the lungs also work, but will depend on how persistent and driven the attacker is.

Either that, or the person who is cut will stop fighting as soon as he sees that a significant amount of life fluid is escaping his body. Effective? You've got that right!

The saying, "Don't bring a knife to a gunfight," only shows that the person saying so doesn't know much about the damage a knife is capable of. In very close quarters, the knife is a much more effective weapon.

It won't jam, it won't run out of ammo, and it's nearly impossible to take a knife away from someone that knows what he's doing. Against someone with a gun and at close range, the person with the knife has the advantage.

If you have a gun and you are facing a guy with a knife, don't doubt a SECOND about shooting him if he's within five yards or moving towards you. Maybe you don't know it, but at that range YOU are the one with the lesser weapon.

The "Tueller drills" used in police training prove what anyone with street experience already knows: An average attacker will cover seven yards in 1.5 seconds. If your plan is to just stand there, draw and shoot, even if you can do so accurately in 1.5 seconds, you have a wounded guy at contact distance attacking you with a knife.

If you didn't manage to make that shot, all he has to do is use one hand to keep the gun pointing away from his body and stab at will. Unless you drop the gun, now each of you has just one hand available.

One of you has an empty hand, the other has a blade. Guess who's not going home tonight?

For this chapter, I'll be using the book "Esgrima Criolla" (Creole Fencing) by Mario A. López Osornio, first printed in 1942.

It's a rare gem, since it contains lots of "Gaucho" fighting information. Since Gauchos were terrific knife fighters, I found this very valuable and was glad to see a lot of it verified with street and prison fighting information.

I also used "Put 'em down, take 'em out! Knife fighting techniques from Folsom Prison," by Don Pentecost. I was glad to see how it also confirms many of the things I learned on my penitentiary visits, in spite of a few minor differences I'll refer to later. It also confirms how similar basic human behavior is all around the world, and how instinctive fighting is usually the best.

Dear reader, the information on knife fighting isn't something an overly sensible person would enjoy reading.

I'll describe effective yet brutal techniques in full detail because that's what works and that's what will be useful to you if you ever have to defend yourself with a knife or other improvised edged or stabbing weapon.

Having said that, lets get started.

HOLDING YOUR KNIFE

"You know how you can tell if someone knows how to fight with a knife? My Ninjitsu master taught me."

We were waiting for our "Concrete Structures" teacher to arrive, at the Architecture University of Buenos Aires. My classmate, real estate dealer during the day, ninja wannabe two nights a week, was ready to reveal to me his ninja secret.

"How?"

"You hold it like this, see? With the blade coming out from the bottom of your fist and the edge towards the outside. The blade shouldn't be on the top side of the fist like you see most people do! If he's holding it that way, the guy doesn't know the first thing about knife fighting!"

As excited as I was about learning this mystical ninja secret, I couldn't avoid pointing out something: "Dude… that gives you NO reach at all with your blade. Rather the contrary, it gives you less reach than an ordinary punch or kick. Other than an overhead stabbing attack, it's also hard to stab and slash holding the knife that way"

Of course, my classmate reassured me I was wrong.

People, forget about intricate stupid tricks taught by "dojo ballerinas." Hold your knife as if you are going to cut someone to death with it. And you're not eating steak with the Queen of England either, so the "thumb rest" on some combat knives is only good for when making yourself a thong with the skin of the leopard you probably killed in your wilderness survival class.

Other than that, grip it as if you plan to have a corpse hanging on that blade. That means you're gripping the handle firmly with your balled fist, blade up, your fingers and thumb wrapping the handle as tightly as if your life depended on keeping hold of that knife. And it kind of does.

THE KNIFE-FIGHTING STANCE

Gauchos fought mostly for honor, and as terrific fighters as they are, this is something that shouldn't affect you as a practical fighter.

It's not about looking manly as you fight, but trying to get cut as little as possible while running off, wounding or killing the other guy, and being the one that lives to go home and kiss the wife and kids goodnight.

A Gaucho would stand fully erect and rely mostly on amazing reflexes, honed by endless hours of knife practice with sticks and true combat. It was cowardly to not stand fully erect and offer the gut for the other to come and try to stab it… if he had the balls. Oriental martial arts also have similar "honor" and "protocol," inherited from 1,000 year old traditions. You don't need that macho bullshit.

So, how should you stand?

You want a natural boxer's stance. That means feet at shoulder's width apart. If you are right-handed your left foot will be slightly forward, the right foot a bit behind and a bit perpendicular to your left foot. You are not looking for an exact 90° or 45° angle or any other angle for that matter. Everyone has a different body; you use what feels more comfortable for you.

Knees slightly flexed, well balanced on both feet. Eyes fixed on the opponent, but with your chin low, covering your neck. Your torso is slightly bent forward, so that your gut is a bit behind and less exposed, with your hands and forearms in front of you in the guard position. The important thing is to feel comfortable and well balanced.

One thing to keep in mind is to not hold your hands and forearms with the inside of the wrists forward, like some Thai kick boxers do. This exposes the veins in your wrists to a potential knife attack. You want a typical boxer stance with the knuckles forward.

There are a million little variations of the boxer stance and this is pretty typical and what works best for me. This stance is your all around stance for knife fighting and very similar to the hand-to-hand (H2H) boxer's stance.

Learn how to move around fast and without getting yourself tangled with your own feet. You'd be surprised by the amount of people that fall when trying to move fast. It's very common for people to fall when trying to hurry backwards, when you rush in and attack them when sparring.

Guys, there's no magic here. The key is sparring and more sparring with non-cooperative partners. I know a little about knife fighting and H2H combat in general, and I know that much for sure.

For knife practice, get rubber knives and chalk up the edges. If you're going to improvise wood knives, make sure they are not pointy or you'll impale yourself with it when practicing. Wrap it up with rubber, foam or cloth to avoid injury. It will also make the chalk hold better. You can even use felt-tip markers and old clothes for practice.

Check your local stores and EBay. The best thing is to buy practice knives. I'm just giving a couple of ideas in case practice knives aren't available to you.

KNIFE ATTACKS

There are martial arts where you can spend years assisting classes and learning a thousand different techniques. The saddest part is that someone that uses three or four simple moves and concentrates more on sparring instead will easily beat you none the less.

So don't devote you life to the Gods of Philippine, Chinese or Japanese martial arts. Just take a couple of knife fighting classes, learn the basic attacks and concentrate on two things and two things alone:

1) Stabbing and slashing the other guy when you have a knife.

2) Disarming the opponent with a knife.

These are the core tools of your knife fighting toolbox. These you'll practice with a NON-COOPERATING partner. Keep it VERY basic and concentrate on practicing these two things.

Learning the "Eagle's Claw of Destiny" ninja trick you use when fighting four guys, and one must be standing over here, the other one over there, and the other two must be holding hands and standing on one foot while looking East at your right is a total waste of your time and money. And if that isn't bad enough, you are not keeping things simple and basic as you should, and that can get you killed.

This is most likely a folder or smaller knife you carry around with you.

Typical small knives such as the ones used in prisons are very primitive. Some are effective because one thing prisoners have is lots and lots of time. They can spend days rubbing a piece of metal against the cement and getting it pretty sharp. But in most cases it's just a piece of plastic, wood, or even a pen or a screwdriver. They are just as deadly but mostly they are only good for stabbing.

This is not the case with a well made folding knife.

So, some pointers for fighting with your folder:

1) Keep it hidden for as long as you can. Hold your knife close to your body while you keep your "sacrifice" hand ahead, jabbing and creating openings.

2) Attack like a whirlwind. Slash and stab as fast as you can. Be brutal and quick. If you are lucky and your opponent is caught by surprise, you'll get a few good stabs in before he realizes there's more to those punches than your fist.

There's no "touch of death," and for God's sake, you have two hands so use them both! Only in BS fighting schools does an attacker stay put, while the defender works on disarming his knife hand. Just like in boxing, create an opening with your first attack, and strike with your second one.

3) Jab with your left hand, and kill with your right. (For right-handed fighters.) It's a basic boxing one-two. The guy you are attacking will move his hands to block your first strike, and you'll dig in with your knife in the second, quick strike. This should be a very fast one-two move.

The first jab goes right to the face (aim for the nose), where the person is instinctively inclined to bring his hands up for protection. Don't be a sissy; make your jab a powerful one, hopefully smashing the nose. The second attack, the knife thrust, goes right to his guts.

4) As noted in the book "Put 'Em Down, Take 'Em Out" by Don Pentecost, prisoners using a basic stabbing weapon will furiously work at quick multiple stabs when there's an opening. Don calls this "the stitching machine" and I couldn't agree more with the name.

It's a very instinctive, very effective attack. It's best applied when using knives that are good for stabbing but bad for slashing. Its efficiency is similar to a shotgun wound pattern, saturating the target with several puncture wounds.

5) There's a big difference between the prisoner's "stitching machine" or stabbing attack, and the classic Gaucho trick called "dropping the guts."

The convict usually fights with a crappy weapon that is just good for stabbing.

The Gaucho fought with the love of his life: A razor sharp "facón" knife.

The Facón is a very impressive weapon. Usually more than 14 inches long, it has a narrow tip and even if it's only a single-edged weapon, it has a few inches of the other side sharpened for better stabbing penetration.

What do you have in common with a Gaucho, that separates you from the prisoner?

You also have access to knives that can both slash and stab extremely well. Your folder isn't as big as the Gaucho's Facón, but if it's kept razor sharp, you can still achieve similar results.

For "dropping the guts," ("bajar las tripas" in Spanish) the Gaucho would slash a horizontal cut in the lower abdomen.

You stab to one side of the abdomen and furiously slash horizontally to the opposite side while the blade is still buried inside. This won't work with a prisoner's screwdriver, but it will work with a razor-sharp, high quality folder. What does this achieve? Cutting the abdominal muscle walls drops the guy's guts; it disembowels him.

That pretty much ends a fight, but it doesn't stop there. You adversary will now try to keep his guts from coming out with his hands, meaning he's no longer guarding his face. Attack the face, eyes and neck to put him down quickly. You have alternatives now, so be creative.

6) For weapons that combine good stabbing and cutting characteristics, you might want to use a different technique than the prisoner's "stitching machine" attack.

I'll call it "Stick and rip". After stabbing as deeply as you can, pull with strength in the direction of the knife's edge. This will create a deep and wide wound that will bleed freely, and hopefully will cut muscles and tendons as well.

This kind of attack is similar to "dropping the guts," but it can be applied to other parts of the body for different results. Since you don't know the exact location of veins and arteries, this increases your chances of cutting something that really matters, which will lead to the swift incapacitation of your enemy.

We'll cover that in more depth in "Where to strike."

7) Attacking the upper torso and above (the rib cage, neck and head) was done by the Gaucho when the intention wasn't to kill, but to "mark" his opponent, mostly to settle matters of honor falling short of a demand for his death.

Of course the neck is a very delicate and dangerous area, and so is stabbing through the ribs. But a slash to the face or chest, as serious as it was, would generally not be lethal.

Of the nine people killed by Juan Moreira in knife fights, three of them were wounded in the chest, while six were wounded in the belly. This goes to show how the abdomen can be a better target in general terms.

LARGER BLADES

By larger blades I mean around twelve inches and up, as well as short machetes.

I've insisted on the efficiency of the modified short machete a lot.

I do so because it's easily available, and very effective. Unfortunately many situations in Latin America and Africa show us how deadly machetes are even today. The Rwanda Genocide and the Congolese civil wars come to mind.

Larger machetes such as the Latin machete can be excellent choppers but poor stabbers. Shortening the length a bit and adding a clip point is easy to do and increases the weapon's overall efficiency.

Short swords and large commercial knives are also good weapons. Even larger butcher knives are very effective and require no modification. They also pass the supermarket test, meaning anyone can buy one in stores around the world.

Unlike the big butcher knife, the machete is specifically made to chop wood, so it's generally more resistant to breaking. It's cheap, easy to acquire and can be found in any store in the gardening section.

There are similarities with the smaller blades, but the larger blades have some characteristics:

1) Any woodsman knows that a bigger knife is better for chopping. This is also true in knife fighting.

The Gaucho used his facón (large blade) for one of the most effective attacks in his arsenal, called "achazo" (axing), or "Dios te guarde," (God save you).

A quick overhead downward chop to the head. Given the weight and size of a larger blade, there's really little that can be done to protect oneself from it.

Either moving aside or closing in fast are the only alternatives, and getting hit will cut deeply through flesh and bone, including your blocking arm.

2) Horizontal, vertical and diagonal slashes to head, torso and arms are very effective with long blades, and with practice it's easy to swiftly change direction and not lose momentum, with a fast series of "eights" being made in the attack.

3) Stabbing is slower than with the smaller blades, and doing the "stitching machine" requires lots of stamina. It might not be possible with a blade that is too big, but the heavier blade makes for much more deadly deeper stabs.

WHERE TO STRIKE

Knife fighting, just like in any other form of combat, requires a good knowledge of the human body. While all wounds should be treated seriously, some are more serious than others. The smart fighter will know where and how to strike.

The Gaucho considered the attacks to the gut to be serious business. Ironically, it was considered worse than a slash to the face.

The abdomen has no bone protection like the upper torso has, and a deep slash opening the abdomen and letting the guts pour out is a horrible way to die. Stabs to this same area may have less immediate "stopping power," but they are even more deadly, and the internal bleeding caused by several gut stabs assures a painful death.

Stabbing the liver is a serious wound. The liver is under the ribs in the right side, or you can reach it stabbing under the chest bone. Kidneys are also serious organs to wound and they will require quick medical attention. Kidney stab wounds are supposedly so painful that they cause immediate incapacitation through shock. Some special operations units teach stabbing the kidney as a method of killing a sentry from behind, because after being stabbed in the kidney a sentry will not even be able to scream. The left hand pulls the sentry backward off balance, while the kidney is stabbed with the knife in the right hand. Even in boxing, a strong, well placed "kidney punch" will result in KO and urinating blood later on.

The kidneys are located in the lower posterior part of the abdominal cavity. There are two, one on each side of the spine. For attacks to the chest you'll have to work your way through the ribs, or strike below the sternum.

I want to remind you, none of these are "death rays," so you still need FAST and MULTIPLE strikes, but at least you'll know what to stab and what to expect. There is NO quick and silent death in knife fighting, unless you push a dagger into the brain through the back of the head where the spine begins. This is easy to say, and about impossible to do in a fight.

Attacks to the chest are more complicated since you need to get through the ribs. The heart is a relatively small and hard to get target, mostly under the chest bone, but it can be reached by stabbing to the left of the sternum between the ribs. Also, a long enough blade can puncture the lungs if it gets through, and lungs filling up with blood will eventually stop your attacker. (Read "eventually." You'll still have to keep him away from you until that happens.)

Contemplating this clearly shows why a folder with a five inch (or longer) blade would be preferable for defensive purposes.

A favorite knife target of prisoners is the neck, where they'll stab repeatedly. Now, the neck is a pretty big area. Cutting the windpipe or neck muscles is not a joke. These muscles keep the head erect and the neck will bleed a lot, but it's better to know where to strike more precisely. The targets here are either the spine (protected by small bones), or the carotid artery (protected by flesh).

To find the carotid artery, feel with your fingers at the side of your windpipe and check for your pulse. The pulse is your blood pumping through the carotid.

The carotid separates into two braches as it goes up on both sides, so it's better to stab or slash the lower neck where the carotid has a greater diameter.

Veins and arteries are good knife targets. They bleed a lot and a person wounded in such a way will be more worried about stopping the hemorrhage than fighting, and if not the blood loss will stop him for good. The veins visible in the wrists and inner side of the elbow are relatively easy to access and bleed a lot. You have the brachial artery on the inner side of the arm too. These are good slashing targets when your enemy is trying to block you with his arms.

The femoral artery can be reached when stabbing the upper inner thigh, or the center of the thigh when closer to the pelvis. A person with a cut femoral artery will bleed out. Many times they die even with immediate with medical attention.

Then you have major tendons to cut as well. Cutting the tendon isn't just painful, it renders the muscle attached to the tendon useless and sometimes completely neutralizes a limb. Behind the knee you have two major tendons, and cutting the hamstring neutralizes the leg, obviously reducing mobility a lot. You can cut the sides of the neck where major back muscles connect (feel them with your fingers). Other good cuts are cutting under the armpit (going upwards towards the shoulder), the inner elbow and wrists.

The face is sensitive but other than the eyes (which are great targets) it's mostly bones and small muscle and tissue. Wounding the face is effective, but more in terms of psychological impact. Stabbing the eye of course causes a serious wound. Cutting the cheeks, lips or nose will scare off most attackers due to the pain and visible bleeding.

Having said that, there are people who, because of drugs or being blinded by rage, will keep on fighting in spite of being cut. So keep the other important targets in mind as well, if your first cuts don't stop the attack.

A KNIFE AGAINST A HANDGUN

When using your knife when wrestling with an opponent with a firearm, one hand will be dedicated to neutralizing the handgun, while you do your damage with your other hand that holds the knife.

Unlike a firearm, your opponent can't just grab the blade, so in this situation you have the advantage.

I would attack the face and neck for distraction, and follow up with a slash to the inside of the wrist holding the handgun so as to neutralize that hand. You want a VERY sharp blade for this.

I was taught that the way you grab your opponent's gun depends on if it's a revolver or a semi-automatic pistol.

The semi-automatic pistol you grab around the frame and slide, (making sure the meaty lower part of your fist is clear of the hole where the projectile is coming out). Of course, you do this while pushing the gun away from your body. Hold it with force and only one shot can be fired. After that, the gun is effectively jammed, and requires the shooter to manually eject the empty case and rack the slide to chamber a new round to keep firing.

I tried this with live ammo in a Glock during a class and it does work. All students did it and no one got hurt, so yes, it does work if you squeeze tightly.

A revolver is a bit more complicated to neutralize, but it can still be done. Here you grab the cylinder and get your fingers over the hammer as well. Done right and keeping it tight, not a single round will come out of that gun. What you are doing here is both keeping the cylinder from rotating and keeping the hammer down. If the hammer was already cocked, you use your fingers to keep the hammer from falling.

A good slash to the wrist will cut veins and tendons, and from there it's easier to get the gun away from him.

GAUCHO KNIFE FIGHTING TRICKS

Besides lots of informal sparring and developing fast reflexes, the Gauchos had a few tricks that could come in handy if you are in a knife fight.

1) Using part of his clothing wrapped around his left arm to slap his opponent's eyes, purposefully leaving a couple feet hanging unwrapped for this.

2) Given that the Gaucho used a long blade, something he did occasionally was to drop his guard and let the tip of the blade touch the ground, then, suddenly he would use it to throw dirt at the opponent's eyes. Picking up some dirt, sand or another object and keeping it hidden in the fist until he threw it with a jab was also a good way to create openings or cause a distraction.

3) Juan Moreira, being a Gaucho well known for his abilities with the knife, was often challenged by other people who wanted to prove themselves better. Moreira was a quiet man that rarely went looking for trouble, and when he didn't want to kill or seriously wound an opponent, he would use his superior skill to slash the opponent's forehead, above the eyes. The hemorrhage would bleed over the person's face and eyes, blinding him and stopping the fight.

4) During a vicious fight, Juan Moreria impaled his opponent with his long knife, and the blade got stuck in the man's spine. Moreira quickly used his knee to hold the now paralyzed and dying man's weight and push him away, releasing his Facón.

5) Gauchos weren't at all fond of throwing their knives in a fight, but they practiced it a lot in informal games, and there are some cases of knives being thrown with efficiency during a fight. The Facón's size and weight made it much more effective than a smaller knife when thrown, penetrating very deeply.

On the rare occasions the Gaucho ever did it, he would either let it fly with a jab when the range was very close, or hold it by the blade between his thumb and remaining fingers, cock his arm over his shoulder and send it spinning with the edge forward so as to not cut himself when he lets go of the blade. After a complete spin and a half, it would hit true at five or six yards away.

6) Gauchos often fought beasts such as cougars, hunting dogs or sometimes crazed horses. Their preferred attack was a slash or stab to the animal's neck, or if the beast was over him, stab him it in the belly and open its guts.

A common method used was to wrap the poncho around his arm and leave it forward, "offering" it to the beast. Once the animal bit, the Gaucho would stab and slash the neck, or sink the facón into the chest going for the heart.

UNARMED AGAINST A KNIFE ATTACKER

Oh, yes, you are in big trouble my friend. And yes, most likely you'll get cut, but hopefully not too badly. But there is no need to drop into the fetal position and let him stab you to death. There's still hope.

If you're caught off guard but you still have range, use objects such as chairs and other furniture to get something between you and the guy with the knife. In the street it could be cars, trees, or whatever you have to work with.

Keep him away from you as much as you can. Throw anything you can reach at him, and try to find a weapon of your own. Try finding an exit and running for a door, and quickly get it closed behind you. Be prepared to turn and fight if it's locked!

Sometimes you can't just escape, and if you can't outrun him you'll just get stabbed in the back, so your only choice is to fight. The odds are, of course, not in your favor. You will get cut, but maybe if you are lucky you can still make it.

Kicks are dangerous to throw but have greater reach than punches. If he closes in fast a good frontal kick to the stomach or a sweep with a low kick might work, or at least it might create a distraction to make an opening to grab him by the wrist of the armed hand.

Keep those kicks to the waist or below, not higher.

Good shoes offer some protection, but the rest of your leg is vulnerable, so be quick with those kicks. Preferably, in a possibly dangerous situation, you'll be wearing leather working shoes with steel toes, and long pants.

Something very common in Gaucho fighting is using the poncho as a shield.

You don't have a poncho but you do have other clothing, preferably a jacket. If not, a shirt will do better than just trying to stop a knife attack with your bare hands. A small backpack or other bag could also be used as a hand and arm shield. I'd readily fight with a naked torso to at least have a few wraps of cloth around my hand and forearm to attempt to disarm the guy.

Gauchos would wrap the poncho a couple times around their hand and forearm and leave the rest hanging. They'd use this hanging piece to slap and whip at the attacker's face or try to get his knife entangled in it, and then close in.

You can also use a jacket or other large heavy garment like a bull fighter would. When the attacker stabs or tries to cut your fingers holding the garment, shift position quickly and wrap his blade and hand with the dangling garment.

(I should mention that the famous W. E. Fairbairn recommended NOT wrapping a coat around your arm in a knife fight. Given that Gauchos have far more real-world experience in this regard, I'll follow their advice instead. If I'm in such a bad situation with no way out, I'll wrap clothing around my arm and hand and use it as described.)

Practice this against a sparring partner with a chalked-up rubber knife or a felt-tip marker and see just how effective it is.

A common Gaucho trick was to leave even more of his poncho hanging, then retreat a bit so the attacker would move forward and step on it, and then jerk the poncho suddenly to make the attacker fall down.

Slap at him with your garment, or if you don't have much cloth (just a t-shirt for example), wrap your hand like a glove. What you are trying to do here is protect yourself as much as possible, while you attempt to disarm the guy.

Once you see the opening or you tangle the blade with one of the methods described, make your move. It has to be perfectly coordinated and usually your best opportunity is when the knife hand is starting to go backwards after a thrust.

Go for his wrist and grab it with your right hand (against a right-handed attacker), but be ready to improvise if an opportunity presents itself to use your other hand instead. Pull with full force towards you to unbalance his footing, and twist his hand and knife towards the outside with your left hand. You want both hands on that arm and fist as soon as possible, since the natural reaction for the attacker will be to pull the armed hand back, and this can seriously cut you.

You want both hands there also to twist the blade away from you as quickly as possible. The attacker may also try to reach for his knife with his other hand. If he succeeds, you'll get cut badly.

You want to quickly jerk that arm with all your strength to put him off balance. If he tries to go for the knife with the other hand, use your body as a barrier. It's better to get punched, and not let him grab it with his free hand.

As soon as he starts moving and you feel his weight shifting, pivot on your left foot to the attacker's right, bending your torso downwards, getting that arm under your armpit as you hold the armed hand and wrist and wrist with both of your hands.

This weight shifting thing is used a lot in Judo to unbalance an opponent and throw him. The trick is to pull in one direction, and as soon as you feel the resistance you pivot and pull in the opposite direction. If you catch him off balance you can easily throw him.

Bend and go low, clenching that arm holding the knife with all of your strength. You want to lock his elbow and shoulder. If you feel the elbow locking, then use your full force to dislocate it. There's your best chance.

Going to the floor is insane if the attacker has friends, but if he's alone, drop all your weight on that locked elbow and dislocate it. Break it and keep rotating as you both go to the ground, trying to rip his arm off, causing nauseating pain.

Of course, you won't do this in training. You'll stop as soon as both of you are on the ground and your partner taps out, having his arm locked while he is unable to reach his rubber practice knife with his free arm.

This is the Gaucho or "criollo" (Spanish for "Creole") method described by Osornio in his book, and it would be the method I'd use to disarm an attacker with a knife. It requires speed and strength, and you should practice it often.

There are other methods out there that you may like better, but remember the golden rule: It must work when trying it with a non-cooperative partner with a chalked rubber knife. That's the closest you'll get to the real deal.

One last thing about dealing with a knife attacker: Do not wait until the knife attacker realizes how much of an advantage he has with the knife. First comes his "knife bluff" to intimidate you, then comes his attack. He won't expect an immediate counter-attack.

If the distance is close enough, throw your car keys or wallet to his face as a distraction and go for it immediately. Heck, even throw him your glasses to surprise him, to get his hands up and grab the armed wrist.

If fights in general are quick and you should be quick at attacking and putting your opponent down, be even quicker when it comes to defending yourself against an attacker with a knife!

This should be an instant reaction. Be on him the second you see the blade. Don't give him time to think, go straight for that arm with all you've got!

This also goes for attackers drawing guns from their waists. At very close distance, a fast counter-attack may be even better than going for your own gun.

A "disarm" is even easier to do against a handgun than a knife, since unlike popular myth, you can grab a gun and if you do it right, one single shot is all the attacker is going to get. (Make sure you are out of the line of fire when that happens!) After that, you can use leverage to disarm him or attack him directly.

At very close "contact" range, the gun doesn't matter. The best hand-to-hand fighter is MUCH more likely to win. You see this clearly in "Force On Force" exercises. If you don't know what Force On Force training is (sparring against non-cooperative adversaries in many different realistic scenarios), then you need to get out and train more! Other than surviving actual life-or-death fights, there is no better preparation for such fights than realistic Force On Force training, using hand-to-hand techniques, practice knives, and "airsoft" firearms.

SPEARS

This is one of the differences between American and third world prisons. In the USA, better prisons require small weapons that are easy to conceal. In Argentina, prisons are much more "third worldly," and convicts will improvise short spears to fight each other.

Spear fighting techniques involve a two handed grip, with one hand closer to the end, and the other hand a couple of feet back. Quick steps forward and forward thrusts are used to try to impale the opponent. The same spear is used with side movements to parry the opponent's spear, knife, club or fist away from the defender's body.

Of course, spears are VERY effective. Impaling a person with a spear usually ends the fight very quickly. Prisoners practice spear fighting with broomsticks as a game. For the real deal, they sharpen the tip, or strap a knife to the end.

The spear is mostly an offensive weapon. Other than parrying with one end while holding the other and blocking overhead chops or lateral arc attacks with the center of the shaft while holding it by both ends, Lopez Osornio describes another technique called "molinete" (windmill). This is performed by gripping the center of the spear's shaft, hands together, bringing it up over the head and rotating it like a horizontal windmill. This was used by both gauchos and natives for defense against foot soldiers and mounted cavalry.

UNCONVENTIONAL WEAPONS

When there's nothing else available, you'll have to improvise in a big hurry.

Chair: A Chair can be an effective blunt weapon. Holding it by the back rest, you can take advantage of its greater reach, using it for horizontal forward "stabs" to the face and chest. This horizontal motions combined with a quick forward step is pretty effective and the leg will cause nice damage to the face or ribs, given the chair's weight and small contact area.

When using a chair with soft seat padding against a knife attack, you can try to get him to stab it, and then rotate the chair to catch his blade. Use the greater leverage in your favor. A smart knife fighter won't fall for this, but it's worth trying. The chair gives you greater reach than any knife. Use that to your advantage, hitting with forward motions from a safe distance.

Using the chair as you would use a bat can also be done, but given the bulk and weight it will be a slow attack and the opponents may rush in as your swing it.

Bottles: Heavy whisky, wine or liquor bottles are nice blunt weapons. Given the short length and usual heavy weight, they can be used as blunt weapons at close range.

Better in my opinion would be their ability to cut and slash. (This is probably the only thing I agree with that usually can be seen in movies.) Hit the UPPER portion of the bottle at a 45° angle against a hard edged surface. If you hit the bottle in the middle it will likely shatter completely, leaving you just with the tip of the bottle inside your fist and maybe cutting your hand as well.

Preferably break it against a stone surface or bar with metal reinforcement. A metal chair would do the trick. If nothing else is available, the head of your opponent can be used as well. Remember to smash with the upper section!

Baseball bat or steel pipe: Forward stabbing attacks to the face give you range, but I'd use such a weapon with immediate and ferocious swings, knowing well that there's little defense for it when doing so with full force. A bat is not a knife, and a smart opponent will eventually try to grab it. It's better to swiftly swing away to the guy's head, with enough strength to crush arms or hands that he may use as cover.

End things quickly. Grabbing the bat with both hands, one in the middle, and one in the grip below, do a couple of quick jab stabs to the face and when you have the range, swing away to the head with full force.

Blunt weapons rely a lot on brute force in real street fights. Beating lightly with thin sticks like many martial arts do only pisses people off. A good grappler or wrestler will tackle you and shove the stick where the sun won't shine.

Pens, pencils and scissors: I once saw an ER doctor from Mar del Plata interviewed on TV. He was asked what weapon was often used that surprised him the most. "A pen," he said. "I never would have though a pen to the neck could do so much damage."

Pens and pencils are only good for stabbing, but they are much better than nothing. I was stabbed in the face with a sharp wooden pencil when I was a kid. It wasn't pretty. Thankfully, I don't have a scar left.

Since it's only good for stabbing, you want to do the "stitching machine," attacking the stomach, face, eyes and neck. Wrap your fist tightly around it and place your thumb on the end, so that it doesn't slip while stabbing.

Umbrella: There are special umbrellas for sale specifically made to be used as a blunt weapon. Other than that special type, ordinary umbrellas will break soon enough in a fight. Use it mostly with stabbing motions, aiming to the face.

Keep this in mind the next time you buy an umbrella. Buy a long one, not the compact folding type. The ones I have all have narrow pointy metal tips…

Against a knife, you can open it and try tangling the knife in the material.

Nail clipper or small file: Using it in your clenched fist, this is just a small stabbing tool. You'll depend mostly on hand-to-hand fighting, but whenever there's an opening, you can try stabbing the neck, eyes or wrists.

Keys: You'll have these in your fist, tightly closed and with the keys coming out between your fingers as a spiked knuckle duster. You punch to the face with these, and hope to tear flesh and injure the eyes.

A particularly long key can be supported with the thumb and used as a small stabbing weapon. There are also small folding knives made to fit inconspicuously on key chains.

Brass Knuckles: Illegal in most countries, "knuckle dusters" are vicious weapons in hand-to-hand combat, especially the spiked versions. I met a guy once who was punched with one by a security guard. It broke his clavicle bone. They're illegal in most countries, but not more effective than a folding knife, especially against multiple attackers. A judge or jury will certainly look at you as a troublemaker for even owning one of these. Unless clenched with great force, it's also very likely to break your own fingers, since the fit is usually poor.

A piece of rope or a necktie: If that's all you have when attacked, I'm sure you wished you had listened to me and carried a folding knife with you all day. But I guess it's better than nothing. Wrapping both ends in your hands, you can keep the rope stretched tight, about shoulder length wide.

It's mostly a defensive tool. You can use it to wrap around a knife or fist and take better control of it. This will require superior H2H fighting knowledge. You can also use a greater length between your hands and try to swing the loop and catch the guy's head. Generally this works best from behind him, as when "sentry stalking." If you try this and you are fast and strong, there are a number of things you can do.

If the opponent is unarmed, you can simply turn your back to him and bend at your waist while pulling the cords over your shoulder and choke him. Turning your back with the rope looped around the guy's neck will close a knot around the opponent's windpipe, strangulating him. Keep that tight for a few seconds and he'll go unconscious, especially if you lean at the waist and lift him from the ground.

SEALs use this as a silent "sentry stalking" technique. It's effective but difficult to perform if the target is wearing a hat, helmet or big coat with a high collar. You only have one try. After that the target is alerted and you are only armed with a piece of rope. Keep this is mind, and surprise your enemy if you can.

With a shorter length of rope, after successfully looping the head you can bring it down with force in an improvised Thai head clutch and knee him repeatedly in the face. These are just some ideas for you to keep in mind. If you want to practice any of these rope techniques with a partner, please be careful.

HANDGUNS

This is the method of self defense that certain people will distrust the most.

Firearms have been demonized in such a way by the media (with a lot of support from governments that coincidentally want to get them banned), that some people distrust you as soon as you mention guns as part of a survival plan.

I'm not just going to mention guns. I'm going to make it abundantly clear that if you do NOT make firearms an important part of your plan you are in fact a "pelotudo." That's Spanish for idiot. Why? Because I know for sure how important it is to be armed. In a violent society it's even more important.

Not because you'll go around shooting people like in an action movie, but because firearms are your last line of defense between killing and getting killed. You have to be ready to make up your mind about that now. Are you willing to kill, to save your life and the lives of your loved ones, or not?

Having said that, again, it's not like in the movies. Most of the time, you point a gun at the guy that means to rob you or hurt you in some way, and he'll just leave you alone. He'll leave. He'll take off. He'll run away. According to the National Rifle Association (the NRA), in the United States this happens **nine times out of ten**.

I can verify that indeed this is the most common outcome. Being aware and reacting in time helps a lot as well. You have to sense danger to react in time, even with a firearm.

There are countries where civilians simply cannot purchase firearms, but an American who is reading this book and who is not willing to buy a firearm when he legally could, is simply a naïve fool.

When I first started writing articles, almost all of the feedback was extremely positive. Everyone appreciated the "been there, done that" thing. But most of the comments at first came from survivalists and people that were into guns.

When my writing went beyond that circle, and non-gun folks read what I wrote, some commented that I talked too much about the importance of firearms.

The reason I insist so much about the importance of guns is precisely the same reason why people respect what I have to say: I've been there and done that. Would I be alive today if I hadn't been armed when I needed to be? I don't know. Probably not. But I'm glad I never had to walk that unarmed path.

In Argentina, nine out of ten people, or a direct family member, have been attacked by criminals in the last year! ("La Nacion" newspaper online, July 4, 2009) It's nearly impossible to find an Argentine who hasn't been a crime victim since the crisis. I still haven't found one, and trust me; I ask whenever I have the chance.

THIEVERY, ARMED ROBBERY, RAPE OR MURDER

I'm very proud of the way I've handled many of these situations, where others simply would have surrendered, begging for mercy, or not even seen the attack coming in the first place. The fact that I've avoided being a victim of violence is something I wear like a badge of honor.

I have not left half a dozen corpses rotting at the bottom of the Riachuelo River, (where bodies are dumped around here). My "credentials" are in handling or managing violent situations that most other people couldn't have avoided.

There's an allure about guns and danger that you see on TV, and of course all of that is bullshit. Your gun is just something you'll carry a lot, hope to never draw, and when you have to draw, you hope the other person has better sense than forcing you to take it to the next level.

Maybe the first time something happens, you'll go home and tell your wife, and later tell your buddies.

Eventually when these things happen on regular basis, you just stop telling your family. You know how much they worry about you, and all you hope for is to get home or do your business without encountering any trouble, or God forbid having to shoot any of the bad guys that are so plentiful. Not because of any moral implications (you got over that long ago), but because of the nightmare in terms of money, judges and blood sucking lawyers it would bring along.

DO I NEED A GUN?

I sincerely pity the person who does not love life with enough passion to kill for it, if that's what is needed to survive. I feel similarly regarding parents who won't even consider the possibility of having to kill a violent criminal in order to save their children.

Even if you don't particularly like guns, they are tools, just like a first aid kit or a fire extinguisher. Like them, a firearm may save your life or the life of your loved ones during certain emergencies.

I'm sure you don't look forwards to seeing your house burned to the ground, yet you have smoke alarms and hopefully a fire extinguisher somewhere handy, probably in the kitchen or garage.

In the same line of thought, a sane person doesn't enjoy killing people, but you still learn how to use the weapon effectively, and you have the mindset to use it if necessary.

Don't fool yourselves with politically correct crap about the sporting use of firearms being their primary purpose. Firearms are for killing, and most of them have at some time been used for killing people. Even so-called hunting or target-shooting firearms.

You have a problem with that? Then don't own one. Buy a bonsai kit and take up Japanese gardening instead. Try golf.

That may sound a bit rough but it's the way it is. You may use a .22LR revolver for plinking with your son one Sunday afternoon and having the time of your life, but know that it's a weapon you are holding, and its business is the gravest and most serious one in the world. A tool that has evolved into becoming the most effective hand-held killing tool man was able to create. Humans are by FAR the most dangerous creatures on earth, so it makes a lot of sense to me.

And there's that question again: "Do I need a gun?"

A few years ago I would have said 100% yes. You need a gun, you need to train with it, you need to carry it, and you need to keep a spare gun at home. And if you can't have a firearm, then have some other weapon, but arm yourself!

I no longer think that way. Now I understand that there are people that simply aren't like me, or the people I usually hang around and consider my friends. Some people have been mentally castrated so badly by a lifetime of politically correct propaganda that I doubt they would react even if they had their entire family tortured in front of them.

Seriously, some people actually say that they wouldn't be able to harm another human being, no matter what! That kind of people used to make me sick. They used to make me feel as if I was about to puke.

And they still do.

Those wretched souls, I usually tell them that maybe they do need a gun after all, but in their case only one cartridge will be enough.

There are cases where firearms are not legal or available, or people have peculiar problems like a suicidal family member. In those cases I recommend keeping it in a safe at all times, without the suicidal person knowing the combination. If guns are illegal, find some other weapon but still be armed in some way. We'll go through more unconventional weapons later on.

Having said that, when it's legal to do so, I simply don't understand why a person would choose NOT to own a firearm. A gun is a tool that is urgently needed during the most desperate times a person can possibly go through in his or her life.

WHY OWN A GUN?

1) For self defense. As unlikely as it may be (or not, depending on local crime rates), you never know when you'll need one. And when you need it, it will be to save your life, and there won't be time to go out and buy one.

2) Certain bogus statistics will tell you that a gun in a house is twenty times more likely to hurt the home's occupants than to kill a bad guy. These false statistics have been debunked many times, but they still reappear in politically-correct news stories all the time.

Statistics also say you are more likely to get divorced than to stay married happily ever after, and that car accidents are one of the top causes of death. I'm still married and I drive my car everyday. And in spite of the deaths caused each year, I've never heard of a car ban being proposed.

Know this: If you allow yourself to be categorized along with the most common level of stupidity, you shouldn't even use matches.

3) Owning a gun is a matter of principle as well.

Free men own guns. Dictators and authoritarian governments have always tried to disarm their populations. An unarmed population is as helpless as a bunch of babies. But millions of armed citizens are a force no wise military leader takes lightly, even in today's modern warfare.

An armed population ready to rise against its leaders is the best way to ensure democracy and prevent tyranny.

THE CASE OF ELSA MARIA ESCOBAR, IN NUÑEZ

What happened in the district of Nuñez, Buenos Aires, Argentina, in 2005 may be the perfect example of the sad irony behind the anti-gun movement.

Elsa Maria Escobar was a beautician, living next to a known sex offender in the same apartment building. She had one constant fear in her mind, and she explained it to a client while she cut her hair.

The woman that used to be her client would later say in an interview that, "She was very worried about her daughter, because of her neighbor. Elsa had many locks installed on her door because of this man. She said that he would only get to her daughter over her dead body."

The man had been in prison for rape and robbery, and a few weeks before he had tried to rape another girl. Since apparently attempted rape isn't bad enough, the man still enjoyed his freedom and he lived with his wife (a human rights activist) and their kids. Elsa Escobar knew that her pretty thirteen-year-old daughter was just the kind of victim that scumbags like her neighbor preferred.

The night after Mrs. Escobar said those prophetic words, at three AM her neighbor broke into her apartment through a window, after breaking the screen.

Mrs. Escobar and her daughter woke up because of the noise, but of course they didn't have a gun. The thirty-year-old neighbor armed himself with a kitchen knife and took both of them to the master bedroom, locked the girl in the closet and proceeded to rape the mother. When he finished raping her, he stabbed her to death.

He took his time. After drinking a beer he went back and continued with the daughter. He raped her in the blood-stained bed next to her mother's corpse, and stabbed her in the back until she stopped moving. He left them both for dead, and then went back next door to his family!

But the daughter didn't die. She had only passed out because of blood loss and shock.

Mrs. Escobar's older daughter dropped by their apartment, after noticing that they didn't answer the phone when she called. The poor girl was seriously wounded, but she survived to tell the story, and she recuperated from her physical wounds after a few weeks in intensive care.

Her spiritual wounds, well, those will never heal.

When the cops dragged this beast into the patrol car, his wife cried hysterically, "Kill me! Kill me!" after learning what her husband had done... yet again.

Right. As if killing her would fix anything.

If Elsa Escobar had had a gun, then most likely the outcome would have been very different. No one can argue that. At least they would have had a FAR better chance at defending themselves from this rapist and murderer.

A QUICK FIREARMS INTRODUCTION

All firearms work on the same principle.

A solid granular element, the powder, is ignited and thus turns itself into a gas that should occupy much more space--space that it won't find in the tight confinement of the cartridge case. This increases the pressure dramatically until it violently pushes the projectile down the barrel and out of the muzzle.

Ever since the invention of gunpowder, the working principle has been the same. Until the invention of smokeless gunpowder by Paul Vieille in 1884, people had been using black power.

Black powder creates large amounts of smoke when fired. Maybe in some western movies you can notice this, though most of the time they are not historically accurate and they miss these details.

Black powder firearms were generally muzzle loaded, meaning you introduced the powder and projectile through the muzzle opening, and the powder was ignited either by a flint that created a spark or by ignition primers that contain fulminate, a substance that explodes when impacted.

This of course was a pretty tedious operation compared to using today's metallic cartages, but I guess it worked well when fighting others with similar weapons and their intrinsic handicaps.

Metallic cartridges such as the ones known today have a projectile tightly fitted into the case, a charge of smokeless powder trapped inside, and a small fulminate primer on the bottom.

Metallic cartridge firearms have firing pins, which hit the primer that ignites the power inside. In most cases, a hammer hits the pin, or the pin is mounted on the hammer itself.

Handguns: Handguns are weapons that can be fired using only one hand, even if sometimes shooters use both for added stability and control over the weapon.

Other than single shot pistols, we basically have two kinds of handguns:

Automatics, which use an ammunition magazine, which is usually inserted through the grip. A round is loaded into the firing chamber by pulling the slide backwards and letting it fly forwards. After firing, the slide is pushed back again by the recoil pressure created by the gases of the fired rounds. The spent shell cases can be seen flying away as the gun is fired.

Semi-Automatic firing systems can be single action (SA), double action / single action (DA/SA), or double action only (DAO).

True automatic firearms are usually referred to as fully automatic. In that case, just keeping the trigger pulled backwards will rapidly fire all the rounds until the gun is empty. These are what Hollywood usually refers to as "machine guns."

Single actions such as J.M. Browning's famous Colt Model 1911 need the hammer to be manually cocked to work. The trigger simply releases the hammer that strikes the firing pin. After each shot, the gases push back the slide, leaving the hammer cocked for the next trigger pull. This goes on until the last round is fired and the slide locks back, ready for a new loaded magazine. Each pull of the trigger fires a single round, but they must begin with a manually cocked hammer.

Double action/Single action pistols don't need the hammer to be manually cocked to start firing. As long as there's a round in the chamber, simply pulling the trigger causes the hammer to move back, and as you finish pulling the trigger, it releases the hammer and fires the round. This is all accomplished in one longer and slightly heavier pull of the trigger. A well known example of a DA/SA pistol is the Beretta Model 92, used by the U.S. Army.

Once the first round is fired, the slide goes backward to eject the empty metallic case, and cocks the hammer to leave it ready to work in the single action mode. As it goes forward, the slide feeds a fresh round into the chamber. So you have a double action (cocking and releasing the hammer) trigger pull the first time you fire, and subsequent single action trigger pulls after that.

Double-Action-Only (DAO) firearms always shoot in double action, for every shot. The slide does not cock the hammer, (or the internal striker in some firearms). Every shot, every time, is made in the double action mode. DAO pistol triggers feel much like the triggers on double-action revolvers. Kel-Tec makes several popular and inexpensive DAO pistols in the USA.

Striker-fired pistols such as Glocks use sort of a hybrid between single action and conventional double action trigger systems. In the Glock for example, pulling back the slide cocks the internal striker only half way. Pulling the trigger applies the rest of the pressure to the striker, causing the gun to fire. The Glock trigger is a bit harder and longer than that of a true SA pistol like a 1911, but at least you always use the same trigger system. You don't need to manually pre-cock the hammer of a Glock, the way you do with a 1911. Also, you don't have a transition between the long first DA trigger pull, and the lighter SA trigger pull, that you must deal with when firing SA/DA pistols such as the Beretta 92.

Revolvers don't have magazines. They have a cylinder with capacity that generally amounts to six shots, or sometimes seven or even eight in big bore calibers. Some smaller revolvers (with two inch barrels, called snubbies) have only a five round capacity in their cylinders.

Modern revolvers have double action trigger mechanisms. Each trigger pull cocks and releases the hammer, though you can also cock the hammer with your thumb and barely touch the trigger for a much lighter SA trigger pull.

Older revolvers only came in single action, like the typical "cowboy guns," where it was necessary to cock the hammer with the thumb for each shot. The trigger only releasing the manually cocked hammer.

These are just a few basic notions, so we can get started and know what we are talking about.

GUN SAFETY RULES

The NRA and most gun manuals come with three basic (and very important) gun safety rules:

1) Always keep the gun pointed in a safe direction.

2) Always keep the finger off the trigger until ready to shoot.

3) Always keep the gun unloaded until ready to use.

These are basic gun handling rules we've all lived by for a long time.

The good thing about the three rules is that, even if you break one, as long as you follow the others no one will get hurt. These rules work best for target practice though, and not armed self defense training. When you start training in armed self defense you'll break all of them, but not at the same time. That's why it's important to apply them whenever you can, so that when you have no other choice to but break one during defensive shooting training, the other ones are still enforced.

For the person that packs a gun (loaded and ready to use) I have another set of rules. Learn them, live by them, repeat them to everyone that owns a gun.

Spread the word and save lives.

1) GUNS ARE LOADED. ALWAYS! Unloaded guns don't exist.

When a gun owner first starts shooting he believes in loaded and unloaded guns, just like kids believe in Santa. Then you grow up a bit in the fascinating world of guns, ammo, and lethal weapons, and one day you know the truth.

Unloaded guns don't exist!

Oh, crap! Cry a river! Yes, just like Santa, fairies, leprechauns and Chileans that know how to play Football well, none of them exist. There is no such thing in this universe as an unloaded gun.

Since unloaded guns don't exist, it's easy to understand how supposedly unloaded guns have killed more people that loaded guns do in household accidents.

My brother told me about the Santa-gate scam.

About unloaded guns I learned myself. I was dry-firing with my trusty little Rossi .38 once. I don't like Brazilian revolvers much, but that older Rossi was very nice.

I would dry-fire at a photograph on my night table. Nothing to read between the lines, I just used it as a focus point while practicing point shooting.

The phone rang, I answered, and went back to dry-firing my empty gun.

BANG!

Shooting a gun without ear protection is pretty loud, especially with a three inch barrel .38 Special, and especially inside a room.

"Man," I thought, "that was supposed to be a click!"

I looked at the picture and my face was gone (which shows how well dry-firing works), replaced by a perfectly cut round circle.

There was also a hole in the wall.

My son was sleeping in that other room.

While I took those few steps into my son's room to confirm the trajectory, I thought I had killed my own child.

It's funny how the human mind works. In just fractions of a second, I knew that if my son was dead, I would simply blow out my own brains. I couldn't live with that.

Indeed the trajectory was perfect, it was even perfectly aligned with the head of my son, that wasn't moving or making a sound at all…

Sleeping like a baby.

I owe one to the Big Guy above.

The apartment had old-school masonry walls, so uncommon these days but still fairly common in Argentina. It had penetrated one side, but stopped inside the hollow brick wall, with just an inch of material left to go through.

Had it been an average interior dry wall, I could have shot him right in the head.

Why am I writing this, and letting everyone know how much of an idiot I am? Because it's worth it if it can spare you from making the same mistake.

I once had a smartass question this rule. Supposedly a hunter and someone well versed in weapons. "What do you mean unloaded guns don't exist? Stop fooling around. I just checked this revolver, and it's unloaded. Come on, let's go to the range."

"Wait a second," I told him.

I grabbed the gun, went downstairs for a second, and then went back up and into the room with him. "Here's your 'unloaded' gun. Would you put this thing to your head and pull thing the trigger?"

He doubted for a second and I interrupted him as soon as he started with some crappy reply. "Guns are always loaded. If you think otherwise, sooner or later you'll hurt yourself or someone else."

I'm saying this because accidental or negligent discharges are something that eventually happen. It happened to me, and it has happened to men that have forgotten more about guns than I'll ever know, men like Bill Jordan.

Bill Jordan's accidental discharge took the life of a fellow police officer after going through dry wall.

And if I'm even mentioning the incident, its' not to lessen the great reputation the man rightfully has, but to make it abundantly clear that if it happened to such an extraordinary gunslinger as Bill Jordan, it will happen to you as well.

It's not a matter of IF, it's a matter of WHEN. Just hope that WHEN it happens, you at least remember one of the safety rules, so that no one gets hurt.

And this brings me to the second golden rule:

2) BE SURE OF YOUR TARGET

Again, let me share a personal experience that occurred many years ago.

Everyone had left and I was alone in the house. Like in the movie "Home Alone."

Well, not exactly. I was fifteen years old and I had a .45 ACP pistol with me, so my version of "Home Alone" would have ended rather fast. I guess it would have been rated "Rated R" as well.

Anyway, I was home and suddenly I heard noises downstairs. The house we were living in at that time was on a hillside and the entrance was on the top level. "Downstairs" was also at ground level, but only further down hill. We had just moved in, and supposedly we didn't have a key for the service door in the lower level, so I didn't expect my family to come in through that door.

I got the gun and went to check. There were clearly footsteps. I walked as silently as possible, lowered the safety of the loaded .45 caliber 1911 and got ready to shoot…and ended up pointing the gun at my own mother.

She had fixed the lock of that secondary back door while I was at school, something I didn't know she had done, using that door for the first time.

Thank God the potential tragedy didn't occur, because I had been taking defensive shooting lessons with a guy that insisted a lot on target recognition.

NEVER shoot at a silhouette or a shadow or a noise. This type of tragedy happens all the time. Positively identify your target first.

Many years later, using that same gun, a burglar tried to break in for real. As I got ready I kept repeating to myself, "Identify the target. Identify the target." I thought that maybe it was my neighbor that forgot his keys, and maybe was trying to get in. The person was indeed a stranger, a burglar, and thank God he jumped back onto the roof and took off, just as soon as he saw me through the window with my pistol in my hand.

This is SO important, and unfortunately it's neglected in many shooting schools these days. Maybe it's because of the military background most instructors have.

People, when you go to investigate a noise in your house, and if you find someone, 99% of the time it's the cat, the dog, your kid going downstairs to drink a glass of water at four AM, or the mother-in-law that supposedly should be in France, but came home a week early and has a key to your house. It's your son that went away and wasn't supposed to come home for two more days, but for whatever reason ended up coming back early and creeping inside at two AM.

About 99% of the time, especially in your home, it's going to be someone you are not supposed to shoot. So keep that finger off the trigger guard until you positively identify the target.

To recap: **Guns are always loaded, and be sure of your target.** These iron laws are the core for your realistic self defense safety rules.

"Blast that motherfucker's chest! Kill that SOB, kill him!" Shooting instructor Jorge "El Negro" Baigorria shouted this as we went through our shooting drills.

One of the federal officers with us had a malfunction with his gun, so he stopped firing and raised his hand, as he was trained to do in the academy. Baigorria rushed to him. "Exactly what the fuck are you doing?" he asked.

"I have a malfunction, sir."

"Oh, so if you are shooting it out on the streets you'll just raise your hand too!? Clear that malfunction right now and keep fighting! I don't care if you destroy that target by bashing it with your empty gun, just kill it!"

Later that same day, we were doing force on force exercises. I grabbed a guy, spun with plenty of momentum on one of my feet and threw him to the ground. The guy flew through the air and landed pretty hard.

Baigorria saw it, and since I had gone at it too hard on the guy, I thought the instructor would tell me to calm down a little. But instead, he said, "Good! Now that's pretty good! See guys, that's how you do it!"

During one of the reloading breaks, we talked a bit about different scenarios. One of the guys had suffered a home invasion, and instead of getting the gun and shooting the bad guy, he willingly surrendered his Beretta 92 pistol to him. Many of the students agreed it was the right choice, but the instructor didn't comment.

Baigorria went on asking, "Okay guys, the bad guy has a family member hostage. Seriously now, and no Rambo or macho bullshit but for real, what do you do?"

They all said they'd put down the gun and surrender.

"I'd take the shot," I said. Given that everyone else said something different, and many of these guys were cops, I was sure my answer was the wrong one. But what the hell; that's what I'd do.

I was surprised when Baigorria said "He's right. Are you stupid? Surrender your family to those scumbags? No, you aim, and you shoot to the head. Okay?"

After that we practiced some hostage drills. Only a small area of the bad guy's head was visible, and we had to slowly walk towards him as we talked to keep him distracted. The hostage's head was right next to it so we only had less than two inches of bad guy's head to shoot at.

"Put the gun down you SOB! Put it down!" Blam!

I had a somewhat different approach:

"Dude, it's all right, calm down and just tell me what..." Blam!

With that, everyone watching burst out laughing.

Jorge Baigorria's classes are excellent, but it's not just about shooting. It's about feeding that creature inside most of us.

It's not a soldier. It doesn't care about orders, objectives or the chain of command. It's not even a fighter. Winning, losing, even the "beauty" of combat or the martial art means nothing to it.

It's a killer.

It's a bloodthirsty side of you. No matter how sick or tired you are, or how much your body hurts, or how big and mean your opponent looks, you are going to kill him, even if you have to chew the carotid artery out of his neck with your bare teeth. I'll explain the reason for developing this killer instinct next.

BEING SCARED

Come on. Of course we all get scared. Being afraid is good because it's instinct, and it helps keep us alive. You hear better, you see better, and you are more aware of your surroundings. Your adrenaline pumps, making you ready either to fight or run for your life.

What you should fight against like a bad habit is "freezing up." This is something that often happens to people when they confront violent or dangerous situations for the first time.

You hear something, there's someone in your house. You are barely awake, but you heard it clearly.

And you freeze, like a horizontal statue, right there in your bed.

Caught between dream and reality, you know it's real enough, but you can't get your body to move. Fight that inaction with hate, and a powerful desire to destroy the SOB that dared to break into your home!

Freezing up can be a dangerous natural reaction. You lose time, valuable time, and you can't afford that. You have to program your brain to react quickly.

Asleep or awake, sick or half dead, you should react decisively to danger.

I know a bit about being scared. I've been scared for a long time.

When neighbors, friends, relatives or even your own family suffer from violent crimes, when every time you turn on the TV you learn about people getting killed on the streets, you can't avoid being worried for them.

Fearing for your own life is also very natural. And, do you want to know a secret? It gets to a point where nothing really surprises you that much any more.

You see, being scared is an extraordinary circumstance. It's not supposed to happen on regular basis. When it does, you no longer react like scared people usually do. You control it.

Combine this control of fear with high levels of situational awareness, and you'll be well prepared to face danger and violence.

The feeling that you should fuel is a desire to destroy those that mean to harm you, so that instead of retreating in fear when surprised, you react aggressively against the threat.

Soon after we got married my wife had this wonderful idea. We were living in a small apartment and I got up to go to the bathroom in the middle of the night. After that I went to the kitchen looking for a glass of water.

Apparently my wife was thirsty too, and she went to the kitchen before I did. When she heard me getting close, she had no better idea than to hide in the shadows and say "BOO!!" when I passed by.

Before I realized who she was, I had pushed her against the wall with such force that I knocked the air out of her. We talked about this, and how dangerous those types of "jokes" could be.

This was a completely involuntary action. A simple reaction.

You have to get used to reacting in such a way.

WHICH FIREARM SHOULD I GET?

Some people are just now beginning to understand that owning a gun is actually a pretty good idea. "What gun should I get?" is a common question that people often ask me.

This question usually generates year's worth of debate, and it's the reason for thousands of magazine articles and books. Millions of trees could have been saved by just admitting one thing.

The answer is, of course, "Buy a Glock."

I've fired and am very familiar with most of the proven and successful handgun designs. The 1911, SIGs, Hi Powers, Beretta 92s, Glocks, CZ75s, Colt and S&W revolvers, just to name some of the designs that have passed the test of time.

I own and regularly fire many types of pistols and revolvers, and I enjoy researching the different designs and mechanisms. It's no secret that I like guns and have been shooting since I was fourteen years old, and took my first defensive shooting class when I was fifteen.

I'm not a sport shooter, and I don't participate in action shooting or target shooting. My interest is mainly in their use for self defense.

The first serious handgun I had was bought by my father when I was fifteen years old. After doing a lot of research and reading magazines and books, I decided that within the budget proposed by my father, a Norinco 1911 .45 ACP was the best deal. Right until this day I think it was the right choice.

The Norinco is a well made copy of arguably the most successful handgun design of all times, the Colt 1911 Government Model.

Man, that was a nice gun. It fired big fat .45 ACP rounds, it was accurate and I knew that even with ordinary 230 grain full metal jacket (FMJ) "hardball" ammunition, it had very good stopping power.

That gun served its purpose as a house gun for many years, and I still have that same Norinco. I had it refinished, and I changed a few internal springs with custom ones of better quality. I added new sights, a target trigger that can be regulated for a crisp trigger pull, and a skeletonized hammer. I also got some Hogue rubber grips, although I later replaced those with walnut ones.

I also discovered the joy of owning and shooting fine weapons such as the Browning HP-35 "High Power."

My Colt and Smith & Wesson revolvers are dear to me, especially my Lightweight and Detective versions of the venerable Model 10 and Model 12.

It was interesting to learn why Colt's "Police Positive" and Smith's "Military & Police" are held in such high regard.

Along the way I learned to appreciate the virtues of "underdogs," such as the Ballester Molina .45 and Bersa pistols.

WHY BUY A GLOCK?

After all of that experience, I have verified time and again that the handgun that both new shooters and myself perform the best with is the Glock pistol.

Guns are a great hobby, but if your intention is purely owning and learning how to fire a gun for self defense, **just buy a Glock pistol.**

If you take its reliability, durability, performance track record, accuracy, great magazine capacity, light weight, mechanical and operational simplicity, unparalleled corrosion resistance and parts availability, combine all these characteristics and no other gun comes close to the Glock.

WHICH GLOCK?

For most people a **Glock 19** is the way to go. It holds fifteen rounds in the magazine plus one in the chamber (15+1), and 9mm is very effective with modern jacketed hollow point (JHP) ammunition.

The Glock 19 is accurate and small enough for easy concealment. The amount of "been there, done that" people around the world that choose the Glock 19 is something that doesn't go unnoticed by "gun pros."

The Glock 19 would be my number one recommendation for new shooters in warm regions where mostly all you normally wear on top is a t-shirt.

Tip: Wear slightly larger clothes to help conceal your gun better.

The original Glock that made Glocks famous was the **Glock 17**, introduced in the 1980s. The G-17 is slightly bigger than the G-19, and holds 17+1 rounds. The model numbers refer to the order of Gaston Glock's gun patents, not to their ammunition capacity or anything else, as many people mistakenly think.

Though considered a "full size" handgun, the Glock 17 is still smaller than a 1911 Government Model, a gun that people have been carrying and concealing for decades. It's also a lot lighter since Glocks have polymer frames.

For people that want a bit of extra stopping power, you can also buy Glocks in .40 Caliber S&W, .357 SIG, 10mm and .45 ACP. But for a first gun I recommend 9mm since its easier to shoot, it's accurate, and ammo is cheaper so you can afford to shoot and practice more. With premium grade ammo such as Gold Dot, made by Speer or Corbon, you still have good stopping power.

If you are really committed and can afford a bit of extra ammo cost, **.40 S&W** is more powerful than 9mm, but still offers high magazine capacity. Ammo is commonly available, because the .40 caliber has become the most popular choice of police departments across the USA. The Glock 22 in .40 caliber S&W is the choice of more police departments across America than any other handgun, bar none.

.357 SIG is an even better caliber in my opinion, but you'll have to buy another weapon in 9mm or .40 S&W, or a spare .40 S&W barrel to be able to afford to practice, because .357 SIG is an expensive cartridge.

The good news is that **all Glock .357 SIG autos can also shoot .40 S&W** just by changing the .357 SIG barrel for a .40 S&W barrel. This takes only seconds and spare barrels are not that expensive.

There are also 9mm barrels for the Glock .357 SIG and the Glock .40 S&W that work very well. In this case, you'll need Glock 9mm magazines as well. In other words, you can buy one Glock pistol, and with three barrels, you can shoot three different calibers! "Lone Wolf" is a very good company in America that makes many types of Glock barrels and other aftermarket parts. These include extra-long threaded barrels for attaching suppressors, if you ever decide to purchase one.

Keep in mind that the very simplicity of the Glock design is a two-edged sword. The safety is on the trigger itself. There is no secondary external thumb safety. If the trigger is accidentally pressed, for example when carelessly holstering a Glock pistol, the gun can fire when you don't mean it to. If you decide to own a Glock and to keep a round in the chamber, the loaded pistol MUST be kept in a holster that covers the trigger at all times. A loaded Glock left loose in a bag, for example, is a tragedy just waiting to happen. A good holster is an intrinsic part of the Glock safety design. You NEVER pocket carry a Glock, or carry it "Mexican Style" without a holster. You always use a good holster with a Glock.

Revolvers: Having said all of this about Glocks, for someone that still wants to be armed but who frankly isn't going to dedicate as much time as they should to learning to shoot well, in that case a revolver would be the best choice.

This is borderline territory, since if you are not committed, then maybe you shouldn't own a firearm in the first place. But there are cases where people fired the first round they ever shot in their lives into a bad guy, thus saving their lives.

For people who want a handgun, but who can't take the time to become proficient with a semi-automatic pistol, a revolver is far more forgiving in terms of its operational simplicity.

You just load the cylinder, point and pull the trigger. There's no empty chamber, safety or failure to fire to worry about. This comes with a few disadvantages as well, some of which we'll be going through later on.

For a house, a four inch barrel .38/.357 revolver is the best choice.

For a smaller house or apartment, a two inch snub nose revolver in a similar caliber and loaded with .38 Special+P or .357 Magnum would be my choice.

Still, at a minimum, a gun safety class is required for any new gun owner.

I'm not alone in this line of thought, and I found that Argentine security and firearms expert Alejandro A. Reynoso shares similar views in his book "Manual de Armas y Tecnicas para la Defensa Personal y Domiciliaria."

SELF DEFENSE SHOOTING

Here again, I'm going to recommend that you get training in defensive shooting. I can give you a few pointers that have worked for me in the past, or for others I know, but that does not replace going out there for yourself and taking real training courses taught by professional instructors.

Here are a few tips you should keep in mind:

1) Develop Your Awareness

This you won't learn in any shooting school, and if I could somehow bottle and sell the level of awareness I've gained by living here in the suburbs of Buenos Aires since the crisis, I'd have a good gig going on. But I can't. The best thing I can do is repeat my "lessons learned" in this book until I drill them into your brain. Awareness is THE most important thing you have to learn about self defense.

Situational awareness isn't cool. You can't brag about it to your buddies like a new gun or knife, but it's hands-down the thing on which you have to concentrate the most in terms of self defense.

Most action movies, where the hero spends hours shooting and killing and firing hundreds of rounds, would end in three minutes if the hero, seeing trouble coming, simply turned around and walked away.

I agree, that's not the kind of movie I'd like to watch, but in real life it's by far the best outcome you can expect or hope for.

Get this engraved into your brain: what you learn in shooting school is what you end up using when you failed at situational awareness.

Gunning down bad guys sounds macho, but being aware of trouble coming your way a few seconds before it's too late can allow you to avoid the potential risk and subsequent legal fees and court visits, or even your ending up in jail.

How do you develop situational awareness? By being fully conscious of your surroundings at all times. While walking on the street, who's fifty yards in front of you, and who's behind? What are those guys doing hanging out on that street corner? Are they doing something wrong? Are they just doing nothing when according to their age they should be in school or at work?

Study people's hands. Are they carrying something? Are their hands visible? Are they trying to keep their hands behind their backs as if hiding something?

Check their waists. Is a gun or other weapon "printing" through their clothing?

Learn to smell and listen to your surroundings. No, you won't "smell" the scent of your attacker. But sometimes you can smell gunpowder after hearing sounds that sounded like shots, or you can smell a fire before you hear the fire truck going that way.

I've gotten used to paying special attention when I hear a **motorcycle**, since this is a favorite transport method for criminals.

Your vision is of great importance. See and be aware of people all around you. Don't worry about looking silly if your gut tells you to **"check your six."** (That's your back, or six o'clock in the language of fighter pilots.) Your human instinct has been around for a long time, so you should pay attention to it.

Don't worry only about people that look "poor" or like bums. Criminals will also dress very well to go unnoticed and attract less attention. I've heard it a million times. "They looked like 'normal' people. With a fresh haircut, and better dressed than you or me."

Don't underestimate women either, young ones or older ones. In Buenos Aires since the crisis we've seen fourteen-year-old girls being gang leaders and stabbing cops, and fifty-year-old mothers robbing shops with their sons. Maybe in the old days "pre-crisis" it wasn't that common. Today, the female "bad guy" is even more likely to pull the trigger than the male version, out of pure hatred.

Force yourself to think this way for a while, and eventually it will become second nature to you.

Think this way for a year or two. Then read this book again.

You did that? Alright. Now touch the back of your head. Feel a little bump? That's a little red light that grew in your skull. It will start flashing when something just isn't right, even if you can't tell for sure what it is.

That, my friends, is situational awareness. Develop it!

2) Carry Your Gun

I can't emphasize this enough. And apparently it's something of a novel concept to some people, even within the survivalist community. They take it to the range, take some shooting classes, post pictures of it on the internet and yet they never carry the damn thing. They'll start carrying it on daily basis "when the SHTF." Yeah, right!

People, the gun does you no good sitting in the safe, and there's not going to be an "Official SHTF Day."

One of those stupid "internet rules" about gun fighting goes, "The first rule of gun fighting: Bring a rifle, and bring your friends with rifles."

Things must work very differently in the USA, because in Argentina you sure as hell don't receive an engraved invitation to attend a gunfight.

Dear Mr. or Mrs. Potential Victim,

We're going to ambush you tomorrow morning at 7:12 AM, when you exit your garage. Please call your friends tonight and let them know.

PS: Remember to bring your battle rifle and wear a chest rig with lots of loaded magazines. Your friends too. See you tomorrow.

     —Mr. Bad Guys.

No my friend, it won't happen that way. Let me give you a few reality-based pointers.

*It will happen when you least expect it.

*It will happen when you think you don't need to be armed.

*You'll be wearing your ordinary clothes, not your IPSC or IDPA gear vest.

*Most likely, there will be your kids, your wife and innocent bystanders nearby.

*You won't have a rifle with you. If I convinced you, or if you already carry, you'll at least have an adequate fighting handgun.

*Your friends will be home watching American Idol, they will not be with you.

Take for example what happened to Mr. Aldo Rico (a man with a long but dark military career), the Mayor of San Miguel here in Buenos Aires.

He was taking his girls to school in the morning, when he noticed a car outside with armed people in it. Rico didn't wait, he didn't hesitate. He just lowered the window and started shooting. The guys in the car just took off.

Keep this in mind when choosing a handgun. A revolver won't allow you to put a steady amount of dissuasive firepower downrange.

3) A gun in your hand ten seconds earlier beats the world's fastest draw.

Do not take any chances. When your gut feeling tells you something is wrong, it probably is.

Why are those guys walking towards you in the parking lot a ten PM, especially considering that yours is the only car in that direction?

Why are those guys in a car just waiting in front of your house, hanging around and doing nothing as you arrive home from work or the store?

Someone knocks or rings at your front door. You check through a window or peephole and find a stranger standing there. Get your gun ready before even talking to him. Of course, do not open the door. Home invaders usually talk you into opening the door for them. Don't do it!

Brandishing a gun for no good reason is a crime, but getting killed is worse. When in doubt (especially after the SHTF), it's better to keep the potentially dangerous stranger at gunpoint, or at least draw your weapon and keep it ready.

If the guy or guys have no ill intent, you'll probably just scare them a bit and they'll turn around and leave rather fast. No one got hurt, and everyone goes home. If they are bad guys and you have the drop on them, they might just turn around and leave as well, since criminals mostly prefer helpless victims. If they start pulling guns at least you already have yours ready to shoot first.

4) Carry Your Gun Where It's Easily Accessible

Being right-handed, I was taught to carry at four o'clock (considering my belt buckle to be twelve o'clock). Some people like it more towards three or five o'clock. Every person is different; just do what's more comfortable to you. Spare magazines go at eight o'clock, though some like them better at ten o'clock. This may be handier for sport shooting but the spare magazines are more visible for concealed carry and can stick into your belly when seated.

5) It's Not Target Practice

As multiple IPSC and IDPA champion Rob Leatham said, half joking and half seriously, "accuracy is overrated." It seems it's true for IDPA and it's especially true for self defense shooting.

Yes, it is true that when learning marksmanship that when you "aim small you miss small." However, shooting a target that isn't standing squarely in front of you, but is moving or running and shooting back at you is very different.

In that case, you shoot to center of mass, and keep on shooting as much as needed. Hitting first and repeatedly matters much more than grouping two inches at fifteen yards.

The way I was taught was to shoot was with both eyes opened. As the hands come together and the gun is raised to eye level, shoot as soon as you see the front sight cover your target. This sounds a bit sloppy but it's fast, it's still pretty accurate and it works well if you take the time to practice it slowly at first.

6) Eyes On Target, At All Times!

You never take your eyes off your attacker. When drawing, shooting, reloading and reholstering, your eyes are always on your attacker. Once he's down you look for his friends nearby, then turn 180° degrees and check your back. Then look back to your enemy on the ground.

But remember, keep your eyes glued to your attacker.

7) Learn To Shoot and Draw With Either Hand

A guy attending a shooting class I went to had been the victim of a carjacking attempt. He had already taken Module One of the course, and had learned how to shoot weak-handed.

The carjacker just climbed into his passenger seat, and this student kept the bad guy's weapon at bay (I don't remember if it was a knife or gun) with his right hand, cross drew with his weak hand, and shot him several times in the chest.

Instructor Jorge Baigorria explained that this is precisely why we trained to draw and shoot with our weak hand. You never know how a gun fight will turn out.

Also important to mention: This student was in overall good shape. A couple of students had rather large beer bellies and little flexibility. For them, it was harder to draw weak-handed, since it requires you to bend your torso forward towards the ground as much as possible and put your weak hand around your back and grab the pistol's grip in the opposite end (for a four o'clock holster position).

8) Gun Fighting Isn't About Shooting, It's About Fighting

Some people learned that on the day when they saw for themselves how they were disarmed and beaten by unarmed non-cooperative partners (attackers) when the attack occurred at close range.

It's not about target practicing, it's about fighting, and the Tueller drill clearly shows the dangers of an attack at close range.

Guns aren't magic wands and most attacks occur at very close range. If the attacker closes in fast and grabs your gun hand before you can shoot him, then the best hand-to-hand fighter wins.

Can you fight hand-to-hand?

"No I'm a couch potato, but that's why I carry a gun."

Wrong! Maybe you'll get lucky, but you are also risking getting your gun used on you as an improvised prostate exam tool if the attack occurs at very close "sidewalk" range.

9) Shoot First, and Shoot As Much As Needed

It's not a Clint Eastwood Western movie. As soon as you see the bad guy with a gun, unless he's already dropping it, you put him down. Waiting until he aims and shoots you might be the worst and most stupid mistake you'll ever make. And probably your very last mistake too.

I was taught to shoot a bit high, to the sternum where the heart is. If the first couple of shots don't get the job done, keep shooting but move the gun a bit up to the neck and then the face. "Zipping it up," as they call it here.

This should be practiced a lot when training, since you shouldn't expect your attacker to drop with the first shot. Also, it works when the attacker in under the influence of drugs and alcohol or is wearing body armor.

10) If That's All You Have Left, Use Your Gun As a Blunt Weapon

Maybe you ran out of ammo or suffered a jam you can't clear. At close range you still have your pistol and you can use it as a blunt weapon. Don't go for a fancy grip. Just hold like you usually hold it, in a single-handed grip.

In the good old days guns had frames made of steel, and just hammering with it over the head could easily break a person's skull. Colt 1911s and Hi Powers are still very capable of doing this, even if you may bend the magazine a bit.

Doing this with lighter polymer framed guns will certainly be less effective.

Another attack that also applies with polymer framed guns like the Glock is simply slapping with the slide into the face. Glocks have nice square slides and this should work well. Preferably aim for the fragile cheek bone, the bones around the eye, the nose and the teeth.

11) Your Handgun Is Your Main Weapon

Rifles are terrific, but they are not your main weapon. Again, there's an important difference between a soldier or a SWAT member, and you.

A soldier carries his rifle because it's his job to do so while at war. The SWAT cop carries his rifle when doing his thing as well, but both the soldier and the SWAT cop do NOT carry their rifles when they go pick up the kids at a friend's birthday party. And yes, the bad guys will attack you at that birthday party, or some other ridiculously unlikely circumstance.

That's the way it is my friend. Understand that while I'm writing this tonight there are thousands of bad guys staying awake in their beds thinking about possible plans and ideas to rob people like you and me.

The attacks occur mostly when people enter or leave their homes, but they also occur when least expected. Plan on having to rely only on your handgun, because more than likely, that's all you'll have.

There won't be an "Official SHTF Day" declared.

You won't get up one day, watch the news while having breakfast before going to work, and the announcer says: "Today it will be a bit cold, so take a light jacket. Also, remember that today the SHTF started, so don't forget to take your battle rifle to work."

Even in countries where there's open war going on, people still have to show up for work. Unfortunately that doesn't change, and you won't go to the office with your AR-15 hanging from your shoulder.

Stuff just happens. Hurricanes, floods or other natural disasters; a market crash and economic activity slowly grinding down as crime gets worse and worse. One day you get up and go to work and you think, "Damn, when did we start living like this?"

You don't get to carry a rifle, but you can get away with a concealed handgun.

Even after Hurricane Katrina, the National Guard disarmed people they saw who were armed. They even went house to house confiscating weapons. A handgun would have stayed out of sight and out of mind while you boarded a boat to evacuate, or simply walked away, getting lost in the crowd.

12) Carry A Handgun With Maximum Fighting Capability

"My handgun is too big and heavy to carry around all day."

Unless you are referring to a .44 Magnum revolver with a twelve-inch barrel, you can conceal it. Carry it in a quality inside-the-waist-band (IWB) holster, and just get over it.

"I got tired of carrying my Sig 226, so now I just drop a five-shot .38 Special snubby into my pants pocket and that's it."

Newsflash, people! It's not supposed to be all nice and comfortable. It's not a hanky or an extra pair of panties. It's a weapon you decided to carry to protect your life and eventually to kill people if that's what it takes.

Some people will even complain about guns as small as the Glock 19, and end up carrying mini pocket guns in some of the weakest calibers ever made. Guns like a NAA .22LR single-action mini revolver just because it's more comfortable.

Sorry, but to me that's irresponsible and unacceptable.

It falls into the same category as:

"I don't like my Glock. It's black and ugly. I want one with moons and stars, just like the drawings "My Little Pony" has painted on his ass."

No guys, seriously. Some shooters out there just sound like big sissies. An unwieldy gun was something like those old flintlock single-shot pistols. Those things were pretty much a rifle with a chopped down stock and barrel. People had to carry a bunch of them around if they wanted any amount of firepower.

Something as small and light as a Glock 17, and you can fire 17+1 rounds? That's a wonder of modern technology. Unthinkable 100 years ago. Modern self defense handguns are all minuscule in comparison, and quite capable of being carried concealed with an adequate holster and clothing.

Compact or sub-compact size versions are for backup, or for deep concealment where failing to conceal your gun perfectly can get you killed. For example, an undercover narcotics cop. This isn't the case with law abiding citizens who can legally carry their guns concealed.

Worrying mainly about your comfort, instead of worrying about magazine capacity, accuracy, sight radius and ergonomics for ease of shooting means you're not serious about carrying a firearm for real-world protection.

13) Nine Times Out Of Ten, the Presence of a Gun Defuses the Situation

The American author Robert Heinlein said that, "an armed society is a polite society." He was so right.

Carrying your gun doesn't mean that you end up shooting people on weekly basis as crime gets worse. It may happen eventually but it's not likely, especially if you draw first and take control of the situation.

When states in the USA started to issue concealed carry weapons licenses, certain people cried out that it would turn into "The Wild West." Of course those people are full of BS and have no idea of what they are talking about.

If they had carried guns themselves and used them to thwart mugging attempts, they would know that even potential sadists turn into the nicest people.

You point the gun at their face and they seem to remember the smell of roses, the kiss of their first girlfriend, how beautiful it sounds when birds sing on a summer day and how pleasant it is to be able to chew food, and how that might get complicated if you pull the trigger and blow a new hole into their faces.

To you, it just looks like the dumbest expression you've ever seen. But they seem to remember other important matters they had to take care of, and they leave in a big hurry.

That's the general outcome. It doesn't mean it will always be like that, and you have to be ready for those that don't appreciate the little things in life, like being able to breathe without the assistance of a machine.

Then it's you, your mindset, your training, and a large amount of luck.

But we are all big boys and girls here and we live by the decisions we make.

14) Guns Do Not Increase the Size of Your Penis

If you consider your penis to be too small, visit your doctor. There seems to be some confusion in this regard. A gun, no matter how big, won't fix your problem. This one is especially intended for the guys. Women don't have this problem. Well, maybe it applies to some manly feminists as well.

If fantasies of shooting people make you feel all warm and tingly, then you don't need a gun. You need professional help. Or maybe what you are looking for is to play some first-person-shooter videogames. That's fine as long as you understand one thing: The difference between videogames and reality.

The idea is to get back home each day in a world that has become unbelievably dangerous compared to what you were used to 10 years ago.

The idea is that at the end of the day your wife still has a husband and your kids still have a father. It gets to the point where you don't even tell you wife that someone tried to rob you, so that she's not nervous the next time you come home late at night.

Don't worry: if you want to find trouble, you'll find plenty after the SHTF.

What I'm writing about here is how to prevent these things as much as possible, and then doing what you have to do to stay alive when prevention fails.

If someone calls you a "son of a bitch," even if you are packing, you walk away.

If someone starts looking for trouble you don't allow yourself to get involved BECAUSE you have a gun. If a person just can't control his own temper, then he should not carry a firearm.

If carrying a gun makes you feel all brave and cocky, then you should CERTAINLY stay the heck away from firearms. Since the SHTF, we had people that confused their handgun with their penis. They are all either dead or in jail.

I hope that was clear enough!

CALIBERS AND STOPPING POWER

Here we are once again entering a common gun fanatic dispute that has cost the lives of many brave trees, dying to provide tons of paper for articles and debates that will never end, so I'll try to keep it simple.

Terminal ballistic effects in live tissue is a very complex field of study, and there are several competing schools of thought.

Some seem to believe that nothing short of a central nervous system shot (spine or brain) will rapidly stop a man. The problem with this line of thought is the enormous amount of evidence that proves otherwise.

Others simply analyze the temporary and permanent cavities created when firing different types of ammo into ballistic gelatin. The permanent cavity is the actual "hole" left, and the temporary one is the cavity created momentarily by the hydrostatic shock. Overall penetration depth, and the expansion of hollow point rounds are also taken into consideration.

This helps to quantify ballistic effects, but there are a few inconsistencies in the way the data is analyzed. Some simply concentrate on the permanent cavity, wrongly supposing the temporary cavity has little or no relevancy in stopping power. This is proven wrong in the field, when you see ammunition such as .45 ACP FMJ that performs well against people in real shootings, but in gelatin tests they make a permanent cavity similar to 9mm FMJ, with the faster 9mm even penetrating more deeply.

I take the ballistic gelatin tests into consideration, but to me the performance on the street is more important.

Gelatin is also very homogenous and of constant density, while the human body is composed of muscle, flesh and organs of different densities and resistance to shock. Not to mention that the entire bone structure is not taken into consideration at all in ballistic gelatin tests.

There are many things that come into play regarding stopping power:

The projectile's speed, diameter, weight, shape, material, weight retention after the impact and where in the body it actually impacted are some of the factors.

A shot in the shoulder may not sound too serious, but if a main nerve is destroyed the arm may require amputation and of more importance, the pain may be so overwhelming that it can rapidly incapacitate the attacker.

Every caliber can kill. The humble .22LR is the most popular round in the planet, and also one of the smallest, and it still kills people every day.

Having said that, the idea isn't just to kill. You need your opponent immediately incapacitated so that he can't harm you or keep shooting.

There used to be a time when apparently people thought that shooting someone was some sort of "ray of death" that exterminated people right there on the spot. This is, of course, not true. Back in those days even police departments and the British military issued weak calibers such as .32 Long and .38 Short.

In many cases people are still able to fight or shoot back after getting shot.

Today, things have flipped around completely. Many people who are into guns seem to think that most rifle and especially handgun rounds will usually fail to stop a person. According to some of them, shooting anybody with anything less than a cannonball straight to the head just won't get the job done.

It turns out that neither extreme vision is correct. As usual, the truth lies somewhere in between.

Take for example 9mm Full Metal Jacket (FMJ).

According to most "experts," it's an inadequate rapid man stopper, even if it kills after some time. The problem isn't its energy, but its lack of capacity to transfer its energy to the target. Usually 9mm FMJ goes through the body and keeps on going.

But since stories tend to be exaggerated, "inadequate man stopper" isn't enough, and if you allow yourself to believe everything you hear or read, then you'll end up thinking 9mm FMJ is completely useless when it's not.

Here in Argentina, 9mm FMJ is the only round issued to every single police department in the country.

Is it perfect? No. Is it even an adequate option, considering the ammunition available today? No. But that doesn't mean it's worthless either. Cops use it to kill bad guys every day. Some of the horror stories are true. Since it lacks rapid stopping power, more than one shot may be needed. So cops keep shooting, something you are supposed to do no matter what caliber you use.

Before 9mm, the issued caliber was the .45 ACP 230 grain FMJ. This round has always proven to be very effective. It's been used effectively in WWI, WWII, Korea and Vietnam, and some of the older local cops here in Argentina remember well the greater stopping power the bigger caliber had.

Yet today, we are supposed to believe that FMJ .45 ACP isn't a good stopper.

It is true that hollow points are better because they expand, transferring the energy more effectively, but don't think that FMJ ammo (9mm or preferably larger), won't get the job done if you do your part.

In spite of a few horror stories, 9mm or larger, such as .40 S&W, .357 SIG, .357 Magnum, 10mm and .45 ACP (just to mention the most popular calibers), will perform very well if you choose the right ammo.

Ed Sanow, co-author of "Handgun Stopping Power: The Definitive Study" and other books, is considered an expert on the subject. He has researched hundreds of shootings, determining the percentage of one-shot-stops when bullets were fired to center of mass, and all the calibers mentioned above have at least one variety of ammunition that is rated above 90% for "one-shot stops."

For this reason, I feel confident in recommending 9mm to people. I know that if you use good quality, high velocity 124 grain JHPs, it will do well enough.

ABOUT PISTOLS AND REVOLVERS

I don't think it's even worth discussing this anymore. Anyone that still hasn't made up his mind about what's better for self defense can just take a shooting class and see what everyone is using.

Then take a couple of dozen other classes with other instructors and see what THEY are using. While doing that, check every military force on the planet, and every police department.

Maybe a few decades ago you could still argue about it. Today, real-world gunfights dictate a new reality. It's no longer just one or two shots fired. It can go up to fifty or a hundred rounds exchanged. A lot of lead ends up flying both ways these days during shootings.

Once you study it a bit more deeply, you can see why this happens.

Take four criminals using 13+1 round autos (Browning High Powers), shooting it out with two cops armed with Bersa Thunder 9s that hold 17+1 rounds each, and you have 92 rounds fired, with none of them even reloading!

People, after the crisis in Argentina, it's not uncommon to hear about eight or more bad guys working together. Sometimes they just take over one house, use that as a command post, and spend the rest of the night robbing the rest of the houses on that block.

The days of one or two bad guys armed with revolvers have been replaced by an average of three bad guys armed with high-capacity semiauto pistols.

Carry a revolver, and you are putting yourself at a huge disadvantage regarding your firepower capability, compared to the criminals you may be fighting.

You only carry a snub nose .38 revolver, because your small town is very safe? I still don't understand it, because there are similar-sized autos that offer much more firepower, accuracy, reloading speed, and easier follow-up shots.

Of course maybe one shot is possibly all you need…or maybe not. More than likely, you might never fire a single round in your life for self defense.

But that's the point, you never know. And today, the possibility of needing more ammo has increased significantly. Why then choose a revolver that, at equal size and weight, provides you with one-third the ammo capacity of an auto?

Your handgun must be everything it can be for its size.

As much as I like the .45 caliber 1911, when I take everything into account I clearly see that today a Glock is a better option.

The 1911 is well proven and very accurate. But it's still a heavy 8+1 auto. Glocks, though not as accurate as a tricked out 1911, are still pretty accurate. They are also more reliable and resistant to abuse, and carry far more ammo.

My personal choice, as the best all around package a handgun can offer, is the Glock 31 in .357 SIG.

The disadvantage is that 357 SIG is expensive and not as popular as other calibers, but this point can be solved quickly since any .357 SIG can also fire .40

S&W by using a spare barrel. A new barrel isn't that expensive and it allows you to fire .40 S&W, which is popular and relatively cheaper.

The .357 SIG replicates the .357 magnum load that made the caliber famous as the undisputed best man stopper for decades: A 124 gr. JHP projectile flying at 1400 fps. The .357 SIG out of the Glock 31 exceeds those specifications.

The 357 SIG is being used by the United States Secret Service and Federal Air Marshals as well as many police departments and agencies across the United States. Every police department and agency that uses it is very pleased with the caliber's performance. Once you study the specifications and analyze the cartridge and bullet design, it's easy to see why. And the street reports by officers that use it are very encouraging as well.

It's not just that the caliber has very good stopping power, but the bottle-neck cases feed extremely smoothly into the chamber, and failures to feed are not as common as in straight-walled cases. It's also more accurate than other calibers.

Shooting it from the Glock platform, you can verify how easy it is to make fast follow-up shots, in spite of the gun's loud bark. There's a visible flame as you fire, but I tried this shooting in the dark and it doesn't blind me in any way when using quality ammo. You have 15+1 rounds of ammo at your disposal, and it's easier to shoot fast and reload than any .357 Magnum revolver.

I'm getting into too much detail regarding my personal caliber of choice, and that's not the intention here.

What I want you to understand is that no matter what kind of auto pistol you choose, high capacity is very important after the SHTF, when crime increases and commando-style robberies and kidnapping become much more common.

I'm not trying to fool anyone here. If you ever face such an attack, your chances aren't very good. But there have been cases where the victim did manage to fight back and either kill or repel the attackers, and they couldn't have done it without a high capacity semi-auto pistol.

I remember a judge that repelled an attack with his Glock. The two bad guys ran and he shot one in the back of the head. He got out of that one because he's a judge. Any one of us would end up in jail for shooting a robber in the back. That unequal treatment will still be the reality even after the SHTF.

I also remember a forensic doctor that used to live in my neighborhood, who got ambushed by five or six men when he exited a restaurant. They did kill him, but he managed to kill four of them and he severely wounded another.

This doctor used to practice with his Glock .40 S&W at my local shooting range. I don't remember exactly how many rounds he fired during the attack, but I remember that it at least doubled the capacity of most revolvers.

LONG GUNS

Even if your handgun is your main weapon, there are other guns you should also consider.

SHOTGUNS

The shotgun has always been considered one of the best all around, general purpose firearms. Pump-action shotguns are reliable, tough, and have tremendous stopping power at close range with the right ammo.

Most of them can also accept a longer barrel with variable chokes for hunting birds and other small game. With a shorter barrel with rifle sights, you can hunt big game using slugs or sabot projectiles.

The caliber of choice is usually 12 gauge, and the top choices are the Remington 870 and the Mossberg 500/590.

For self defense, 00 buckshot is one of the most common choices. Some prefer to use slugs instead because of the great knock down power and acceptable accuracy up to seventy yards.

Bird shot is intended for birds, but armchair warrior wisdom aside, the amount of dead people killed with birdshot clearly shows there's more to it than shooting pigeons. At indoor ranges of less than five yards or so, birdshot will almost act as a solid projectile. At greater ranges stopping power drops significantly because of the very small pellet size. If you keep your shotgun for self defense and plan to use it indoors, this might be an advantage if your house has dry wall construction.

One of the things I like about the shotgun is its ability to shoot a variety of ammunition, including less than lethal (LTL) rounds.

I keep my fourteen inch barrel Mossberg 500 loaded with four shells of Federal 000 buckshot, and one of Number 1 buckshot to avoid over penetration at close range. Fourteen inch barrels are legal in Argentina, but in many countries the minimum is 16" or 18", so check the laws of your country and State to be sure.

Since this shotgun has a capacity of six shells, there's space for one more round in the tubular magazine. This is called a "hole," and leaving the chamber empty allows a shooter to feed one round into the tubular magazine, pump the action, and send that round into the chamber ready to fire. This allows me to use "special" ammunition I keep in the shell holder on the stock. There I have a couple of LTL shells, two slugs and more buckshot. This setup allows me to deal with a variety of situations, including the use of LTL ammo, something almost impossible to do with most other firearms.

Maybe it doesn't seem likely to be deployed by civilians, but during the riots of 2001 many shop owners bought all the LTL 12 gauge ammo off the shelves, to be used to dissuade potential looters.

I'm not saying that LTL ammo is a good self defense alternative. I'm just saying that it can be handy in specific situations, such as when dealing with looters, when killing them might get you arrested later on. Maybe a LTL round will convince them to change their mind. If not, lead buckshot is just a pump away.

At least it's nice to have the option. It's another tool in the tool box.

As handy as the shotgun is, capable of performing different tasks, it wouldn't be my first choice as a fighting long arm.

SHOTGUNS FOR DEFENSE

I like shotguns because of their reliable mechanics and unparalleled stopping power at close range, but I've always thought that they are not the best choice for home defense. The lessons I've learned during defensive pistol classes have reaffirmed this notion even more.

Even though many consider the shotgun to be THE best home defense weapon, they have a few inherent problems when compared to what I consider to be more capable weapons for close quarters combat (CQC), which is the kind of fighting you are most likely to engage in inside of your home.

First, most long arms are too big and unwieldy to move easily through and around the tight confines of a house.

It takes a lot of practice not to bump into every wall, door or piece of furniture, especially if you are under stress. Next, in case an attacker grabs hold of your barrel, it gives him just too much leverage to use against you.

In spite of the maneuvers you can learn in case this happens, the truth is that a long arm does provide him with more surface to grab and more leverage. If you are up against a physically stronger attacker, the odds are not in your favor when fighting over the weapon.

In a big isolated house or farm, where the fight can be easily brought outside, I'd much rather have a pistol caliber semiauto subgun, like a Beretta Storm, or a short carbine chambered for a rifle round.

For an average size house or apartment a big bore handgun would allow you to move around better, open doors and have a leading "sacrifice" hand ready to keep an attacker at bay.

The pump shotgun also has another disadvantage that was made very clear to me while practicing retention drills and hand-to-hand techniques during the class. The pump shotgun obviously requires both of your hands to work the action. This is something that is fast to do when no one is giving you a hard time, but you still need both hands none-the-less for each shot.

What I mean is: if you fire your weapon and your attacker happens to twist the barrel away from his body, you are now in a pretty big pool of fecal matter. You are fighting over a weapon that requires you to also use the hand that you are currently using to defend yourself from your attacker. Putting both hands on your shotgun allows your attacker to use one hand to keep the barrel away from his body and the other hand to punch, stab or shoot into your face at will.

You'll probably be locked together as you fight, so you'll also lack the space needed to put the muzzle of the barrel against him.

A handgun allows you to use your "sacrifice" hand to keep your attacker at bay, open doors as you move around, and punch or push to gain more separation distance. You can easily fire round after round with the pistol held close against your ribs, slightly angled down with the muzzle pointed at your attacker's chest.

Trying all this out for real is very enlightening. Remember to take the necessary precautions, please! Both participants must check for themselves that the weapons used are empty before they exercise this.

Sure, cops use shotguns (though lately AR carbines are becoming more popular), but they choose shotguns because of other reasons.

1) ALL cops carry a handgun as well, something most folks that recommend a shotgun as the one and only weapon for defense seem to forget.

2) They have other bystanders to worry about, and the shotgun's limited range is a terrific bonus regarding this issue. God only knows how many innocent bystanders are alive thanks to this wise decision.

3) Cops work as a team. They won't go anywhere alone if they can help it, especially when facing an armed attacker. Meaning, if an attacker grabs hold of an officer's shotgun barrel, his partner will either shoot him, Taser him, or crack his skull open with his baton.

These are BIG differences. You are much more likely to be alone when handling something like that. A short barrel AK would be much better than a pump shotgun regarding the ease of putting rounds down range just by pulling the trigger. They also have much higher capacity, thirty rounds versus six to eight rounds in most pump shotguns.

A rifle round is very effective due to its high speed, but for home defense I'd go for JHP ammo to avoid over penetration, something that can easily happen with military FMJ ammo.

The carbine advantage becomes more evident when the fight is brought to your front lawn or back yard, defending against attackers at longer ranges like Alejandro Reynoso mentions in his book regarding defending isolated retreats or farm houses. He says that in these locations, the minimum gun battery should include two or three handguns, and at least one shotgun or better yet, a pistol caliber carbine or subgun.

The rifle cartridge turns most cover into concealment, since it penetrates much better than most pistol and shotgun cartridges.

The Saiga-12 shotgun, based on the Kalashnikov rifle pattern is also worth mentioning. The magazine-fed weapon has a capacity or two, five, eight or ten

12-gauge rounds, and a 20-round capacity drum is also manufactured. It's a devastating short to medium range weapon. Care must be taken though regarding leaving magazines full, since shotgun shells are more likely to deform under pressure, unlike metallic rifle cartridges.

RIFLES

Though most of the time the handgun will be what you use to defend yourself, sometimes you are lucky and you are able to get to use your rifle. Either when defending your home from attackers or while carrying a rifle in the trunk of your car, if you can get your hands on it, it's certainly a force multiplier.

More range, more power, greater magazine capacity…what's not to like?

Too bad you can't carry one under your shirt…though with a short barrel and a folding stock under a big jacket, you can somewhat keep it out of sight.

Also, I must admit, a rifle is far more intimidating. If drawing a handgun scares most criminals and sends them running, bringing a short barrel FAL (Fusil Automatique Léger) out from under your coat will likely make them piss their pants.

All firearms are deadly, and no one wants to get shot with anything, but certainly rifles are more intimidating. Besides, if intimidation isn't enough, well…you have a rifle to deal with your problem!

In my opinion, the survivalist is best served with a short barreled rifle.

Though 5.56 is widely popular around the world, .30 caliber rifle ammunition has proven to be more effective. There's still a debate going on regarding whether or not 5.56mm (.223 caliber) is an adequate man stopper. Some people like it, mostly theorists, while a lot of people that actually have to use it for fighting don't like it much.

As eventually lethal as 5.56 may be, it does not have the stopping power of the AK-47's 7.62x39, or the 30-06 caliber the legendary Garand rifle fires, or the 7.62x51 fired by the FAL and the M14. These are all .30 caliber rifle cartridges and have a proven track record of immediate stopping power and penetration.

Don't underestimate the importance of powerful penetration, where the 7.62x51 is a winner among the common battle rifle calibers. It may be sufficient for Army soldiers to employ a weaker caliber such as 5.56mm to pin an enemy down, while more powerful weapons such as machine guns, grenade launchers and mortars are brought to bear. You are not a soldier and you will be alone, without heavier supporting arms behind you. Your rifle will be the most powerful weapon you have, live or die, all the way to the end of a fight.

A weapon that can "turn cover into concealment" will give you a very big advantage in a fight. For example, 7.62x51 will punch all the way through both sides of a car from many angles, to reach adversaries shooting at you from the other side. It will also go through small trees and many common types of walls.

Usually, 5.56mm will not be able to penetrate these obstacles. Thus, the 7.62x51 can end an engagement decisively and in your favor, in situations where the weaker 5.56 allows your enemy to continue to fire away at you from cover.

While the 5.56x45mm may have been adopted by military forces because of a number of reasons, but some of these advantages don't apply to you as a survivalist. The 5.56 is light, accurate, easy to fire since it has little recoil, cheap, and the soldier can carry a lot of it. This also makes logistics much easier in terms of fabricating ammunition and transporting it all around the world.

Tip: 5.56x45mm NATO cartridges look just like .223 Remington, but they are not completely interchangeable because of certain small differences. The ability to shoot both rounds will depend on each firearm. The same happens with 7.62x51mm NATO and .308 Winchester.

Most people who are into armed survivalism are usually better trained than the average boot soldier. Many have been shooting or hunting since they were very young.

The survivalist doesn't have to worry about arming a wide variety of people of all sizes, so unless you are sensitive to recoil, it won't be a problem for you.

The survivalist should certainly not care that much about the cost of the ammunition fired to save his life. While cheap ammo is preferable to allow more training, it's hard to go cheap on the ammo that will be used to protect yourself and your family.

For all of these reasons, I believe .30 calibers offer much more, even though it comes at a more expensive price. I'd go for a folding stock AK with a short barrel and a quick-detach electronic red dot sight. Other than maybe getting a better trigger for it, I'd keep it as simple as possible.

At greater ranges, beyond 300 or 400 yards the more accurate AR rifle will outrange the AK. If your terrain or situation dictates such ranges, seriously consider an M1A or fixed stock FAL chambered in 7.62x51 mm with a quality gun mount and scope. This is basically what the US Marine Corps does with its DMR (Designated Marksman Rifle). The Designated Marksman is issued a scoped M14 rifle, chambered in 7.62x51mm. This is an effective long range weapon firing an effective long range cartridge. The Designated Marksman isn't a true "sniper" but is still the one doing the more accurate rapid long range shooting in its squad. He's the one doing the killing at long range, while the rest lay down mostly suppressive fire that isn't as accurate and the affectivity of the cartridge isn't as important.

My favorite rifle caliber is 7.62x51 NATO, and here I'm partial to the FAL in the "Congo" configuration, with a paratrooper folding stock and a short barrel. The FAL is a pretty accurate rifle and can take advantage of good optics with the right type of scope mount.

The semiauto M1A is a top of the line rifle. One of the most accurate semiauto rifles available, it's a descendent of the M1 Garand rifle and is the civilian version of the M-14. One of the things I don't like as much about it, is that it's hard to get a good folding stock for it, and those that are available don't look very practical compared to the FAL PARA stock. The mechanism of the FAL is more simple too, in my opinion.

My configuration for a M1A would be a Scout Rifle set up, short barrel and forward mounted scope.

Though Red Dot sights are fast and great for close range, you might want something else to squeeze out the extra accuracy a FAL or M1A can provide.

For hunting and long range shooting, a bolt action rifle will be nice to have. Even if your AK, FAL or M1A are very capable of hunting and long range shooting (200 yard range with a scope), bolt action rifles are even more accurate.

How necessary is this? Unless you hunt, not much. The idea of an ordinary person that is into survivalism and prepping needing to do long range "sniper" shooting is something that borders on fantasy. Remember, you always shoot in self defense, and you can't claim self defense when you blow a hole into someone 200 yards away.

So the bolt action rifle will mostly be used for hunting and getting rid of troublesome animals.

Though the 30-06 has more variety of bullet types and weights available, I would keep things as simple as possible and get a bolt rifle in .308 caliber.

Many people like the Remington 700. Slightly modified, it's been a standard police and military sniper rifle for decades. The Savage Model 110 is a great value for the money, a superb rifle that costs a fraction of more famous brand names.

Here in Argentina, most hunters get their rifles built by a gunsmith using the actions of old Mausers. This also allows the shooter to choose a wide variety of calibers, if .308 isn't right for the game they have in mind.

Tip: There are chamber adapters that allow you to fire .32 Short, .32 Long and .32 H&R out of your .308 bolt rifle. How can this be? Well, the .32 caliber is actually 0.30" in dimension. Similarly, the .38 Special is actually 0.357". (This is why you can shoot .38 Special ammunition from your .357 Magnum.) There were no "truth in advertising" laws a century ago, when many new calibers were introduced. Some companies misnamed their calibers, to separate themselves from their competitors.

These handgun rounds have to be manually fitted into the rifle adaptor. The adaptor has the exterior appearance of an empty rifle case. The advantage is that you can carry a pocket full of .32 Long ammunition, and shoot small game with your big game rifle.

The little .32 caliber projectiles kill rabbits and other small critters with authority, and due to the long barrel and the ammo designed for handguns, it's a very quiet combination as well. This is one little inexpensive adapter that has a lot of applications...

Try finding one online, or ask a friend that knows how to work metals to make one for you. He will need a lathe, and the correct dimensions.

I like the ruggedness of a rifle built around a Mauser 1909 action. My advice is to play it safe and stick to Remington 700, Winchester M70, Savage 110, or rifles built on the M98 action by a reputable gunsmith.

The barrel length should be around twenty or twenty-four inches for hunting and for general purpose shooting. Twenty-six inches will be reserved for longer range shooting since it squeezes a bit more velocity out of rifle cartridges.

The CZ 550 in .308 with the full length Mannlicher-style stock that goes all the way out the barrel is not just a beautiful weapon. The action is very strong and has a single set trigger. This means that it can be fired with a conventional amount of trigger pull weight or may be "set" by pushing forward on the trigger. This takes up the creep in the trigger and allows a much lighter trigger pull for more accurate shots.

One last thing about rifles: Be ready for when your scope or Red Dot sight breaks or fails you. Especially with your combat rifle, make sure it has quick release mounts and that the iron sights are properly sighted in. You must know how to use your iron sights well, for when your optics fail you. As a quick alternative, you can also practice using your turned-off Red Dot sight as a large "ghost ring aperture" and still attain pretty good combat accuracy using it and your front sight.

YOUR FIREARMS BATTERY

For a bare minimum defensive battery you need:

Two Handguns. Your handguns are your most important self defense weapons for after the SHTF, and you need a spare one.

One AK-47 or other carbine length rifle, preferably with a folding stock. The idea is not to shoot people at 200 or more yards away, but to take advantage of the greater power the rifle ammo offers. This is your minimum defensive set up.

For anyone looking for a more complete battery, you should include:

One .22LR rifle. I recommend the most popular .22LR rifle in the world: the **Marlin 65**, which has a tubular magazine. There's a detachable magazine fed version as well, but the tubular magazine version has a much slicker profile. If the budget allows, get a stainless steel version with a laminated stock.

Some people like the **Ruger 10/22**. They sure are popular and accurate, though I don't care for their magazines much. It's mostly a matter of personal choice. Having said that, the Ruger 10/22 is the most popular and common 22LR rifle in USA. There are a thousand "after market" devices made for the 10/22, including 25 and 30 round magazines.

One .22LR handgun. There are .22LR adaptors for Glocks, 1911s, CZ75s and Hi Power handguns. These will usually include a replacement slide, barrel and magazine. The adaptor allows you to shoot cheap .22LR for target practice and training using the same platform you carry all day for defense.

Another good alternative is a four inch barrel "kit" revolver in .22LR. These have a capacity of eight or nine rounds in some models, and are very practical guns for the trail, plinking, and pest control. Because of their larger capacity (for a revolver), they can perform a marginal role as defensive weapons. Don't expect much stopping power, and be ready to empty the cylinder into your attacker.

The revolver advantage is important in this case because "bulk" .22LR ammo is usually not as reliable as center fire ammunition. With a revolver you just pull the trigger and fire the next round.

In the USA, the Ruger Standard Model is the most popular 22 caliber pistol by a very wide margin. They are rugged, accurate, and not too expensive.

There are plenty .22LR pistols but most are of the "target" variety. While very accurate, they aren't designed with self defense shooting in mind.

One of the few exceptions is the Bersa Thunder 22. It's a small pistol, accurate and very durable. The shape and mechanism is somewhat similar to the Walther PPK pistol seen in the old 007 movies.

Bersas have a lifetime warranty and you should snatch one of these .22LR pistols if you find one around for a good price. You won't be disappointed, and if you are you can sell it for a profit to someone that is willing to send it to Bersa for repair, free of charge. The magazine capacity is ten rounds plus one in the chamber.

When using these small caliber pistols for defense, be ready to manually rack the slide, because you often find duds in bulk .22LR ammunition.

One backup handgun. Like any other tool guns can fail as well, so a backup firearm makes a lot of sense.

For many years, the two-inch-barrel "snubby" revolver in either .38 Special or .357 Magnum filled that niche. With a covered or bobbed hammer, the little revolver allows a fast, snag-free draw.

Tip: If you pocket carry a snubby, and the revolver's hammer has a spur, get used to placing your thumb on the spur as you draw so it doesn't get caught on your clothes.

Today you have much better options, especially if you make a Glock your main everyday concealed carry handgun.

The subcompact Glocks are about the same size as a snubby revolver. They come in big bore calibers, have a higher magazine capacity, and they are easier to shoot rapidly and accurately than any snubby revolver. If you pack a Glock as your main gun, you can also have ammo and magazine interchangeability. Many of the spare parts are also interchangeable. For all of these reasons, a full size Glock and a subcompact Glock as a backup are an ideal combination.

One pump action shotgun, with a short barrel for defense and a longer one for hunting. Either a Remington 870 or Mossberg 500/590 in 12 gauge.

One pistol caliber carbine or semiauto sub-gun of some kind. While having full auto as an option is a big plus in my opinion, in the USA it's just too expensive. The Beretta Storm is a good example of a semiauto pistol caliber sub-gun. It can use the same ammo as your primary handgun, but gives you more firepower and greater range. Kel-Tec makes some other pistol caliber carbines that are available in the USA and are not very expensive.

Per family, or for every four persons, you might want to add:

One bolt action .308 rifle. Mostly for hunting and long range shooting. Though not that important for self defense, if you live in a deserted area or your place is surrounded by large expanses of open land, you might want to keep a scoped bolt rifle handy. To take full advantage of this weapon, you'll need good optics, and don't go cheap on the scope either. Leupold is a good brand that makes reliable products. Trijicon is expensive but their scopes are top of the line. They have some nice "tactically" oriented products.

If you're going to use the rifle a lot for hunting in harsh climates, a synthetic stock Remington 700 or M98 Mauser action-based rifle will do better in the long run. For extreme weather, stainless steel rifles with synthetic stocks such as the Ruger KM77 or Savage 110 are a good alternative.

This is strictly a personal option, but I have a weakness for classic lines like the Ruger M77 RSI international or CZ 550, both in .308 Winchester, and both with full length Mannlicher-style stocks. These are rough, accurate and functional yet beautiful rifles.

If your region has large predators such as bears or you are planning on serious big game hunting, maybe a 375 H&H is in order as a general purpose big game rifle. This may also be an issue if the local authorities suddenly lack the funds or resources to monitor and control wild life like they used to do during the times of prosperity. Wolves, coyotes or wild dogs will require a less powerful weapon, but one capable of quick follow up shots and enough magazine capacity instead.

One air rifle. This one you'll need for cheap training. .177 caliber is more common, but I like .22 caliber better since it has more knock down power when shooting small game. You can also use your .22LR cleaning kit on it. Buy thousands of pellets, they sure are cheap enough. Plinking, pest control, target practice and even silent small game hunting can all be done with an air rifle, and it's the cheapest and quietest weapon to fire.

One sub-gun. I would add an extra one for every four family members.

These are sub-guns such as the MP5, Uzi, Beretta, Kel-Tec, and other long arms that shoot pistol ammunition. Full-auto is extremely expensive for most people, or they may not even be legal to own in many countries. For this reason in most cases they will be semi-automatic weapons.

Some people will say that they are simply oversized handguns that offer no real advantage, and you should get a rifle caliber long arm instead. While these weapons don't offer the power rifle calibers provide, there are a number of benefits you should consider.

1) Just like in the old west, ammo interchangeability is a big bonus. Your supply of handgun ammo works for your sub-gun as well. With soaring rifle ammo prices, this is a strategy that looks very attractive.

Even today, people that have a lever-action carbine in .357 Magnum (and .38 Special) or .44 Magnum (and .44 Special) will also carry revolvers chambered for the same round. A 9mm pistol and 9mm semiauto carbine, with 3,000 rounds of ammo, has a lot of potential and doesn't cost that much.

2) Full auto can be a waste of ammo, but it's clearly a force multiplier in the hands of a level headed person that knows how to use it. Unless it's too expensive, you might want to have that option, if legal where you are.

3) Sub-guns and pistol caliber carbines are also more accurate than their handgun counterparts, and give the same bullets greater range.

4) The longer barrel will add about ten percent to the projectile's velocity, making it hit harder. Your 9mm +P ammo will hit like a .357 Magnum when fired from a sub-gun.

5) It's also more controllable. Follow-up shots are easier to perform and the capacity is greater, usually thirty to forty rounds.

6) One of the most important advantages is that many of these subguns will fit right into a backpack, briefcase or a messenger bag. You can go on foot, not carry that much gear, keep everything concealed and still have a handgun and a long gun for more serious situations.

SOUND SUPPRESSORS

Let's talk in "hypothetical" terms here.

A day may come after the SHTF, when things just don't work as they used to. After an economic and social collapse, a person threatening to kill you and your family for his own gain may believe that the level of anarchy is high enough for him to carry out his evil deed without any fear of legal retribution. And he would be right.

Also, in not so hypothetical terms since this actually happened here in Buenos Aires, dogs may roam the city on their own, because the owners can no longer afford to feed them. Eventually they form large feral packs and they even attack people. This happened in my neighborhood and it was a serious problem until someone…got rid of them.

For all of these reasons and many others, do yourself a favor and get a sound suppressor in an effective caliber. A good choice would be .45 ACP, since most of the ammo is already subsonic.

9mm and .22LR subsonic ammo are also available.

After you get a major caliber sound suppressor, you can look into getting one in .22LR for informal plinking and even small game hunting without alerting the neighbors. This can also be done with a good quality air rifle.

Remember the "tip" on the chamber adapter for a .308 bolt action rifle too.

BODY ARMOR

After your first handgun, body armor should probably be your next major purchase, even before you buy more firearms.

Of the things I take along most frequently for "serious business," my handgun is number one, and my body armor is without a doubt number two.

Fantasy: You strap on your body armor and your tactical load-bearing vest, and go scrounging through the remains of what was once your city. You are looking for some canned food left behind by looters and the zombies that came after them, with your faithful pit bull "Dogmeat" running alongside. Oh yes, don't forget your beat-up leather jacket and your sawed-off shotgun.

Reality: First, start by accepting that Fallout is just a role playing game, and Mad Max was a fun movie, but there's no connection whatsoever between them and reality.

Crime has become a problem. A HUGE problem. You try not to worry too much or else you'll go nuts, but you also can't stick your head in the sand and pretend nothing is wrong.

Before I go on, I'd like to say that this is what I do. In no way can this be considered common practice for most Argentines, just as you can't consider it to be common practice for the average American "Joe Six Pack" to make a risk assessment analysis of his personal situation, become proficient in armed and unarmed self defense, stock up on food, have cash savings in case the SHTF, worry about investments, and have an emergency contingency plan.

What I personally determined was that there were certain situations I couldn't avoid, that were very risky given current events, and that based on what was frequently happening to others, there was a much greater possibility of being targeted by criminals than before the crisis. Things like moving large amounts of cash for whatever reason, receiving payments for real estate transactions, meeting potential clients for the first time, or even meeting people to sell your car to, are examples of situations you can't avoid that involve a much higher than usual temporary security risk.

Body armor is not something a lot of people think about. Even most people that carry guns don't own or consider they need body armor. This is foolish!

But as violence gets worse, as the possibility of a gunfight gets closer and you hear about neighbors and people you know personally getting shot or stabbed, you will you have a much clearer picture.

You understand how ridiculously stupid it is to think that someday you'll get into a gunfight, and you are even carrying a gun for just such an event, but for some mysterious reason you think you will never be the one getting shot.

Granted, if things get SO bad after a crisis that you need to use body armor every day, of course you better start wearing it. But to have it ready to wear AFTER the crisis, you need to buy it NOW. Believe me, affordable body armor will not be in your neighborhood store after the SHTF.

Next, you must also find a way to move out of that dangerous area, because it's certainly not safe to continue living there. But hey! You still need to have body armor to survive until you move out of there, don't you?

Unless you live in an extremely dangerous neighborhood after the crisis, I'm not talking about wearing body armor all day, but only on certain situations, like the ones described above that are known to be particularly risky.

Your body armor should be in your closet or another handy place ready for immediate use, with only one side closed. The other side is left open for putting it on fast. If something "goes bump in the night," or if there's trouble of any kind, you get your gun and flashlight and put on your body armor. Practice this getting ready drill in the dark until you can do it very fast, like a firefighter getting ready for a fire.

Other situations where you might want to wear body armor would be while evacuating a city for any given reason when violent encounters are more likely, or during times of civil unrest, looting and outbursts of violence, or when social protests and demonstrations have gone out of control.

Just like your firearm or your fire extinguisher, body armor is the kind of "insurance" you must buy before you need it. Body armor won't be readily available or affordable after the SHTF.

What kind of body armor?

Soft body armor can be concealed under regular clothes. Level II armor is an ideal balance between concealability and protection. It will stop most handgun rounds, except for FMJ 9mm sub-machinegun ammo (higher velocity) and .44 Magnum. You'd need III-A for that kind of protection.

But if you are worried about that kind of threat, maybe hard body armor ceramic plates are better for your situation.

Level II, II-A and III-A is soft body armor made from flexible material. It's more comfortable and will stop most common handgun calibers, but it will not stop rifle rounds, which will zip right through it.

Level III and IV (stops armor-piercing rounds) are hard ceramic armor plates, and these will stop rifle rounds. American soldiers wear them in combat.

In my region, rifles are not that commonly found being used by criminals. It happens, but it's not very common.

Ideally, get good level II soft body armor and then get some armor plates. If things turn ugly, you'll be glad you bought it.

Even in much more common home burglaries, taking a couple of extra seconds to put on body armor can make the difference between life and death. I cannot understand people who own a dozen firearms, but no body armor.

ABOUT NIGHT VISION GOGGLES

I don't own any and I have no experience with them.

Having said that, I've been in isolated places where there was trouble and I can tell you, at night you don't see crap. It's frustrating trying to find people running around you when you can't see. You feel very vulnerable.

A flashlight helps of course, but NVGs are another level. I can understand how they could be a terrific advantage in a place where there's poor or no light at all. I'd seriously consider getting NVGs, in spite of their cost, if I didn't live in the city. Even in the city, when lights go out it's like a tomb. I can clearly see how it could be a serious advantage during troubled times.

Tip: American combat soldiers have found that single-eye NVGs work better than goggles that cover both eyes. Covering both eyes for extended times results in "tunnel vision" and a dangerous loss of peripheral vision. A good helmet mount should allow the single-eye night vision device to be quickly flipped up out of the way. The tube is flipped down and used only when needed. A single-eye device will also be much cheaper for you to buy.

MAGAZINES, CLEANING KITS, SLINGS, PARTS, ETC.

Get at least six ammunition magazines per weapon. Preferably twelve, especially for your fighting rifle. Guns aren't of much use without their magazines, and every gunsmith can tell you that magazines are the part that causes the most malfunctions. Magazines are also the one part that needs replacement the most.

And dear God, don't bet your life on the cheapest magazines you can manage to find! Buy only quality mags, and when possible, go for military specification magazines. Put a number on them to identify each one in case there are malfunctions. Make sure to try them out well before you trust them with your life.

Destroy and discard any mags that cause malfunctions. If you identified the part causing the problem (deformed magazine lips, bad follower or weak spring) maybe you can save the rest for spare parts. Beaten lips or weak springs are the most common source of problems with magazines.

Research your weapons, then find out which parts break, fail or wear out the most, and buy spare parts now while you can.

Since you need a spare pistol, it's a great idea to buy two of the exact same models in case one breaks, gets lost or stolen. You can also then share magazines between them.

Remember to report any weapon that gets stolen or is simply lost, so there's proof you no longer have it in case a crime of some sort ends up being committed with it later on, or if confiscation is enforced and cops show up at your door demanding a gun you no longer own.

For your rifle magazines you'll need either a chest rig (draws a lot of attention but its very practical) or a shoulder bag to carry your magazines and other gear. Fanny packs can also be modified to carry rifle magazines in a low-key way.

You'll also need gun cases and slings for your long arms.

A tactical light and/or a laser that can be mounted on the rails of your pistol is also a great idea. Visible green lasers mounted on rifles have been proven by American "contractors" in Iraq and Afghanistan to be highly effective in low-light situations out to 200 yards and beyond. The key is to only flick the laser on momentarily, just before firing. Don't worry too much if you can't afford top quality night vision goggles, and can't buy military infrared lasers to go with the NVGs.

A visible green laser and your own two eyes works almost as well, and some "contractors" who have access to both NVGs and infrared lasers prefer to use the green laser and their eyes instead. I am told that "if you can see an enemy, you can hit him." Total darkness is a rare condition, especially in and around cities. A green laser mounted on your rifle will greatly multiply its effectiveness at night. Red dot sights also work, but green lasers are even better.

TIPS AND MISTAKES I MADE REGARDING FIREARMS

I didn't take advantage of the opportunity of buying several FAL rifles when I had a chance for a ridiculous low price. I thought those weapons would always be available, cheap and easy to buy. Big mistake. Later they became almost impossible to buy and cost ten times as much as before the crisis.

Learn from my mistake.

Buy a couple of fighting handguns and a fighting rifle as soon as you can. Then buy a third handgun and a second rifle. They are a safe investment. You can always sell them and get your money back (and more) if you later regret the purchase or need the money.

Being the gun fanatic I am, at first there was no order to my purchasing. I bought and sold dozens of firearms as time went by. I always had a small collection, but I constantly bought and sold guns to try new stuff.

The good part is that I learned to handle and fire pretty much any firearm, and I understand most gun mechanisms rather well. This is an advantage in case you end up with your attacker's gun under your control, or someone has to loan you a weapon in an emergency.

The bad part is that my little collection was a mess by the time the SHTF, and I had to get busy putting things in order and getting what I really needed.

Do yourself a favor and follow my suggestions. It's experience that cost me a lot of time and money, so learn from my mistakes and build an organized collection before you buy more exotic firearms simply because of their looks or their historic appeal.

Contrary to what you see in movies or read in books, once the SHTF people won't start selling and trading guns and ammo in the streets like fruit. Rather to the contrary, the government will try to take control over them very quickly, no matter what laws and rights you previously enjoyed.

Know that firearms are confiscated when there's a tyrannical government, and also when governments panic after a crisis. Americans, I'm especially talking to you guys here. Remember Hurricane Katrina in New Orleans? Over a thousand guns were confiscated, just when there was no 911 to call. Just when people were defenseless, and needed them the most. It has happened before, and one day it will happen again.

Hidden or buried firearms with enough ammo are a good insurance policy.

Don't waste your money, but get the essentials that you will need. Buy holsters, slings, the means of carrying a couple of extra magazines, rifle and pistol cases, and cleaning gear. It is one thing to take your guns to the shooting range, and it's another to actually carry your pistols concealed, or carry your rifle tactically with a sling. Be ready to do that if needed. Buy a good holster, so that the gun doesn't fall even when you run or jump. Test it to make sure the gun is secured. You'll need a good gun belt as well. A good holster is of little use when you combine it with a poor belt.

How much ammo? Measure it by the thousands. Though 200 rounds of handgun ammo is enough for someone on an extremely tight budget, if possible get at least 1,000 rounds of ammo for each pistol and rifle you own. For each

.22LR, buy 5,000 rounds. .22LR is very cheap, and it's a great general purpose cartridge.

Maybe this sounds like overkill. It isn't. A firearm is just a poor club without ammunition. If you can afford it, I'd multiply those amounts by five in each case. Only then would I consider it truly enough ammo for after the SHTF.

I remember once not that long ago when I helped a friend of mine open up some packages that his grandfather had left him when he passed away.

He had left him a Victor Sarrasqueta double-barrel shotgun, along with a double-barrel 14mm "Safari" shotgun pistol. There was also a big package wrapped in plastic. When we opened it we found eighty 25-round boxes of ammo for the two firearms. Those old paper shells were almost fifty years old. Most of them fired just fine.

My friend's grandpa sure knew the importance of ammo.

If today's ammo prices scare you, just think about your grandchildren opening those cases up in a world where that same ammo costs ten times more or simply can't be purchased at any price. Unlike paper shotgun shells, metallic cartridges can last a hundred years if they are properly stored in a dry, sealed ammo can.

Do dry-fire practice. This is maybe the most underestimated post-SHTF training method. Don't use up your valuable ammo after a crisis just practicing at the range. Practice at home with "snap-cap" cartridges without wasting live ammo, just by running dry-fire drills. Only fire live ammunition at the range once or twice a month, as your money allows you to buy more ammo, but don't use up your "SHTF" stash. Do dry-fire training instead.

SHTF GUN CLEANING

I don't have enough money anymore for fancy gun cleaning stuff. Not at the current prices. I have some H&R bore cleaner still left, but mostly I use much cheaper stuff.

Grab a pen and paper and buy plenty of these the next time you go to the hardware store:

*Red High Temperature GREASE

*MOTOR OIL

*KEROSENE

*WD40

*LIQUID SILICONE

Oil: Synthetic motor oil works just fine. Some people like it better than your favorite Hoppes. I have heard good things about Dexron Automatic

Transmission Fluid too. The best part is that you can buy large amounts of it for very little money. Refill a smaller bottle for ease of handling.

Unlike expensive cleaners and lubricants that come in tiny bottles, and cost a fortune when you calculate how much money it's worth per ounce, here you can buy quantity too. How much would a quart of Hoppes cost?

Kerosene: Kerosene has many uses. It's very cheap, and it cleans barrels as well as most stuff. Maybe a bit better than most. I use it just for the barrel, but some people dunk their entire gun. I worry about plastic frames and the metal finish, so I don't. But for cleaning bores, it's fine.

Red high temp auto grease: Red grease is great stuff. You can almost clean the whole gun with it, and it will keep your rails lubricated four time longer than Hoppes oil. I sometimes use it to scrub and clean, then leave a bit on some contact surfaces for lubrication.

Cotton Rags: Hoppes Cleaning Patches are what Angelina Jolie uses to clean her H&K. After the SHTF, real men use cotton rags cut up from old t-shirts. Don't waste your money on fancy, expensive stuff made "just for guns."

A couple considerations:

1) This is all VERY cheap.

2) Buying large amounts not only saves money, but it ensures that you will have many years worth of cleaning supplies when the SHTF. This is something that the guy who has all of those expensive little "gun boutique" bottles won't have.

THE WAY I CLEAN GUNS

After basic disassembly, I put some kerosene in the barrel and let it soak in for a few hours. Scrub it well and run some tight fitting kerosene-soaked rag patches through it, the tighter the better.

After that, and if I won't be using that gun for a while, I put a few drops of oil on clean rags, and run them through until they come out clean and dry. Some people say residual oil creates a micro film that increases the pressure... but I'm heterosexual, so I just dry it up well and forget about it.

My guns work fine this way. I dry them well mostly to avoid oil getting to the primers. Even though sealed primers are safe, I prefer not to risk deadening them.

I clean the slide and frame with an oily/greasy rag. Use a screwdriver to clean the rails and other groves. I put some grease in the rail and contact surface of the barrel/slide, and a drop of oil for springs and smaller parts.

Try not to overdo the grease and oil, it attracts dirt and might do more harm than good. I put a bit of grease on the exterior and rub the entire surface with the oily rag.

I try to avoid chemicals getting into much contact with plastic, but I don't worry that much either. Plastic is usually better left alone. Just rub on some silicone once in a while. This is also cheap and found in auto shops in quantity. ArmorAll brand, Original Protectant will also add UV protection to plastic parts.

That's basically it. Scrub the barrel, protect all surfaces with oil or grease and dry everything up nicely, then put small amounts of oil and grease where necessary.

If my gun gets wet, I spray it with WD40. I used to clean everything with WD40 (drying it up with a rag) but it's getting too expensive as well, so I only use it when water or a lot of sweat is involved.

Tip: Read your firearm's manual. Some guns need to be cleaned in a certain way, or require you to avoid getting oil or grease into some places entirely. Don't lose the manual. If you ever disassemble a firearm down to the small parts and can't put it back together, you will be glad you kept the manual with the exploded diagrams and assembly instructions.

Ed's Red Bore Cleaner: Some people say pure kerosene can ruin a gun finish.

For those that want to try it (and it's also very cheap), there's Ed's Red homemade bore cleaner:

1 Quart Dexron II, IIe or III ATF (automatic transmission fluid).

1 Quart Kerosene - deodorized

1 Quart Aliphatic Mineral Spirits, Federal Spec. TT-T-2981F, CAS #64741-49-9, or substitute "Stoddard Solvent" CAS, or "Varsol" #8052-41-3, or equivalent.

1 Quart Acetone, CAS #67-64-1.

Notice: CAS registry numbers (Chemical Abstracts Service) are unique identifiable numbers for chemical elements and compounds.

Mix together in a well ventilated area. Store in a metal can with a tightly sealing cap, to prevent the escape of the solvents. You now have a lifetime supply of cheap, effective bore cleaner. Pour what you need into small empty bottles of "gun boutique" bore cleaner for easy use.

AFTER THE FIGHT

(Thanks to my sexy lawyer—my wife—for her help regarding legal issues.)

If you are ever involved in a gunfight and you are still standing at the end, the first thing you should do is thank God. Even though it could have been worse—you could be dead—in reality your problems have just started.

If wounded you need to lie down, apply pressure to stop any hemorrhage, and call for help.

Hopefully you'll have a cell phone to call for help.

Here in Argentina it's a matter of luck and location. Ambulances will not go into some of the worst parts of Buenos Aires. You are better off calling family or friends.

If your area was hit by some natural or man made disaster, you are not likely to get help. Medical services and police may not be available at all, or your phone may not even work. All the assistance you'll get will come from the people in the area, if there are any at all.

You should still try to contact the authorities.

If cell phones are working, your attempt to call the cops may be registered, and that will be more evidence supporting your version of events. You are a law-abiding citizen that just used lethal force to defend his life.

If you are still able to do it, the next number you want to call is your lawyer.

Check the list of "people to be friends with." This is one of the many situations where a lawyer is priceless. If possible, make friends with a criminal lawyer now!

Do not talk to the police. "Hi" and "Thanks" should be the only words you say to them other than, "I was in fear for my life." In answer to any questions that are asked, such as "what happened," all you should say is that you'll wait until your lawyer arrives.

If you say the wrong thing at the wrong time, you may be the only one to blame when you end up in jail later on. Shut up! It's better not to say anything than to say the wrong thing, because it WILL be twisted around and used against you.

Let's suppose for a moment here that you just confronted some robbers or violent looters.

After refusing to stop when warned, they keep walking onto your property, and you shoot the one that seems to be in charge. Generally, he's the big mouthed one with the wrong attitude, the one located in the center of the pack surrounded by his buddies.

It became common here for looters to ask you to simply give up the goods. I was once in a supermarket called "Auchan" in Avellaneda, Buenos Aires, when I saw this happen.

The main mob waited a bit farther away. The big fish and a couple of his tougher buddies did the talking with the supermarket manager. The employees had made a barricade by tying together lines of shopping carts (not a bad idea), and they looked terrified.

As I was leaving, I saw some employees bringing out bags of groceries and setting them on the ground. I suppose they reached some sort of agreement.

Now, this is NOT what you want to do when it's your home under threat. Once you let these animals inside, you and your family are totally at their mercy.

Maybe they initially talk you into just giving up your material goods, but then later they may decide to take a piece of your wife, your daughter, and then finally your lives in order to leave no witnesses to their crimes.

So, no, do not negotiate with looters regarding your private property. Like an animal that smells fear, they'll try to take you down. They'll want more.

So instead, you shoot their leader. Everyone else suddenly becomes a genius and figures out that it's better to escape and live to loot another day, than to risk getting shot through the chest like that great leader of theirs did.

I remember one particular cop that appeared on TV during 2001. He defended an entire supermarket single-handedly from a mob of looters. The camera showed him standing in the middle of the parking lot in front of the store, with the right attitude and a determined face.

When the looters tried to cut some distance and slowly move forward, up came his pump 12-gauge shotgun and he shot a couple of them with LTL (less than lethal) plastic buckshot. The looters moved back and then left the area.

The cop had his body armor on, and his vest contained big fat red 12-gauge shells. Those were 12-gauge triple-ought lead buckshot, while the LTL ammo available here is green, so the looters could easily tell the difference.

But back to you.

The other looters left, but now you have a nice dead looter in your front yard.

You called the cops at 911, and this being after the SHTF, no one answered. Your lawyer friend can't be found anywhere either. Maybe the phones don't work at all when this deadly situation occurs.

So what do you do?

This gets a bit more delicate, but there are still things you can do to legally protect yourself when and if the authorities finally do come.

First, go and get a couple witnesses. Not just one, but two or three. Remember the "3 is 2, 2 is 1 and 1 is none" rule that people apply to gear and supplies. Well, my lawyer-wife tells me that it especially applies here.

You need at least two witnesses to back up your story if you want to have any credibility in court. Yes, eventually you will be in court. It might take a long time, but finally you will end up in court. Try finding neighbors or bystanders. Your close relatives or best friends won't work as well, but they are better than no witnesses at all. Get their full names, phone numbers and addresses. After that, take some pictures.

Take some close-up shots of the corpse to show any details, two full body shots, and a couple of more pictures from a bit farther away. This is in order to indicate the general location, and the distance of the body from your home and other significant buildings.

If the cops don't even answer the phone and you don't expect them to show up any time soon, you have to do something about the corpse. You can't leave it there rotting for days, for the kids to poke with sticks, or for animals to chew it up, or for it to spread diseases near your home.

Don't touch anything on the body. Not even his pockets or his ID. You shouldn't care about his name or where he comes from. Unless it's the end of the world and there are only a dozen humans left on the planet, all you'll be doing is planting your fingerprints and DNA in places it shouldn't be.

Just wrap the body up in a blanket or plastic sheet and move it far away.

Anyone that ever smelled a rotting man-sized dead creature knows how badly it stinks. In a humid or tropical climate it's intolerable. Get it at least 300 yards away, more if the wind blows in your direction, or if there are large wild animals or feral dogs that could follow the smell.

If possible, find some small shed where you can leave it locked up and out of the rain. You don't want the family dog showing up a couple of weeks later with the dead looter's rotting arm.

If this isn't an option, wrap it up in plastic and bury it. The problem here is that the authorities may confuse this with an attempt at hiding the corpse or destroying the evidence of a crime. Let your witnesses know you are doing it, and why, so that later they can back up your version of the story.

Again, it helps if you know the local authorities. It helps a lot.

I remember when I was little, things were safer and a burglar getting shot was something the entire neighborhood commented on for weeks. The owner of a nearby candy store, where kids bought candy after school, had shot a burglar.

The word was that the cops dropped a gun or a knife next to the burglar's body. Supposedly they carried them in their patrol cars for just such occasions.

In another incident, a home owner that shot armed home invaders ended up in jail. Apparently, he saw them and waited for them upstairs until they turned to leave. He then shot them both in the back with a .44 Magnum lever-action carbine that he used for wild pig hunting. He killed them both.

The judge determined that since the armed robbers were already leaving, he was not in reasonable fear for his life.

Note that the gun used was a lever-action carbine. This is a weapon many survivalists recommend because according to them, it's more politically correct, and a judge or jury will go lighter on you if you have to use it.

That doesn't hold an ounce of truth. A firearm is still a firearm. Don't worry about the way it looks; worry about using it under the correct circumstances.

If police do answer and show up, what do you do about your own gun?

In some movies the good guy drops his gun right after the shooting, waiting for the cops to arrive. No my friend, that's not a good idea. You don't know if the bad guy's pals are still lurking nearby.

One thing you learn in self defense shooting classes is to always look for your enemy's friends after a shooting. So no, don't drop your gun and leave yourself unarmed and defenseless against a second attack.

Simply reholster your weapon, or get your holster or pants if you didn't have them on and then holster your weapon. If it's a long gun, carry it across your back. If you have no sling, then yes, leave it on the ground or somewhere nearby and try to stay close to it. (This is yet another reason to have a sling on your long arms.)

You don't want to appear threatening in any way to the nervous cops that arrive and see a dead guy on the ground. Having your gun in your hand at that moment is a pretty bad idea. Make sure you show your empty palms when they get close. No need to stick them up like in the movies (unless the officer asks you to do so). Just keep your empty hands visible in front of you.

That's the first thing a trained cop (or a smart armed citizen) will check.

There are other cases where things won't turn out this neat and tidy.

Say you are traveling and someone tried to carjack you, or you are traveling on foot and you are attacked, what do you do then after shooting your attacker?

In these cases, if the area you are in is too dangerous, secure your family and yourself first. Don't stick around, because you may be putting yourself at even greater risk of further attacks, especially by the friends of the dead criminal.

If you have a cell phone with a camera (a good idea), you may be able to take a couple of quick pictures. If some bystander saw what happened, try to get his name, phone and address before leaving. Doing this or not depends on how dangerous the area is.

If you are in reasonable fear for your life, you don't have any obligation to stay around until cops show up. Go home or to some other safe place and then yes, call the cops and tell them what happened.

FINANCES, NETWORKING AND THE NEW WORLD YOU LIVE IN

YOUR FINANCES AND YOUR MONEY

When I first started writing about our crisis in Argentina in 2002, and how important money and finances are during and after SHTF, people didn't pay much attention.

"Don't you know?" they would write, "We'll all be bartering once the economy crashes. We'll trade ammo, pelts and other goods for whatever we'll need. Paper money will be worth nothing at all. We'll light fires with fifties and wipe our butts with hundred dollar bills."

Many even swore that gold would just be a "shiny, pretty metal," with no value.

Trying to explain to them how gold and silver have been an unquestionable form of currency and value for thousands of years didn't seem to change their minds. Somehow they had magically seen the future, and they had already decided that gold and silver would have no value after the SHTF.

It was a bit frustrating, mostly because the wounds of my country's economic collapse were still very fresh. I wanted people to listen to what I had learned by hard, first-hand experience. Back then, very few were willing to listen. Many even made fun of me, assuring me that "that" only happens in third-world countries and "banana republics."

At that time I never said that the USA would have an economic crisis as well. I have no crystal ball here. I just explained that we were once a rather powerful nation in our region and that we didn't see it coming either. I was saying to just be careful and consider it a possibility, that's all.

"Foolish Latino, what happened with your petty little country will never happen in America."

Oh yes, that thing called irony. Given the world context as of 2010, I think people are parting with the idea of using hundred dollar bills as toilet paper. Yes my dear friends, a hundred dollars will still buy you a lot of toilet paper. Crisis or no crisis.

CASH IS KING

There are places like Zimbabwe, where the inflation rate was reported as 66,000 percent for 2007.

You could see an African gold digger explain on video how the paper currency was only good for wrapping the few bits of gold he found after a long day in the mud. To him, it really was just a small piece of paper.

These things, yes they do happen sometimes and in some places. But do they happen overnight, and do they happen in more developed countries?

Well, no. It's not likely. It is possible, simply because it's within the realm of possibility, but do not expect that kind of extreme hyperinflation to happen in a first-world country. Especially don't expect it to happen overnight.

Our economy collapsed completely in December 2001. I mean, people would stop buying even a single liter of paint for their house due to the economic uncertainty. There was ZERO economic activity for many weeks, and everything was pretty much frozen for most of 2002.

Did our paper money lose value? Yes, by over two-thirds. First it went to one USD to one Argentine Peso, but then it settled for one USD for three pesos. Right now, with the world crisis, it's 3.5 and losing a bit more value to the dollar as time goes by. It's estimated that next year it will reach 4.5.

The point here is, paper money, while still a fiat currency, still holds important value for a long time as the crisis develops. When the economy crashed and all of the banks closed in December 2001, the "cash is king" catch phrase became very real.

The infamous "corralito" was created by the government. Like a "corral," it captured people's money in the banks, freezing their accounts, and not allowing withdrawals. There was a withdrawal limit of 300 pesos per week, and only from accounts in pesos. Dollar accounts were kept completely frozen and you couldn't withdraw a single cent.

You could still use debit and credit cards, but since most shops didn't accept them, things got very complicated.

This "corralito" measure lasted a full year. After that, the USD accounts where "peso-feed," converted to pesos at 1.4 pesos per dollar, when the real value on the street was nearly four pesos for one dollar.

Till this day, many small shops and grocery stores don't accept credit or debit cards. After all these years, many gas stations in the suburbs of Buenos Aires still have "cash only" signs up.

Cash is king indeed. It allows you to keep going when banks and digital money are down, and that alone is a good enough reason to keep enough cash handy for surviving during emergencies.

HOW MUCH CASH SHOULD YOU HAVE?

Having at the very least a hundred USD bill on you at all times for emergencies would be a good idea. Two hundred or more would be even better.

I know a guy that carries a 1oz. gold coin everywhere he goes. I wouldn't do that here due to the high crime rate, but it's still a good idea. Especially if it's well concealed or sewn in your clothes, although that would be easier to do with a number of smaller, thinner gold coins.

I stick to a hundred bucks because I don't have much money, and the risk of getting mugged is pretty high, so you might want to take those two factors into consideration as well.

This is money you may keep in your wallet, but preferably in a separate compartment, just for emergencies. Change sometimes isn't available, so maybe you want that extra hundred bucks broken down into tens or twenties.

Don't forget several quarters for vending machines, phones and parking.

Someone once asked me how much money should he keep at home? This is a bit similar to how much ammo should I have, at a minimum. There's really no right answer.

Let's suppose something very bad happens and you have to leave the country all of a sudden. Let's make it a worst-case scenario and assume you'll be leaving with your family for some other place where you have friends or relatives willing to help you.

A good guideline would be to have enough cash for plane tickets for everyone, and let's say three months worth of cash for groceries, motels, and other expenses. Keep your passport and other important papers handy and updated, in a grab-and-go waterproof container. That's an important amount of cash but sounds like a logical "worst-case" amount.

If this is a bit out of your range, at least have two months worth of bills and groceries in paper money, in case something like what happened here in Argentina happens in your country, and you need money on hand to live on. Remember, your banks and their ATMs might be closed for a long time.

Another way of determining how much cash to keep around is to have five to ten percent of your total savings in paper money.

In my opinion, I'd also keep another twenty or thirty percent in precious metals. Mostly in the form of well-recognized gold coins.

The more you have, the less percentage you'll keep in paper money and precious metal, since it would be better to have it invested in something that makes money for you, rather than sitting around in a backup hidden fireproof safe or a bank deposit box.

Tip: Be careful with banks and bank deposit boxes! They've opened deposit boxes before, in spite of supposed rights to private property. After 1933, not only was most gold banned in the USA, but bank deposit boxes could not be opened without a federal tax agent from the IRS present. Yes, this was the law in America under Franklin Roosevelt.

This may sound a bit too much, but understand very clearly that there are many situations where you may need your money, and for one reason or another it's simply unavailable to you.

Banks going bankrupt, the government freezing accounts, downright stealing them ("nationalization") or even opening private deposit boxes. Kidnaps are also emergencies for which you need to keep money at home. People have also died in Argentina because they needed to pay for medical treatments or life saving surgery, but they could not get their money out of the bank.

I've learned not to trust banks very much. I'd keep a very small amount of my cash and precious metals in the primary safe and most of it hidden in a small secondary fireproof safe, which would be extremely well hidden behind a fake wall or under the carpet or furniture.

Burglars expect to find one safe at most. They will rarely ask for you to reveal a second one if you are taken hostage during a home invasion.

What do I do, as of today? I don't have much money, so I keep what little money I have at home. I can't afford to lose a percentage of my money because I have very little, so I don't take any risks with our local banks.

When I receive transfers and deposits, I usually get the money out fast. Mostly I deposit money to take advantage of some special promotion or discount when buying groceries. Sometimes you can save up to 20% that way. I'll deposit the amount of money I estimate I'll be spending, and use it the following day. This is post-crisis banking, after the SHTF.

THE IMPORTANCE OF PRECIOUS METALS

This is one of the many things I hadn't thought about before the crisis. I learned about it as the crisis developed, and the new reality settled in.

All of a sudden, "I Buy Gold!" signs started popping up everywhere. Especially jewelry stores. They would put up huge "I Buy Gold!" signs. You would turn on the television, and find local celebrities running advertisements for one big jewelry store or another.

"Beat insecurity; why keep those old things at home where they can be robbed? I do all my jewelry business with Triple-A Jewelers! They buy gold, diamonds, Rolex watches and antique jewelry for the best prices."

It became a common sight in improvised "gray market" fairs, called "Ferias Bolivianas," to find stands that bought and sold jewelry—and of course they had a big "I Buy Gold!" sign as well.

Unfortunately, these dealers also do business with thieves and chain snatchers who would rob jewelry from women on the street without thinking twice. It has become such a big problem that most women choose not to risk being robbed, and so they leave their gold jewelry at home. This even created a new market for jewelry made of other "safer" metals.

After the crisis, criminals preferred to hit jewelry stores, since it became a better deal for them than robbing a bank. In Buenos Aires we witnessed that shift, with many robberies and murders on Libertad Street in the Capital District, where many of the top jewelry stores can be found.

When I did a bit of research, I found that the gold buying and selling business had gone up over 500% since the crisis. Most of these gold buyers deal with 18k jewelry gold, and not with .999 purity coins and bars.

For doing business with .999 purity (mint) gold, it's better to find a reputable precious metals dealer. They are available, but the "I Buy Gold!" shops that are interested in ordinary jewelry gold are much more common. I suppose they make a greater margin of profit melting the 18K gold, since they are paying relatively little for it.

But why did this happen in Argentina after the economical collapse? As a matter of fact, why is gold so important in nearly every culture around the world? If you look around, you'll find many cultures (such as India and other East Asian societies), where gold in the form of jewelry is the way in which they keep most of their savings.

For Catholics here in South America, it's common to receive gold chains, crosses or medallions when you are baptized and when you receive your First Holy Communion and other sacraments. But why gold in particular?

When Jesus was born, he received frankincense, myrrh… and gold. People, Frankincense and Myrrh were valuable throughout western Asia, the Middle East and Eastern Europe around 2,000 years ago. They were basically another form of currency, just like gold. They were forms of portable wealth.

You can go back for thousands of years, and ever since trade and commerce were invented, gold has had an undisputed predominant role as a leading form of currency, and that's its beauty.

Paper money can be burned, or ruined by water, or devalued or even replaced by a government. Gadgets and even cars can lose value within weeks of purchase, or just as soon as you remove them from their packaging.

Your internet empire or super trendy money making website can disappear as soon as the electric power goes down. Your stocks and investment portfolio mean NOTHING after your stock broker stops answering the phone, and an "out of business" sign appears in his door. But gold will always be gold, and it's amazing how it has held its value through time.

Gold isn't an investment in terms of it generating profit for you. Its beauty, financially speaking, lies elsewhere. Gold is a wonderful way to store wealth, in a way it's easy to carry and is impervious to a fiat money collapse. Gold is like a time machine, it keeps value through time.

For example, during Roman times, a gold coin would buy you a nice toga, a good belt and quality made leather shoes. Today that same gold coin will get you a smart looking outfit, shoes and a belt. In the 1800's, it would have bought you a quality hand-made pistol, and it will still buy you a well made top of the line handgun today.

Why do you think it has been so popular for jewelry, through the ages?

Not only because of its beauty, but also because it was a way to keep wealth on a person's body at all times. As a gold medallion, chain or ring, it could be carried around with you. If your bag was snatched in a crowded area or your money purse was cut away and stolen, you still had your gold literally on you.

In a time when locks and home security measures where very primitive, and many people even lived in common quarters, this was an interesting concept.

WHAT KIND OF PRECIOUS METALS SHOULD YOU GET?

For the bulk of your tangible savings you are, of course, better off buying precious metal bars and well-known coins of reputable origin.

Minted South African Krugerrands, American Eagles, Canadian Maple Leafs and Chinese Pandas are the best way to preserve your savings—but be aware of the increase in counterfeit precious metals coins from China.

These coins should be kept secured in envelopes or cases so they don't get scratched or nicked, something that people dealing with gold are very picky about. If nothing else, at least wrap it in a small piece of paper or place it inside a small paper or plastic envelope. There are small translucent plastic cases available as well. These preserve the coin and allow easy identification.

This is especially true with .999 fine "pure" gold Maple Leafs and Pandas, which are very soft and easy to scratch. This individual coin protection is less critical with American Eagles and Krugerrands, which are alloyed with ten percent silver and other hard metals to make them more durable. These coins also contain one full ounce of .999 fine gold, so don't worry. They weigh 1.1 ounces on a scale, one ounce of which is pure gold, the same amount of gold that is contained in a 1.0 ounce Maple Leaf or Panda, which are made of gold and nothing else.

Since we are talking about gold coins, I'd like to relate something that happened to a friend of my wife's family. You could say this guy was a bit of a survivalist. He had lots of guns, ammo, food and an important amount of gold coins. He was pretty well prepared for 2002.

Or not...

During 2002, he had a heart attack and spent several weeks hospitalized. Since he's an older single guy and had no one at home, his house was left empty. An empty house in Argentina attracts thieves and home invaders. Squatters are always looking for a place to take. People have come back after a week of holidays, just to find squatters already well settled in their homes. The man's house was picked clean. The thieves robbed absolutely everything. They even took the doors and toilets.

A good idea is to have a big safe, and a smaller fire proof safe that is extremely well hidden. Perhaps behind a removable wall panel, or under the floor. Robbers will settle for one safe. They'll rarely guess that you have a second one.

Preferably you'll keep most of your gold and silver in this second safe, but also have a third or even a fourth hidden location for smaller portions as well. The idea here is to not keep all of your eggs in the same basket, even though you'll keep most of them in the safest location, your second, well-hidden safe.

Then you can also leave some precious metals with a trusted relative, or buried in the back yard or in a cache location away from your property. Make sure you'll be able to find it again, both with physical references and a GPS location. And make sure it's in a place that won't be bulldozed and turned into a building.

Some gold coins could be kept in a safety deposit box in a bank, but realize that governments have sometimes authorized the invasion of such boxes looking for cash and gold during an economic crisis, and that they are also favorite robbery targets during a depression.

PRECIOUS METAL "POCKET CHANGE"

Coins will cover most of the value of your precious metal savings, but what about daily transactions during dangerous times, such as when you are visiting gray or black markets? Do you really want to go to one of these places with a shiny gold coin, or even minted silver coins? Let me answer that for you. No, you don't!

I see people often selling jewelry at these places or on the street at jewelry stores. But I never saw anyone stupid enough to sell a gold coin at a black or gray market store.

Go to the "La Salada" gray market in Buenos Aires, and you'll know what I mean. Well, actually don't go, because it's kind of dangerous. For those who are a bit "doom inclined," yes, it pretty much looks like Mad Max's "Barter Town," only it's ten times bigger.

I can only imagine what would happen to someone trying to use a gold coin in the "La Salada" market. You might as well paint an "I'm Rich, Please Kidnap Me!" sign and hang it around your neck.

For this reason, I've recommended in the past to have a small amount of "junk" or scrap jewelry gold. Scrap gold jewelry can be found cheap in pawn shops. Used gold wedding bands and gold chains are particularly useful. The less intricate the better, since you don't care about their artistic value.

Stick to 14k (58% gold content) or preferably 18k (75% gold content), and make sure it's marked as such. Remember that 24k gold is 100% pure gold. Be careful not to confuse it with 24k "plated" gold. This means it just has a very thin outer layer of real gold, and the rest is lead or some other metal. "Plated" gold is worthless, and few people will be fooled into believing it's the real deal.

It might be worth investing in an acid gold testing kit. These allow you to estimate the purity of unknown gold. Testing kits can be found on EBay for about twenty dollars. This is money well spent for anyone interested in gold.

The idea here is that during the first periods of a severe economic crisis, when the more serious gold dealers who would normally buy your .999 fine gold coins are closed or are just not safe to go to, you'll get by with your bag of junk or scrap gold jewelry.

Imagine replacing your real wedding ring with one of these, going to the "I Buy Gold!" guy or a pawn shop, and pulling it off of your finger. Then, with your pitifully sad Oscar-winning face you ask, "Please sir…how much can I get for this?" You look like just another poor soul and you are not attracting unwanted attention to yourself.

Ask around at two or three gold dealers to make sure you are getting a fair price. This is MUCH safer than trying to buy directly with minted gold coins. Remember, showing a gold coin in public will be like flashing thousand dollar bills to people who are desperate, and who may be willing to kill you for much less.

While conducting a little experiment regarding gold on Libertad Street, where most jewelry stores are in Buenos Aires are located, I came by a sweet tip. I was wondering how much I could get for a small chain bracelet I had, marked as 18k gold. I asked around at several places and was pleased to learn they all offered very similar prices. Oh! The wonders of capitalism and the free market!

They all pretty much offered 100 USD, which was a bit more than what I had purchased it for almost twelve years earlier. One guy who was buying my amateur acting attempt said, "Hey, if you don't need to sell it all, you can just sell me a few links…"

Brilliant!

That's a new use for junk gold chains right there: they are easy to divide into small segments, to accurately fit the amount you want to sell at the time. Imagine trying to do that with a one-ounce minted gold coin. Impossible.

But with an 18k gold chain, you can simply break away a few links, have them weighed, sell them, and just go buy the few groceries or whatever you need.

Imagine pulling out of your pocket your grandmother's antique heirloom bracelet (BS, you bought it on EBay as scrap), and with your multi-tool you cut away a couple links, sell them, and go buy a few groceries next door. While the guy weighs it you might add, "I'll keep what's left of grandma's bracelet, but I need to sell a bit to buy food…" Academy Award, here I come!

It's no wonder that SOE agents (British secret agents parachuted into Europe) and American OSS agents during WWII were given what they called "gold kits." These were used for bribery and to buy goods and information.

Their gold kit included .999 gold coins (small ones), a bit of gold jewelry, mostly rings, and…(drums)…a gold chain. Cut a couple links and pay for a sandwich and a coke. Undercover agents had hidden compartments in the soles of their shoes. Two small gold coins were concealed in each shoe for last resort emergency use. Some agents sewed pieces of gold chains or coins within clothing or under insignias.

Nazis fleeing to South America after World War Two found that a gold coin slipped into the correct bureaucrat's hand made crossing international borders much easier. Historically, gold coins have been the ultimate form of "flight capital." When a persecuted refugee does not have his papers in order (or any papers at all), a gold coin often opens the door to a new life in a new land. Many Vietnamese fled their country in 1975 with enough gold coins and jewelry sewn into their clothing to start new businesses in America and other nations.

In the USA there's another alternative for precious metal "small change." Pre-1965 dimes, quarters and half dollars are made of 90% silver. Already people are buying these coins for their silver content value. Especially in the USA where people are familiar with this, a few rolls of pre-1965 coins are well worth having just in case.

The 90% silver content of these old coins will never change, and they are a nice way to buy a few goods if the currency collapses, without attracting unwanted attention. If you're not in the USA, try looking for similar old silver coinage in your own country, and get some now while it's easily available.

If you want to know the current metal "melt" value of US and Canadian coins, you can go to www.coinflation.com .

I was sitting in my pathetic little cubicle, waiting for another customer on the phone. Come to think of it, it wasn't even "my" cubicle. They always rotated us so that we didn't have a place we could call our own, and maybe keep a picture of our kids or our wives, anything that would to help make the situation any less depressing.

My phone headset had no foam padding. Once they got lost, the company didn't consider it necessary to replace them. Given that we were providing technical support for the largest software company in the world, you would have thought they could afford the twenty damn cents the little pieces of foam were worth.

We also had thirty minutes for lunch, and five minutes for a bathroom break. On one occasion I went to the bathroom and was back in five minutes and twenty seconds. The sysop (system operator) told me that it was fine, but try to hurry up more next time.

With 25% unemployment, they can afford to treat you that way. And I was doing that job for a dollar an hour. Man, the salary was humiliating, and the treatment was worthy of slavery. Of course, working in a call center that competes with call centers in India, you can't expect much humane treatment.

What kind of people do that sort of crappy job? Well, there were a bunch of us bilingual college students. There was a female architecture student who had spent the last two years in Thailand, and made the big mistake of coming back to Argentina without getting more information about how things had changed since the crisis. Once here, she soon ran out of money and had to find work rather quickly.

Then there was this Barak guy from Israel, a former sniper in the Israeli Defense Forces. He started traveling around the world after finishing his military service, something very common for them, but he married an Argentine girl before he had time to travel more.

So he was stuck here, but he seemed pretty happy about it. He liked the idea of leaving war behind. At first he worked as a bodyguard for some guy that moved a lot of money around. He was issued a Glock 17, but no body armor. That tells you what his employer thought of the value of his life right there. Apparently his young wife convinced him to take a less dangerous job.

Then we had a guy who was pretty weird, a "vegan" of some sort. I guess he had something against water too, because he usually smelled pretty bad. Overall, it was a pretty strange bunch of people.

One thing I learned from the dreadful months I spent slaving in that call center was the difference between working, and making money.

People sometimes ask the wrong question: "What jobs are in high demand after an economic collapse?" The question they should be asking is, "how do I make money after an economic collapse?"

I'll answer that question as well as I can, but since we're already going through it, let me tell you a bit about the few jobs that you can expect to find after the SHTF, and which ones are worth considering.

Security Guard: Without a doubt, this will be the most common job opportunity available after an economic collapse. It's no wonder, since it's abundantly clear that after an economic crisis crime goes up tremendously.

Mostly security companies look for fit men of at least average height with a high school diploma. Some also require basic gun skills. Occasionally they look for female guards as well.

For years after the crisis, this was by far the most common new job offered.

Still, it paid very little, and it required working very long hours to bring an acceptable salary home. And of course, it's one of the most dangerous jobs you can do during times of extremely high crime.

People with good hand-to-hand training and gun skills will often find better paying jobs as VIP bodyguards—but these are also very risky.

Telemarketer: It seems that poor nations around the globe have this job niche in common. A second language allowed educated people such as me to work for multibillion dollar companies…for one USD an hour. The working conditions were very bad. The idea seems to be to exploit you as much as they can until you quit.

Long working hours, constant pressures to reduce the amount of time spent with each customer, a minuscule break room with no A/C in the summer, when it's hot enough to boil eggs outside. The "break room" was like a sauna.

And we were the lucky ones! Those poor souls who didn't have English as a second language worked in the Spanish section, and they got paid even less, only about fifty cents an hour!

Unemployment is so high that companies can afford to hire people for pennies, and put them on a phone all day, bothering people with promotions non-stop.

This will become a very common job after an economic collapse, but due to the low wages, the lack of promotion possibilities and the terrible work atmosphere, it's the kind of job I'd avoid as much as possible.

Promoter: "Wanted: Female, eighteen to twenty-five, slender, good looking, must send full body picture." What's this about? They want hot looking women for promotions and special events.

When unemployment is very high, it's been proven that pretty young women handing out pamphlets and doing other live promotions is an effective form of advertising. Usually it's too expensive. But after an economic crisis, you'll have girls that could be fashion models literally begging for work. With sky-high unemployment, promoters can afford to audition lots of girls.

Marketing is important after SHTF because it's one of the few ways in which sales can be increased, and hot girls sell. Even the girls working at gas stations are forced to wear clothes that are too revealing. Anything to sell.

Police: In Argentina, cops get paid very little. It's one of the worst paying jobs, and it's also the most dangerous one. In Buenos Aires several cops die each week. It really is a high-risk profession.

Of course this is one of the differences with first-world countries like the USA, where being a police officer might be a good idea. Crime will inevitably go way up, and law enforcement officers will be in high demand in first-world countries. With the unemployment rates also high, the government finds it can kill two birds with one stone: Put more officers on the dangerous streets, and create more jobs.

With good salaries and benefits, a career in law enforcement is pretty SHTF proof, and something I'd seriously consider as a very good post-SHTF job in any first world country. Of course, if the economy crashes the local governments might not be able to pay their police as much as they did before the collapse, but it will still be a good job, relatively speaking.

Paramedic and Emergency Medical Technician: Not as safe as being a cop in terms of employment security, but it's still something well worth looking into. With higher crime and poverty, more people will need medical attention and the "satellite" services associated with it. And of course, being trained in emergency medicine is always a valuable survival skill in itself.

Military Career: This can provide a secure income during SHTF, especially in first-world countries. The skills learned can also be applied in personal business such as starting a security company or training security guards for other companies.

Medicine: Doctors and nurses always seem to have jobs and make good money. Their salaries may decline after a crash, but like police, they will always do relatively well. One of the added benefits is that you can also work in other countries since doctors and nurses are usually sought after all around the world.

MAKING MONEY

There are a number of ways in which you can do this. None are 100% certain, even though smart planning can get you pretty close to an almost certainly profitable business.

Some people (very few) have made millions. Most applied the ideas I'll mention here to make nice money. In most cases they made enough to survive, and in other cases even a bit more than that.

EXPLOIT YOUR POTENTIAL

What are you good at? What do you have to offer? Is there a market for it? Is it just your mom and dad that think it's a great idea or is it something that more people would be interested in?

It doesn't take a genius to figure out that's exactly what I'm doing with this book. As the owner of bulletproofme.com told me in an email, "You are the kind of guy that, when all you have is lemons, you make lemonade".

When, of course, it doesn't make any sense to try to make orange juice.

I have valuable knowledge regarding a situation that, due to the current world economic crisis, is suddenly of interest to thousands or even millions of people. That knowledge is something I can use to make a profit. I can write a book that provides real experience that others can benefit from, and sell it for a small amount of money.

When the SHTF, many people who lost their jobs opened their own offices at home. Accountants, lawyers, whatever you can think of. People have something to offer and if they can't find a job, it's natural to start your own business.

I know a woman that teaches Structural Engineering for architect students. She prepares them for some of the toughest exams. For a relatively small amount of money, she coaches students for the national tests that take place a few times a year. Instead of giving private lessons, she set up a small classroom in her home… and teaches thirty students instead. Two shifts a day, and the numbers start looking pretty good.

She doesn't even work too many hours. Two hours in the morning and two in the afternoon, three times a week. The Architecture University provides all the clients she needs.

That, my friends, is being smart and knowing how to make money.

EXPLOIT THE ABANDONED MARKET SECTORS

This is a business strategy that many have exploited with wonderful results in some cases. The idea here is to replaces the services the government isn't providing any more, or is failing to provide well because of lack of funds.

Transportation business: Owning a bus line is a very good business. There's more poor people, fuel is more expensive, thus, there's more need for public transportation. It doesn't take a genius to figure out why bus companies are making nice money here these days.

"But I'm not Bill Gates, and I can't afford this BS you're talking about."

Well, that happened to some people here too. But they didn't cry a river because they didn't have that kind of capital. What they did was offer another alternative: Combis. These are minibuses that transport commuting passengers to the Capital district for a small fee. You can stop them on the street, just like a cab, but they only stop if they have seats left.

For five bucks per passenger, this minibus takes people from suburbia to downtown where people work, everyday. Pay another five bucks and they drive you back to the suburbs at the end of the day.

It's a bit more expensive than the ordinary bus but it's faster, safer, you travel seated, it doesn't smell like urine, it has working AC, and it still costs half of the price of the fuel you'd need to do that trip with your own car.

These guys started with one or two minibuses, then added more, then hired drivers, then started selling the "brand" to people with their own minibuses using the brand name and logistics, for a fair percentage, of course.

Now that's smart. That's learning to exploit the needs of the new market. Give the "Nobel Prize for Economics" to the guys that came up with "Lomas Express" and "Adrogue Bus."

In the poorest parts of the country, there's also money to be made this way. But instead of minibuses, theses are generally thirty-year-old rust buckets that are falling apart, and the price is one peso. Still, some people make a living this way.

Private Security: More Crime + Not Enough Cops = Business Opportunity.

I've said it a million times. Private security will be the greatest gig once crime goes way up. If you are young and fit, becoming a cop will be an alternative, given that in the USA the police are well paid and there will be a growing demand for them.

But for those with the vision, a private security company can mean a lot of money, or something for police to do when they retire from law enforcement. You'll be offering security to some high-end neighborhood. You set guards on a few strategic corners.

It's obvious that if you are getting paid by say, three blocks, and you only set guards on those three places, criminals will start hunting out of the "guarded" territory. Soon the word gets around, and others will want guards of their own to keep an eye on things.

Be serious, be professional, and as crime goes up a private security company will be a good money maker for you. Think like a businessman. You won't make much money standing guard yourself, even though you can be your own employee in a one man company, driving around the neighborhood all day and keeping an eye on things.

But the best way to make money is to think bigger. Train a few guards, and set them covering strategic points. Eventually when crime gets worse you'll need one in every corner. Make a good business plan and you'll sure make money with private security after the SHTF. This is a guaranteed growth area when crime takes off.

Education: As public education goes down and the government indoctrination gets worse, people will want better education for their kids in a safer environment. Mom can't afford to home school any more, she has to work now. As salaries keep going down, due to salary reductions or indirectly through inflation, both parents working becomes more and more common.

A respectable neighbor that parents trusts can set up a private school. One that's not expensive, but offers a safe atmosphere and a good education level. I've seen it done a number of times, and I know of several people that did very well with their own private schools or daycare centers.

This would fall both in the "market need" and "things you love doing" category, since starting a school and teaching has to be something you enjoy doing. If you do it just for the money, chances are you won't be good at it.

Health: As public medical care decreases in quality, people will find private health care plans and insurance more appealing. This requires greater investment but if you work in the medical field, you can organize with other professionals and set up your own small clinic that offers health plans.

Lending money: There's no credit after the SHTF, so lending a little money (usually 1,000 or 2,000 USD tops) is a good deal for some people. The interest rate is of course very high. 100% annual interest is something you see often. In some cases even more.

The greatest problem here is that you need a "collector" that will help with those that want to get off the hook without paying back what they owe. Either that or use a collection agency that employs real sharks. Anyway, lots of new places in Buenos Aires are lending money, so I guess it's good business.

Tourism: Remember how I insist that life just goes on after SHTF? This is a good example. Of course most people that once could travel, can now no longer afford expensive trips to other countries.

This creates an interest in cheaper tourism. You might think that people won't want to spend a single buck because of the crisis, but as the crisis becomes a permanent lifestyle, people need to find ways to relax and get rid of that stress they live with.

Local tourism becomes an interesting option, and we certainly saw our local tourism go up since the crisis. You want to go for affordable-safe-relaxation-for all-the-family. Market your idea well and the results will be good.

The possibilities go from renting your hunting cabin, setting up a camping space if you have some acres where that could be possible, or building a few bungalows or cabins with a few friends that might be interested in the project.

AFFORDABLE LUXURIES

As people get poorer and they have to abandon some of their previous expensive luxuries, they move on to more affordable ones. These "affordable luxuries" as I like to call them are things that even though not at all indispensable for life, they still make the owner feel good about himself. He gains a bit of status and the product is something he or she can afford.

We see it clearly here in Argentina and it can be seen in most poor countries around the world: Even poor people need gadgets or trinkets that make them feel good. The trick is providing things they both enjoy and can afford.

Unfortunately a good example of this is the way in which drug use and alcoholism increases as the SHTF. You can find far less harmful business opportunities.

Cell phones: Oh, of course they are already everywhere and the market is terribly saturated and very competitive.

But I still want to mention that in most of the poorest "barrios" cell phones are big sellers. It's affordable, modern, flashy, and in spite of the person's poverty, he can still brag about his new toy.

A friend of ours along with her boyfriend opened a "cell phone and accessories" kiosk in the commercial area of a rather poor part of town. Soon enough they opened two more. They are still doing well.

Clothes: I know a guy that made good money with clothes. He knew the neighborhood well, knew that there was still some people with money. They were middle class, but a middle class with a tighter budget.

They couldn't afford the fancy brand name clothing they once did, but he expected to do well if he offered good clothing, nice fashionable designs, but at an affordable price. The store had to look cozy with a sprinkle of high class, and a designer was required for the store.

He hired a professional graphic designer for the advertisement displays and labels used in the clothing. This was how the "Snowball" brand was created. He ended up opening over a dozen stores in the southern suburbs of Buenos Aires.

Need a present for someone? Most of the time women do the buying, and most of the time they buy clothes. Snowball is affordable and people like it. Many other clothing brands started in a similar way.

Jewelry: Gold is too expensive, and it gets stolen a lot. This means there's an entire market for silver and steel jewelry, as well as for accessories made of all kinds of materials.

HOME BUSINESS

I know people that make aromatic candles, soaps, and salts for bubble baths. They are sold individually or as a kit. The clients are mostly people they already know and this kind of business requires a lot of "people" skills, and a fat phonebook.

Another woman makes presents for events such as weddings and baptisms or First Holy Communions.

My wife's best friend is a chef, and she quit her job at a hotel to start her own catering business, cooking for weddings, birthdays, etc. Some offer special breakfast gifts as well, mostly for birthdays or Valentines day.

There are many, many other stories and niches that were exploited.

People, just do some research, sit down and think until you come up with ideas. All the ones I've mentioned are very common and there are enough success stories for me to feel comfortable recommending them.

Analyze your assets, both physical and intellectual, and see if there's a market for your idea. Another way is to find an unsatisfied niche and work to provide for those needs.

INVESTMENTS

A friend of mine in the USA asked for a bit of advice regarding business ideas the other day. He told me a bit about what he had in mind, and at some point he said he had a buddy that offered him a percentage on a car sound system installation shop, also doing tinted windows and car alarms.

He said that he didn't think people would want to spend money on a fancy sound system during a depression. We talked about how car alarms and security film for windows would go up in demand, and also tinted film for security reasons.

When we got to the sound system part, he asked what I thought about that. I told him, "well... there's a few things people will still want after the SHTF: booze, drugs, religion, prostitutes, gambling...and a loud car."

I told him that it's common here to see total rust buckets from the 1970's with maybe 2,000 bucks worth of sound system, maybe more expensive than the car itself. Of course any business can fail, but if his friend does things right and he is a smart business man, he has a fair chance of success.

My friend said, "Man, people are stupid!"

I told him "YES, dude, they are." It's not that they are stupid, actually; it's the "affordable luxury" thing I talked about before.

Owning part of a business that does well is a good idea for an investment. Of course there's a risk. You should know what kind of risks you are talking about and if it's worth taking them. Something like this would be a medium to high risk investment.

You investments are things that make money for you. You'll hear survivalists sometimes talk about buying lots of tools or food as an investment. They are not. Even when people talk about "investing" in gold, they are using the word incorrectly. Even if you can make a profit buying and selling gold, it does not create money by itself so it's not an investment.

REAL ESTATE

My family has been into real estate for as long as I can remember. It's one of the best forms of investments. Slow profit, but the risk is low. It's also very "SHTF" proof if you buy when the market price is low, since you'll always have the bricks and the land they sit on.

Remember location, location, location? Well, after the SHTF, it's location, location, location, LOCATION!!!!!!

It's extremely important to know the overall area like the palm of your hand, because one block of distance may be the difference between a very sweet deal and a rather bad one where you lose money.

It's a "nice" neighborhood, you say? I ask, "how" nice?

Are the people there new "nice people" or is the place full of well-off older guys too, families with their own businesses going well, so that the kids of these older guys will stay there and carry on the family businesses or practice their professions. The doctor has his kid that is also a doctor and is taking dad's place. Is there a good school near by so that solid middle class families might be interested in moving there?

Are those blocks becoming fashionable, with trendy bars, boutiques and restaurants and cultural/social life? Do you see the place going somewhere? Did you get to know the place well so as to make an informed opinion? Did you visit on weekends? At night? When it rains? Does it flood?

How solid is the general income in that neighborhood, post SHTF?

You want people with solid finances, not rich but solid, such as an older guy that has had a business that survived lots of downturns over several decades. You don't want a place full of twenty-year-old internet wizards, who are the first ones to lose their jobs when things turn bad.

How can you tell the kind of people, the target of the place? Do your research.

Old nice neighborhoods that have been nice for a hundred years and still have business owners, politicians (like roaches, they never die, even after the nuke), judges, people with money still living there. That's a good place.

A new development, even if nice, that was built just years ago and where most of the people don't even own their own houses, that's not so SHTF proof.

What happened here was that the more exclusive "nice places" that had been "nice" for a hundred years managed okay, even keeping their pre-SHTF prices, while just a block away (I swear, just one block away from the nice places), the prices dropped like a brick. Those houses are worth maybe 75% or even 50% of what they used to cost.

But prices won't drop much more than that. A 50% loss is pretty bad I know, but maybe you can hold on until the price goes up, or you can look hard for the proper person to rent to. So that's the key point in real estate after the crisis. The place must have a well rooted community.

You might explore the new market. That's going to be people that can't afford a "nice place" anymore and move to a duplex or an apartment right next to their job opportunities downtown. So, it's got to be easy on the pocket, a small place but nice, and it should be located downtown or just next to it.

Just a small example. A little true story. Yesterday while waiting for my turn under the claws for that demonic sadist otherwise known as dentist, I overheard the conversation two young women had. The TV was on in the waiting room and the news was about another home invasion in a homestead in Pilar.

I heard them comment, "See? We're going to be just two women living alone. We can't live in a house, we need to move to an apartment. It's much safer."

The other woman shook her head in agreement right next to her with her eyes glued to the television.

People just don't die by the millions after an economic collapse, like they do in the movies and books. In the real world they survive. And that makes things much more complicated. Because, where do they go?

The demand for this kind of real estate will create a new kind of "nice place" demand, in or right next to downtown, simply because that's where more job opportunities can be found. That's a niche in the market you'll be able to exploit.

Before, it didn't matter. A family lived in the suburbs, had a home surrounded by nice trees, lots of vegetation, and drove a long distance to work.

Now he has no work.

Now he can't afford the big house.

Now he can't afford the gas or maybe even the car.

See where I'm going? Don't start splitting hairs and going for far-fetched theories. These things, they actually happened here in my country. It's not something new, we're nothing special, it's the typical urban-suburban dynamic that has been going on forever.

An economic crisis means a fresh churning of this old dynamic, and this means fresh opportunities in real estate and rentals.

Having said that, be careful of the places' downtown, which are destined to become rat holes. Walk around the place a lot, day and night. See what kind of people live there. Are there book stores and cafes? Nice. Triple X stores or industries that just went bankrupt? Maybe a larger investor can buy a few blocks and redesign the city, but not you.

So be smart, and do a lot of research until you know the place very well. Don't just go along with whatever the real estate agent says.

Generally speaking, when property drops 50%-60%, investors (bigger investors than the average folk) start buying because they see the opportunity. That alone prevents real estate prices from going down much further.

Old time real estate investors in Argentina estimate that 50% down is about as low as property gets until it reaches its floor. I've seen exceptions a bit above and below that number, but it's still accurate, as a rough average.

ADVICE REGARDING RENTING AND DEALING WITH TENANTS

1) It's business, okay?

If you let them cry you a river, you won't even have to water the lawn anymore. At first I went a bit soft on a guy, until one day he told me that he was glad because that way he could pay for all the other things that didn't cut him any slack.

"Dude, I'm getting fooled by you, just so you can keep paying for your credit cards and buying God knows what else?"

I told him that I was sorry, but he had a month to get updated with his rent or he could start looking for another place within his means.

These are the words you must use: "I'm sorry Mr. or Ms. X, but you'll have to find something you can actually pay for, something more within your means. I can't rent this place to you for 1,000 bucks a month, when I have people that would be happy to pay the real market value, which is 1,200."

That is it. Don't be best buds with your tenants. It's business.

2) Be careful what you sign.

Get a lawyer to read and check everything you sign before you actually sign it.

I was looking for someone to fill an office downtown. The real estate company wanted me to sign something before they started looking for a tenant. They had six months exclusivity, and I had to pay them a 5,000 USD penalty if I found a person to rent it to on my own, etc, etc. Man, that was great. I started laughing at the guy right to his face. I called my wife who's a lawyer, so we could both laugh at the same time.

I'm not kidding or exaggerating, I laughed at the guy in his face and after wiping away a couple small tears I handed him back the paper and told him of course, I wouldn't sign that.

He looked at me with a face made of stone. "Sir, everyone we work with signs this. The owner of the real estate agency requires it to begin working and finding a tenant for you."

I told him, "That's fine. I'm glad you find idiots to sign that for you. That only proves how many stupid people there are around. Tell you what. I'm not signing that; its ridiculous, but I'll offer you this instead. I'll give you half the commission you're asking for. I don't pay anyone more than that, ever. And I'll give you, say, two months. This is the downtown capital district and you should find someone fast. I'm not asking for more than the market value."

"You have no exclusivity over anything. I'm going to contact at least a couple of other brokers. If you find a tenant, then you get the commission, if not, then that's too bad. If you're not interested, let's just stop wasting each other's time."

His jaw hung pretty low. I don't know if he was pretending to be shocked or if he really was. I don't think everyone falls for what he wanted me to sign, but I'm sure that many people do.

He asked me to hold on a second while he talked to some guy on the cell phone, and then offered me the deal for 75% of the commission they had asked for before. I told him I was willing to round it up to 60% of the commission he asked. He talked on the phone again, and then he said okay.

Know the market. Don't let anyone push you into paying more than you should. And just don't sign anything until you and your lawyer are sure.

Tip: Whatever contract you sign, make sure it includes some kind of protection against any jump of inflation in the market in general.

My contracts have the possibility of breaking off the deal after six months if inflation has increased and the parties don't reach a new agreement on rent. Others contracts include approximately how much the rent will go up, again, with the possibility of breaking the agreement after six to twelve months.

3) Find the right tenant.

The real estate firm ended up finding a tenant for the downtown office, a gay psychiatrist. The place had two offices and he'd use one. A woman (also a psychiatrist), would work in the other office.

That's perfect. Not only one, but two professionals. The guy will never have a divorce or childcare to worry about. That shrink will be paying rent for the rest of his life, and one thing people need during a crisis is therapy. He's going to have lots of work for sure.

Don't rent to any chunk of meat that walks and breathes.

Kids are a reality, but take a good close look. A shabby looking guy with five obnoxious brats running around, with an equally shabby looking wife, is not someone you want as a tenant.

You want somebody who is clean looking, with a secure job, and who preferably does not have twelve kids. Their appearance is important when you interview them. If a person can't keep his own self clean and neat, how do you think he will treat your rental property? You want someone that sounds reasonable when you talk to him. Check his background as well as you can.

There are lots of scams going on and once a tenant is inside, it's harder to get rid of them than ticks or fleas.

BARTERING: FIRST STEPS TOWARDS REBUILDING COMMERCE

At first after the crisis no one wanted to buy or sell even a brick, the future was so uncertain. The banks had closed, and no one knew how much the paper currency was going to be worth tomorrow, or even in the next couple of hours.

I vividly remember being at the local Home Depot (called "Easy" in Argentina), and buying a few tools. The clerks would run around like crazy, replacing the old prices with the new ones, which sometimes changed within the same hour.

It was depressing to see a price and notice that after peeling it off, the old price was still there. There was no time for the clerks to remove them. There would be a five layer sandwich of ever increasing prices that were maybe just a couple of days old.

After a few months, people found that they were in a very delicate position. Many were without a job, and those who had a job were paid in a currency where the value was dropping by the hour. Sometimes you had the problem of reaching the cash register and finding out that the price had already changed.

The value of a peso was dropping like a brick, and finally food as well as all other product had gone up 200-300% or in some cases much more. Certain items went up even 600%, such as a certain famous brand of corn flakes.

The solution?

Of course it didn't take much time for someone to suggest, "Hey, I manufacture product A, and I really need B and C, so how about bartering?"

A few months later the "Barter Club" concept spread throughout the different districts, and people started to organize, trying to barter with goods (food, clothes, and crafts mostly), and services (plumbing, electrical work, general masonry, private tutoring, psychiatric sessions, you name it).

It sounds like a good idea.

Survivalists spend endless hours discussing which products to stock specifically for post-SHTF barter. Tools, needles, candles, shoes, and sometimes the most ridiculous suggestions are considered the wisest "investment" for after the SHTF. This or that item "will be worth its weight in gold."

Well, no, actually. Only gold is always worth its weight in gold. Bar none.

Let me explain. Only a little time passed until a problem with these "Barter Clubs" showed up. A problem with no solution, which would eventually doom most barter clubs.

Aunt Margie would show up with two dozen sweaters that she had made. Very nice ones which would sell for at least 100 Euros in Spain, when they were truthfully advertised as "custom hand-knitted" sweaters.

Hey, Aunt Margie should be loaded by those standards! She has 2,400 Euros worth of goods, right? But the problem was that she had no market for her product. The guy who liked one of her sweaters had scented candles to trade, but Margie wanted some of those good looking eggs. Her husband Bob loves omelets, but the egg guy was looking for someone to fix his water heater, and he had no use for her nice sweaters. And Margie already had enough candles.

See the problem? It turned out that it was practically impossible to find someone who had something you wanted, who at the same time wanted exactly the goods that you had available for barter.

This is not just some armchair expert from Argentina making a prediction about bartering after the SHTF, this is what actually happened. All around the country, over and over.

Rural towns had it just a bit easier because these small communities had SOME degree of barter in place already. The guy who sold honey already had an arrangement with the man who sold eggs, but this was limited to a small number of goods. Currency was still indispensable to subsist, rural town or not.

How about Uncle Bob's ammo stash? He read somewhere that .22 LR would be "the new currency" after the SHTF, and it would be the best barter item, so he thought ahead and bought a few cases of 500 round "bricks" of ammo just to be ready. Again, his surprise was huge when the egg guy told him that he didn't need any .22 ammo. He doesn't even like guns. He simply needs a plumber.

Since he was at the "Barter Club," Bob checked around to see what the actual market for his .22 ammo stash was, and he was disappointed by the few offers he got. It seemed that each person wanted a different item, and those that were interested in bullets...many of them looked like people from the wrong walk of life, and Bob wasn't sure he wanted to give them ammo. Ammo that would end up being used in delinquents' guns, and possibly against him and his family.

Though few, there were some folks interested in his .22 ammo—at least more than the number of people interested in his wife's sweaters. Besides, ammo prices had gone up along with most dollar prices, and now ammo cost three times more. He found a guy that was interested in a 500 round brick of .22, who had some nice cured ham to trade. They traded and Bob walked back home feeling pretty good about his .22 LR "investment."

The problem came a week later, when reading his "Magnum" gun rag. Bob saw a notification from RENAR (our ATF) warning everyone that from now on, .22 (the only unregulated caliber until then) was also regulated, and required an ammo card as every other caliber did, signed by the registered dealer that sold you the ammo. Suddenly, it was a felony crime for Bob to sell even his humble .22 ammunition.

People, Uncle Bob and Aunt Margie are fictional characters, as you all realize, but the Magnum gun magazine is real and so was the article announcing the new law. Shortly after the crisis, RENAR regulated the only caliber of ammunition left unregulated, the .22 LR, turning everyone selling it who wasn't already a registered gun dealer into a felon.

The lesson would be that, though .22 LR is a good thing to have around, and maybe you can sell some of it to a friend or trade for something with him after the SHTF, still it will NOT turn into a regular item at barter markets, and it will certainly NOT be "the new currency" after the SHTF.

It may be that way in the Middle East, where guns have been sold on the streets like bananas for centuries, but in more "civilized" Western countries it doesn't work that way. In countries like the USA, you can count on the government regulating and even banning guns and ammo, especially after a crisis and even more especially after an outbreak of civil unrest.

People, the government will not simply disappear after the SHTF. It may be inefficient, it may be incompetent and unable to protect you, but it will be around to arrest you for breaking the laws the politicians care about. Especially the laws regulating guns and ammunition. Trust me, the government will care even more about them after a major crisis. Remember Katrina?

We live in a world of currency, of paper and plastic money. Several centuries ago things might have been different, although even pre-historic civilizations had some sort of currency as a means of exchange. Paper money, precious metals, seashells, and even seeds were used as currency at different times.

In their book "Warriors of Christendom," John Matthews and Bob Stewart describe the following barter equivalents for armor and weapons around the sixth century:

Helmet: six cows

Chain Mail Coat: twelve cows

Sword and Scabbard: seven cows

Leg armor: six cows

War horse: twelve cows

Even though in those days barter was much more common, people had already been using currency for centuries. They would go into the town, sell their products or barter if they got the chance, and buy what they needed.

Today, people are even more bonded to currency, turning true barter into something that is impractical and frankly impossible in most cases.

This occurred in our own Argentine barter experiment. In spite of all the speculations, in spite of the countless hours of internet debate by survival and preparedness experts you may have read, true barter was simply not possible. Some form of currency was desperately needed. But what to use?

The "Barter Club" organizations that spread all over the country came up with the idea of "credits." What are credits? A new paper currency to be used at each individual barter market, in each city. Both in the big cities and in small rural towns, barter clubs started making their own credit notes or local paper money.

These "credits" worked out at first, but there where several inherent problems that could not be overcome.

1) People had trouble determining how many "credits" each product or service was worth. Just who would set the "fair market value" of your goods or service? Is one hour of a surgeon's time worth the same as one hour of a plumber's? Yes? No? Who says so? The owner of that particular barter club?

2) All people needed were a good printer and some creativity and they could easily counterfeit unlimited amounts of their own fake credits. There is a reason why "real" paper money printed by governments today includes so many sophisticated anti-counterfeiting measures. Locally created paper "credits" are a joke by comparison. Any child with a computer and a printer can counterfeit as many perfect copies as they want. As long as computers, scanners and printers continue to exist, locally produced paper "credits" simply won't work as a substitute for counterfeit-proof paper money created by governments.

After their failure with "credits," most "Barter Clubs" returned to the official paper money, the Argentine Peso. Yes, even though the value of the Peso compared to the USD was still determined daily, or by the hour in some cases.

But to be honest, we kind of grew accustomed to it. Every day we would all go to Dolaraldia.com.ar to check the current price of the US Dollar in Pesos. Radio and TV gave us the updated Dollar-Peso price several times a day, along with the traffic report and weather. We got used to it, and lived accordingly.

Eventually most of the "Barter Clubs" evolved into what I generally describe as gray or black markets, where you shop with regular paper money, Pesos in our case. You also find "I Buy Gold!" shops in these markets.

I call them "gray/black" markets because (sometimes) they sell stolen merchandize, and none of these dealers pay taxes.

My brother visiting from Spain used Euros to buy jeans, and the dealer readily accepted them. We've all become experts at discovering counterfeit funny money, either Pesos, USD or Euros.

Keep all this in mind before you buy a cargo container full of condoms (I knew a guy that actually did that, but that is another story), or any other good you think will turn you rich after the collapse.

Ammo is a good barter item within a certain circle of people you trust after the fall, and even if you do not end up trading it or selling it, it is useful in itself to defend yourself, and for hunting. The same could be said of canned and other long shelf life food. If you don't end up bartering it or selling it, you can use it yourself. Crisis or not, you still have to eat, so it's a win-win situation.

Other products such as cigars, liquor and women's makeup that are commonly associated with post-SHTF barter should be considered more as "gifts" to buy "favors" more than as barter items. Although you may find someone willing to pay good money for them after the SHTF, please don't count on it, or you will risk ending up like the condom guy with a lot of unsold products.

What would have happened if things in Argentina had not stabilized, as they did? What if the Peso had continued to collapse in true Weimar Germany or Zimbabwe type hyperinflation? Well, here we are entering into guesstimate territory, but I believe that the "I Buy Gold!" dealers would have become more and more common, until every merchant, no matter what good or service he was selling, would have started to buy and sell with gold directly. Maybe silver would have also ended up being used as well in due time, as a form of smaller value currency. But this is the stuff of movies and novels, not rational preparedness. It is still a matter of speculation at this point.

Do you know who really made nice money with theses Barter Clubs? The guys who owned the places where they were held, and who rented space to people to display their products. The same happened with the "black/grey" markets or other "outlets." The one making the big bucks is the owner of the place.

THE ART OF BARGAINING AND HAGGLING

This has become a way of life here in Argentina. You don't do any of this in a chain supermarket or the nicer shops. You don't barter at the grocery store.

But when you buy stuff on the street, when you go to the black/gray market or "outlets" like "La Salada," which are places that almost resemble Mad Max's Barter Town, then bargaining and haggling comes in very handy.

You also use it a lot regarding services. Dealing with things such as auto mechanic repairs, contractor jobs, and hiring people in general. It's easy to see how some of the things would also apply to bartering or even negotiating deals for your business.

1) Be ready to say "no, thanks," and walk away.

If you look or sound too interested, the price will quickly go up. Take your time. Ask a lot as if trying to make up your mind, even if you already know everything about the product you are interested in.

2) Play poor.

Maybe you really ARE poor and that makes your acting much more realistic.

A dealer will have a hard time trying to take more money out of you if he sincerely thinks you really don't have it. For him it's either reducing the price or not selling at all.

3) Offer half of what you were told and start negotiating from there.

If the price is ridiculously high, make a ridiculously low offer, like 20%. Do so in a way that it doesn't sound offensive.

"Oh, but I was just planning on spending only X. Guess I'll have to pass"

You can combine your low offer with point number 1. The merchant will stop you before you leave with a counteroffer. If he doesn't, well just keep looking and asking around. You can always come back later. Get used to doing this.

You need to have a rough idea of how much something is worth. If you're not sure, just ask around at several other places until you get a better idea.

You need this information because some merchants will offer ridiculously high prices, expecting you to offer half or less. This mostly happens in places where clueless tourists go shopping, not where people that are "in the know" buy.

4) Ask for discounts due to quantity.

If I'm buying two pair of jeans that cost 55 bucks each in a market, I'll offer to buy two for 100 bucks. Most of the time the dealer will go for it.

5) Be picky and ask for discounts due to defects or malfunctions.

For example, I was buying a locket (those that you put a little picture inside) for my wife. One of the inside rims that keeps the picture in place was broken and needed soldering.

"Any goldsmith will solder that in a minute for 15 bucks," said the dealer.

I told him "Not a chance. That will cost at least twenty bucks. Tell you what: discount the twenty bucks and throw one of those fancier velvet cases (worth two or three bucks) and we have a deal." The dealer agreed.

6) Ask around and tell the dealer the price the other guy gave you.

Many times you find people offering similar products in the same market. Ask around before buying and then ask one of the merchants if he's interested in making a better offer.

7) Ask for cash discounts

This is very common in Argentina, and it's a popular way to evade taxes, even in the fanciest places. The shopkeeper or dealer will offer a cash discount, or you can ask about one yourself.

Since the sales tax here is 21%, it's very common for people to offer cash and not demand the cash register's receipt, and go half on the evaded tax, asking for a 10% discount. Sometimes the discount is even higher, but 10% is the minimum if you don't get a receipt and the tax is being evaded.

8) Be polite but firm

Some merchants will say, "Oh, man, you're killing me, this book (or clothing or whatever) cost me 15 bucks and you want it for only ten?!"

Don't let him push you around. If you know you are right, then just say, "okay sir, lets both stop wasting our time," and start walking away. The merchant will surely stop you with one or two better offers before you are gone.

9) Become a "client"

When a shop or dealer is worth it because of the prices or the kind of goods he has to offer, become a "client." That means you buy from that certain guy often, so you stop by and chat a bit from time to time. Eventually the client-dealer relationship brings benefits.

You get discounts, you get offered special merchandize reserved for "clients," and when you buy something you usually get a bit "extra" for free.

My gun shop dealer usually throws in a box of ammo, a used soft case, offers me a mint condition gun that someone just left and wants to get rid of quickly, or offers me premium hard-to-get ammo that he somehow got a batch of.

10) Be friendly

No need to be a prick. You can be firm yet friendly, and you can haggle and bargain without being disrespectful.

Also, having friends in certain circles can be very convenient. For example after a little chit-chat, one of the guys in a nearby supermarket told me about a shipment of energy bars that tasted great and were very cheap. The employees were buying them themselves and not even putting them out on the shelves (where they were supposed to be).

I overheard a conversation (something you should get used to doing to gather "word on the street" information) he was having with some other employee so when one of them left I started talking with the other guy. I ended up leaving with a box of energy bars under each arm.

11) Don't be too cheap

I sometimes lost out on things I really wanted because I was too inflexible when negotiating.

You should set a roof of how much you want to spend before you even start making offers, which should be far less than your roof. But if for example you set your roof at 100 bucks and you finally get it down to 120, when you feel the guy won't go a buck below that, ask yourself, "okay, I'm about to walk away. But if I want it that bad, isn't the extra 20 bucks worth what I want so much just this one time?"

12) Take your time and don't look attached

Work hard at looking objective and impassionate about your purchase. Take your time, even tell the dealer to attend to other customers as you make up your mind. This sometimes works almost as well as the walking away ploy. If you manage to look uninterested, the dealer will offer you a better deal.

It really is an art. For example, after fifteen or twenty minutes of thinking and looking uninterested, I start asking and showing interest in some other, much cheaper product. This usually drives the merchant nuts.

13) Counter-offer for even less.

If the dealer is just too ridiculous, be ready to walk away but try counter-offering with even less.

You: "I'll go a hundred bucks."

Dealer: "No sir! This costs a thousand dollars right out of the factory."

You: "Eighty bucks and not a buck more. I see here that there's a defect that … wait, forget about it. If you want, I'll take it off your hands for fifty. If you are not interested I'll just walk away. This is not what I was looking for."

14) Dress for the occasion.

Again, the "Oh, I'd pay a million dollars but I just have fifty bucks," is one of the most effective tools. It gives the dealer almost no margin to work around if he truly believes you don't have more money.

Still, you have to "dress poor." It makes no sense to say you have almost no money if you are dressing like someone that is doing well.

When I'm going to one of these markets I'll usually go after doing some work around the house and looking a bit dirty and sweaty. An old T-shirt with holes, jeans and work shoes works well. No wallet, just the cash in my pocket and usually just the amount of money I'm planning on spending.

POST SHTF SHOPPING GUIDE

1) Become a discriminating buyer

This is pretty much the core to your new mentality. Regarding everything: Do I NEED another box of 50% saturated fat donuts? They do taste good, but how much do I need them, compared to some beans/rice/lentils/meat that could go into the freezer that would provide real nutritional value?

Donuts, cookies, chocolates and junk food in general. Not only are you wasting money but you are not doing your body any favors. I'm sounding a bit like a "flavorless terminator" here. Man, we like brownies as much as the next family. Cookies and ice cream too and a nice glass of ice-cold Coke.

Just learn to rationalize it to: a) save money, and b) not eat junk food that slowly ruins your arteries and adds more fat to your body. Try your best to find alternatives that don't have saturated fat. That stuff is the worst thing you could eat.

So for example, when I'm buying food, I estimate we'll be having two or three junk food meals. Say, brownies one day, ice cream for desert a couple more days. Yes, that's three junk meals per week.

Sounds like too little to most, given the average person's diet. But once you start adding up other things like soda drinks, you see how much "damage" you are doing to both your wallet and your body.

The point here is that there must be some kind of control. If you don't exercise control, one day you'll stand in front of the mirror and see Jabba the Hutt.

If a 2.5 liter soda bottle disappears at each dinner, that's a lot of sugar you are consuming and a lot of money you are wasting. I go for one small glass at lunch and another one later on during the day. I think 2.5 liters should last us (two adults, my kids don't drink it) two or three days. And cutting down to two bottles a week or none at all is something we've done in the past and were darn glad about it.

Tang orange drink is something we drink a lot of. It's cheap, has vitamins, less sugar, and is way better for your body than soda pop.

Soda pop should be a controlled substance, not by the federal government but by each parent. Uncontrolled consumption of soda will make your kids obese in no time (not to mention making their teeth rot and your dentist rich!).

So, learn to tell the difference between food and junk, and be honest with yourself regarding how much junk you are actually eating. Generally speaking, processed foods and ready-to-eat meals will fall on the junk food side, full of salt, saturated fat and hydrogenated God knows what else.

Add to that that they tend to be much more expensive. Doesn't take a genius to figure how much of this should be in your shopping cart: little to none at all.

2) Discounts and sales.

Discount days, sales, coupons, promotions of any kind, anything goes here.

You lucky guys living in the wonderful USA, you can even print them out off the internet on coupon websites. Do you think this is common in other parts of the world? It's not! Take advantage of these things while you have them.

Of course, buy in quantity when you find good deals. This saves the most money.

3) Become an informed client.

Here we are entering into more "post SHTF shopper" territory.

Quick version: The government that is supposedly in charge of quality control in general lacks the time and resources or is too corrupt to care about what actually ends up on the shelves. The economy crashed, and they have crime and social disorder to take care of. Quality control is something that isn't even on their radar picture. You need to know yourself what you are eating.

Just as an example—tomato sauce. I buy the known brand, called "Campagnola," which is the most expensive you can get but it also lasts for well over a year, so that's a bonus.

Why? Because I learned that nearly all of our other sauces are made from a huge load of tomato sauce that the Chinese sold to the food companies in this country. Later they found out that its quality was much worse than they expected, but since they had it, they had to sell it, mixing it up with the more expensive stuff that's produced locally.

In this case, it's worth buying the safer product.

But in other cases, quality and price do not always go hand by hand.

I'm always asking for references to other products. Take note of any positive comments regarding a lesser known brand. Old ladies usually know better about such things, so talk to them when standing in line, then try some new product out and compare it to what you're already using. This usually leads to some great finds that can cost less, and sometimes even cost less for a better quality.

4) Be careful where you shop.

This is another post-SHTF classic. People have little to no money and are looking to maximize any possible profit. Some grocery store managers figured they'd save some bucks by turning off the fridges at night, hoping that the temperature would stay low enough until the next day.

Do this during the summer, especially with milk, yogurt, cheese and meat, and you might end up sickening your clients, maybe even killing them as we've seen here in some cases not long ago.

How do you know if the chill cycle was broken at some point?

The cup or pack should obviously be cold, less than 5° C or 40° F. The packaging should not be wet, nor should there be water at the bottom of the fridge, nor ice formed there. That's a sign of defrosting, meaning the temperature went up too high at some point. Frozen products should be as hard as a rock.

In yogurts and other cups with soft packaging, look for swollen and inflated containers. If you feel it's a bit more tight or "tense" than it should be, then you better leave it behind.

Take an overall look at the place. A dirty grocery store is a sign of a cheap owner that probably tries to save some bucks by turning off the fridges at night.

This is no guarantee though. I've shopped in a "Disco," which is a well known chain of big supermarkets (our equivalent of Wal-Mart, with one in every neighborhood), and the chicken I was about to buy had gone bad and smelled rotten once I poked the film with a key.

How do you tell if chicken or other meat has gone bad? Smell of course, but also take a good look at the bones. The cut bones leave the medulla exposed. It should be bright red if it's fresh. If it's dark it means the blood is going bad.

If there's no bone visible in the meat you are buying, look for small arteries and spots of blood. Again, you want bright red blood, and a good smell.

Eggs? That's a bit more complicated, but once you are home you can tell by putting an egg in water. A good egg sinks, a bad egg floats.

Also, regarding sales: Is it really cheap? Sometimes "Disco" supermarkets will announce a sale for next week ... but raise the prices a few days before.

These are some commonly known tips, but they are even more important after the SHTF because no one else will be controlling things, at least not the way they should or that you are used to.

5) Checking your change and receipt.

Most people I see don't even bother to check the change. They should. Another thing that has happened to me is that the price I saw on the product does not correspond with the price rung up on the machine at the counter.

I don't check every single thing, but I do look overall for anything that looks odd. A couple times I paid more than I mentally estimated I would. A quick check showed that I was being charged several bucks over the price displayed.

This happens a lot, especially during the worst months of rising inflation. So guys, check that you are paying what you should. A notepad and a calculator is a good idea.

Be careful when coming back home and getting your bags out of the car. Put fancy "name brand" shopping bags into old beat up boxes to prevent their being seen. If you buy any expensive gadgets, destroy the box. Don't leave it out there in front of your house or in your garbage can to be seen by potential thieves.

USING GOLD, SILVER, AND FOREIGN CURRENCY AFTER THE CRISIS

You bought some gold, silver, Euros or other forms of "safe" currency to keep your eggs in different baskets, as they say. So one day you wake up, and people are going nuts for whatever reason and they are quietly trying to close their bank accounts.

Within hours they are not that "quiet" anymore. They are screaming, "You crooks, give me my damn money… or else!" Of course there's no liquidity to compensate for such a demand.

Banks close, ATMs run dry, and absolutely no one accepts plastic or checks. This is a good time to lay low, stay at home to watch the news, eat popcorn and watch that favorite movie with your wife again.

Sooner or later the banks reopen, but they have a new set of rules you may not like that much, like not returning your property, your hard earned money. Some people don't dig that, and they tend to get really pissed off.

The good part is that banks immediately stop advertising on TV. You know, all that BS about the "Acme Bank" being there for you, helping your company grow, and being part of the community. It took nearly a year for our banks to start advertising again, and until last year you could still see angry former clients banging on the front doors of the downtown bank buildings with hammers.

You'll soon find out that it's very hard to pull through with a fifty or one hundred dollar cash withdrawal limit per week, and it may take days or weeks before even that is allowed.

But you have your emergency stash of cash and precious metals at home, right?

What happened here in Argentina was that soon enough "street brokers," or money dealers, started popping up on the busy boulevards and in the highly populated downtown areas. You would just walk by, and see a guy doing nothing but whispering "change, change." That's your man.

It's not really safe to make an exchange right on the street. It worked that way for years, but today most money dealers have a "front."

The guy I deal with most of the time has a drug store. You walk in and you only see pens, candy, office supplies, watches and a few pocket knives, but the guy's "real" business is buying and selling Pesos, Dollars and Euros. I don't buy other currencies, but I'm sure he has Brazilian money too, and there are other guys that will take precious metals. Thousands and thousands of Dollars and Euros go through this guy's hands at his "drug store."

Those that have pawn or antique shops may specialize on dealing with precious metals (PMs), diamonds and expensive jewelry, but your average money dealer works with paper money.

Why not go to the bank or official exchange houses? Well, for many months or even years, there was a limit to how much money you could change (100 USD, if I remember correctly). Even then you had to leave all of your personal information, and the exchange rate was better in the black market anyway, so that's why even today most people still prefer to use the black market.

You won't be buying what you need with gold coins or 100 Euro bills. Many folks will readily accept them, but you won't get a fair exchange rate. That's why you'll usually prefer a money dealer, or sell your gold coins to a reputable precious metal broker.

Here are some tips on how I generally handle things. Please guys, I'm just a regular guy that's simply been doing this for a while now, but don't expect any ninja BS touch of death or 007 secret password. Just some experience and common sense. Take it or leave it, and then come to your own conclusions.

1) Exchange small amounts of currency.

You may get a few points more if you exchange larger quantities of money (it is a temptation sometimes), but you are also risking much more. I'd rather lose four or five bucks and only change 100 Euros or 200 Euros or USD at a time. The same would go for gold and other PMs. Don't be stupid and show up with a pocket full of gold coins or jewelry. Anyone can notice, even the money dealer might be tempted into kidnapping you if he thinks you are loaded. Or he may tell a buddy who is a thief or a kidnapper about your treasure, for a share of the loot. This happens more than you think. Even the companies that install burglar alarms and safes sometimes sell this valuable information to criminals. Not everybody is honest, especially after the SHTF. Remember also that good companies may unknowingly hire crooked employees.

2) Try different dealers.

At least at first, deal with different folks until you find one you like better, then deal with that guy more often, while always checking if you are getting a fair exchange rate. If you have a friend or relative that can advise you on fair dealers, better yet. Once a few months have gone by and you feel you can trust that guy, deal with him the most.

This isn't exactly a walk in the park. Most of these guys are right there on the edge of the law and you should expect to run into some less than pleasant people. Just make sure that you don't go into buildings far from public areas or out of sight from the sidewalk. Always try to stay as public and as close to the exits as possible.

I've dealt with over a dozen of guys like these, and they aren't saints. I've had a couple of risky encounters. Do not do this kind of business while going along with family members (wife, kids). An "able-bodied" buddy... shall we call him... would be a good idea.

3) Spend the collapsed currency fast!

The trick is not having the collapsed currency with you for long. It should burn your hands. Use it up right after you have exchanged your better currency for it.

Example: if the USD crashes and you decide to sell some PMs to buy a month's worth of supplies, do it quickly. Sell the PMs or Euros or whatever other solid currency you have, and use the weakening dollars that same day or the following day at most.

You do this because the collapsed dollar will be like a sand castle. It can fall apart within hours.

Say you sold your Euros at a one Euro to three USD rate, and the following morning on TV Oprah said that she had a dream about a one to six rate. All of a sudden people lose even more trust in the currency and it falls to one Euro to four USD. Any silly or not so silly thing can sink the fallen currency even deeper. Even rumors.

Other than a few hundred dollar bills for emergency use, don't risk keeping large amounts of collapsed currency. It'll rot faster than bananas.

4) Keep your BIG MOUTH SHUT!

Don't tell ANYONE about your savings. While you are better off, there will be people out there who can't put food on the table, and it's not some skinny kid in Africa, it's your neighbor or the guy that works next to you. Desperate times call for desperate measures and some people will do anything. We often hear about people getting tortured during home invasions just to make sure the victims give up any booty they may have hidden. This happened routinely in the Balkans during "ethnic cleansing" in the 1990s. Before being forced out of their homes or killed, those being "cleansed" would be tortured into revealing any hidden valuables. It became standard operating procedure. It seems to be part of human nature during a grave crisis.

5) Be careful and stay alert while doing business.

Leave the car in different parking lots; always take different routes while walking back to the car and driving back home. If possible walk into malls where you may lose people following you or drive through other places, anything you can do to blur any fixed route or schedule a person may notice.

In general, and not only when doing "money business," avoid making your cars into "flags" that indicate if your home is empty or occupied. Once in a while leave your car at home and get a ride to school or work, or have a neighbor park his car in your driveway or in front of your house. Park away from your house and walk a short distance home from time to time.

 Switch cars with your wife. The idea is to prevent watchful criminals from observing a sure pattern in your behavior. A car that is a certain "flag" about your home's occupancy is one of the worst patterns you can make.

Try not to use any clothes that can distinguish you from the rest or attract attention. Apply the "gray man" approach more than ever.

I try not to have any bags or any other objects in my hands when I'm out in public, in order to have both hands available in case someone wants to mug or kidnap me or those with me. Just an old pair of Nikes, worn jeans and T shirt, the car key, pocket knife and the money I'll be changing.

When you have no other option but to sell larger quantities of currency, you may want to use concealed body armor and carry a concealed weapon.

6) Be quick.

Use a calculator to make sure you're getting paid properly. Walk in, say "Hi," make the transaction quickly, give a handshake and be done with it. Try not to stay in there too long. The longer you hang around, the greater the chances of someone spotting you and organizing something against you. Some of the money dealer's other clients may be part-time criminals looking for new victims. Try not to meet them.

Finding like-minded people is no easy task. Survivalists and people that are into preparedness are usually very strong minded and independent. Especially among the survivalist movement, there are people that are indeed extremists or radicals.

My idea of a survivalist is first and foremost a person that is at the very least capable of functioning in a society. This is a basic and necessary skill. If you can't even fit in during "normal" times, after SHTF it only becomes harder.

These extremists are usually loners. Usually they have little family or they don't get along with them well. Some have peculiar views regarding race or religion, and overall they constitute the kind of people you wouldn't want to have around or invite over to your home for some barbeque with the family.

The internet provides a world of information and in many of the survival and preparedness forums you'll find like-minded people. Eventually after some time you get to see better how like minded they really are.

 I visit a number of such forums and in several of them I find a handful of people I'd gladly go get a beer or a cup of coffee with. Minionreport.com is where I spend most of the time. Many of the members there are people that I've known since 2002. My own survival blog (www.ferfal.blogspot.com) is also a place where many like-minded people usually drop by and leave comments and questions.

After a few years of visiting these places almost on daily basis, I've learned a few things that might be of use to the new guy just getting started.

1) Visit a number of forums and read a bit before you register. As a general rule, I distrust discussion forums that require you to register to see what's going on inside.

2) Don't waste much time discussing politics and religion. I've done that before, I still do, and I probably will do it again. I just know it's mostly a waste of time. When I encounter religious intolerance or other dirty business going on in some forum, I just leave. I recommend people do the same when encountering places where moderators or owners are disrespectful of the members, or pretend to treat them like lesser creatures. I don't allow anyone to put a foot on my head in the real word. I don't know about you but I don't plan on letting it happen in the virtual world either. There's more than enough information out there, so you shouldn't allow yourself to be pushed around.

3) Talking about everyday stuff and fooling around is fun and a good way to relax. Just try to learn things too. If all you do is go on line each night just to fool around, you are just wasting your time that could be better spent.

4) Treat people like you would when talking to them face to face. You'll have to understand that sometimes there are kids pretending to be adults on line. Sometimes there are adults who are worse than kids, who insult or provoke you when they never would have the guts to do so to your face. Again, letting this consume much of your time isn't the smartest thing.

5) Learn to forgive. A wise man once said, "You are not a five dollar coin that everyone likes." There's a lot of truth to that. But you can still forgive people. Be man enough to turn the other cheek. (Metaphorically speaking; if someone actually hits you in the face, beat the crap out of him.)

Eventually you may get to share e-mail addresses or even phone numbers. You can go to get–togethers and reunions and meet people face to face. I've always felt a bit of envy in this regard because some of the guys I have gotten to know for many years post photographs of the reunions where they have a great time. Living at the other end of the world makes meeting face to face pretty hard.

Unless you know everyone that is attending very well, then chances are you'll find some people you DON'T want to be associated with. That's why sometimes it's a good idea to know for sure who's going before attending.

My advice is to first know people on an individual basis. Exchange e-mails or phone numbers and go together to the shooting range or have dinner. That is, meet on neutral territory for the first time.

People that live near each other have the added benefit of being able to help each other during an actual emergency if the friendship prospers. It's all very entertaining, meeting people, going out hiking and camping, and going on line each night and debating philosophical issues until two AM.

Now, the bad news.

In case you didn't notice, post-SHTF life isn't about camping, hiking or going out hunting. Count your blessings if you can count with the fingers on one hand the amount of friends that will indeed be there for you when you need them.

Most of these will be life-long friends. You can find them online and build a friendship, but it's certainly not easy or very likely. That doesn't mean you shouldn't try.

I've learned that when the SHTF, of all the people you knew, some of whom were close friends, only one percent will be there for you. Out of that one percent, some may not be able to help you even if they want to.

I've learned this the hard way a number of times.

When people talk about forming groups and all living together in a survival retreat, I can only imagine the problems that will certainly occur. Different individuals with their own problems and ambitions, with their own wives or husbands who have their own unique problems as well. Kids who are educated differently. People who just don't get along with each other, for whatever reason.

Will you stay posted running guard duty on a friend's farm for food and shelter, when they are hiring guards and paying them well in the next town, and there are a number of skills you have that would be much more profitable? Will you (or your wife) tolerate living under someone else's roof and under their rules?

Many survivalists think about forming these groups and communities. They go on with their normal lives and jobs and think that "when the SHTF," they will all live life exactly as they read in books or saw in movies.

Just hold this thought for a second: If complete nutcases such as brain-dead cult followers eventually break up, what makes you think that strong independently thinking people will suddenly all get along well and blindly follow the commands of one person? All this, of course, while the world falls apart.

I don't know about you guys, but my family reunions during Christmas and New Year are pretty wild. Sometimes, everyone ends up yelling and fighting. Many families have so many problems they don't get together in the first place. And we are talking family. Imagine people who are just friends suddenly all living together under the rules of the house owner during extremely stressful times and 25 to 50% unemployment.

What happened here in Argentina was that some people made an extra effort and lived together. The parents, grandparents, and the older children moved back to the folks' place because they couldn't afford to pay for their own place any more.

So you have the eighty-year-old grandparents, the parents, and thirty-something-year-old sons and daughters, all living together and doing their share to get by. Yes, that happens a lot here.

Everyone works, usually getting paid very little, and maybe the grandma helps by making dinner or doing some other chore she's capable of.

I assure you, in most cases people do this out of necessity and there's a lot of fighting and bickering going on.

There are advantages though: The bills are divided by several working family members, and one of the grandparents who is capable of doing so usually stays home babysitting the children.

I've never heard of friends doing this or forming retreats where they could sustain themselves, doing the fabled self-sufficient thing and living off the land.

If I could have it my way, I'd move to a small community, and try to live next to friends and people I believe I can trust for real. But I know better than to think a bunch of families can all live together in some compound under the rules of one or two persons.

If the situation is getting out of control such as a civil war and high levels of social unrest, I'd just move out of the country. My grandparents did that during the Spanish Civil War. They came here and rebuilt their lives. Life just goes on.

My grandfathers worked as carpenters (one in the railroad, the other one building boats), and my grandmothers started their own shops once they saved up enough money. One had a bakery (and she did very well with it), and the other one had a small bazaar/general store.

Counting on your neighbors is pretty hard as well. Generally speaking, you'll be hard pressed finding other survival-minded people.

One thing that happened here was neighbors organizing for security. In some places they started watches. Some people in the country keep contact with their neighbors and talk to each other if they see something.

Being an active member of the community, either church, school, or shooting club is a big help. Try getting to know your neighbors, knowing fully well that even though many are good people, few will be of help when SHTF.

The possibility of needing to set up a watch is very real as crime goes up and police can't keep up with it. Hiring guards is always a choice. Especially when you make an average income and it's not profitable for you to spend half your day just sitting at a guard post.

If you end up organizing guard shifts with the neighbors, know that of those that even have guns, very few will have even basic firearm handling training. This can be very dangerous. You'll find out that you have a dozen guns, but not a single person you can trust enough to handle one, so look for military veterans that have had extensive firearms training.

To prevent this problem that WILL occur if you need to count on your neighbors and friends for security, start now.

If they're not veterans with firearms training, and even if they are, take them shooting and drill them on basic gun safety. Don't pretend they will be SWAT. Just not shooting the neighbor's kid by accident will be good enough. If they can hit a man-size torso at twenty meters with a handgun and fifty meters with a rifle then that's even better.

About rifles though: I'd be extremely conservative about handing those out. There's a reason why cops around the world still use shotguns. A rifle round that doesn't hit its intended target can be dangerous in a populated area. A pump action shotgun with buckshot would be my choice for the average guard. A four-inch revolver chambered in .38 Special/.357 Magnum would be the handgun I hand over to someone that isn't trained in self-defense shooting with autos.

Your real friends, though few, will be people that may be lifesavers when the SHTF. Friends make things much easier during hard times. Try to keep those friendships strong by returning favors and always being thankful.

Sometimes, just help people in your community because it's the right thing to do.

My next door neighbor is a woman that has had a tough life. She lost her husband to cancer when they were a young couple, and was left alone to raise the children.

They've suffered a number of violent home invasions. The last time it happened was last year. She was already living alone and she got home to find the front door broken open.

It was already dark and the poor woman called the neighbors and no one answered. My other neighbor is a pompous bastard and he didn't even answer the widow's call for help. Learn to not count much on most neighbors.

By the time I went out she was crying. My wife made her some tea and offered to let her stay in our home that night and I waited outside until the cops arrived.

As things get worse, these things will occur more often. The weak get targeted and it's our responsibility to help them. In fact it's our duty, if we want civilization to survive.

PEOPLE TO BE FRIENDS WITH

Maybe "friends" isn't the right word, thought having some of them as real friends would be great. Try to at least have a good relationship with them, and eventually get to the point of "you scratch my back, and I scratch yours."

A polite relationship will do at first. You can start talking more to your doctor or pharmacist, people you already know but never thought much about.

After some small talk, sometimes if the atmosphere is right I invite people to go to the shooting range with me. Since it's often something new to many of them, they usually appear interested and end up having a good time.

If you like fishing, hunting or some other hobby or sport you enjoy, you can try that instead. And if eventually you make a friend then that's just great. If not, well, at least you worked a bit to improve your "people skills."

You need to be an outgoing person, someone who knows how to make new acquaintances, if not friends. You don't necessarily need to become best buds. You won't be giving away your daughter to them for crying out loud. All you need is to be friendly enough to be able to ask for a favor if you ever need one. And of course, you should be ready to do the same in return.

These are your "must have" friends and close contacts. People you can trust at a more personal level, and who are willing to go a bit beyond the average client relationship:

Doctors: This should be pretty obvious. SHTF or not, you need someone that you can trust for your family health issues. But try going a bit further. You may one day need something more than the average patient/doctor relationship.

Ask about his or her weekend, and how the kids are. Suggest doing some activity together sometime. This can be shooting, hiking or whatever you think you have in common. Again, you aren't looking for a best friend, though a Doc as a best friend would be pretty handy…and it even sounds cool because then you can call him "Doc."

Just build up a good relationship in case you ever have to ask for a favor, or ask for some extra subscription meds, such as antibiotics. Maybe you will call him someday during a medical emergency, when the normal services aren't available.

Lawyers: When you need one, you'll need one badly!

If you ever get into a shooting, get sued for God knows what, or have to fight some legal battle, a good lawyer you can trust is invaluable. Preferably one who practices criminal law, although you'll need one that knows about taxes and business too.

Believe me when I tell you, because I've gone through this. Get a good lawyer and get one now. Try as hard as you can to build a real friendship with him. If you kill someone or end up in jail for whatever reason, worrying only then about finding a good lawyer is the best way to lose everything you have to a criminal wearing a suit that holds a law degree. He'll pick you clean using your desperation against you, and he'll do so legally. So I'll say it again: get a good lawyer, if possible a relative or a close family friend. Give him a call and invite the guy over for dinner using any excuse you can think of.

Accountants: This is another basic must-have, maybe not as desperately needed as a lawyer but still important to protect your finances. One of the things that happened in Argentina and will surely happen in the USA soon is that the money-hungry government will raise taxes like crazy to "redistribute" the wealth better. Or at least that will be the excuse. You'll see a number of taxes and fees growing all over like fungus.

Your lawyer and accountant will be your weapons against this.

Tip: Doctors, lawyers, accountants and other professionals often don't know much about shooting or other survival-related skills that will become even more important after the SHTF. If you have some expertise in these areas, you can trade your knowledge for the help they can offer you in return. Again, it's all about building mutually beneficial relationships with people who can help you.

Cops: You will need them as friends to know what's really going on. Sometimes this is information that doesn't get spread through the news to avoid panic, or simply because of censorship. You'll know what's really going on in your neighborhood by talking to your local police, if you have built a friendship with them.

I usually like talking to local cops. They are at the front line fighting crime and they know what it's really like. Some of these cops will maybe tell you things that you wish they didn't. One cop told me that people who dumps corpses in the Riachuelo River cut a deep cross in the corpse's stomach, so that it doesn't inflate when it starts to decompose and create gases, therefore floating the body back up to the surface.

Another one once told me that he also carried a revolver besides his issued auto pistol for when he didn't want to leave empty cases behind, which may contain his fingerprints or could help identify the weapon used. When you find such a person just be polite and try to avoid further conversation.

You need to be on good terms with them, so that they respond quickly during emergencies and watch over your house with at least a bit of extra interest.

If you end up shooting somebody in self defense, a cop friend in your district may save you a LOT of trouble. I know of a case where it made the difference. During a robbery attempt, a switchblade materialized next to the dead bad guy's body... You definitely need the cops on your side, for so many reasons.

Judge: A judge is the "Holy Grail" of people to be friends with. He's like a super combination of lawyer/politician/government guy, and he or she has a lot of leverage and connections. "Your" judge will know almost all of the other judges in your area, and if you are in serious legal trouble, they can "put in a good word" with their colleague on your behalf. If you can meet a judge, work hard on your relationship with him.

Below are other people who will help a lot as things get more complicated. It does not hurt to build up these relationships now just in case.

Pharmacist: Having a good relationship with someone that can get you medications is something you should try working on right now. At the very least, try to be in good terms with the pharmacist guy or gal. The guy in the pharmacy nearby will sell me almost everything, even without a doctor's prescription. This is part of normal life after the SHTF.

A Black/Gray Market Guy who can "get things" can save you a lot of money. And when things start getting either hard to find or too expensive, he's the guy you'll want to speak with. Given his..."trade"...you won't be building much of a friendship. But still be polite, say "Hi" and maybe chit-chat a bit. Try to have him on your side in case you need him.

Currency Broker: Someone that buys and sells different currencies and precious metals. I have three guys from whom I buy or sell. When one tries to screw me over, I go to the other one. That way none of them thinks he's got me tied down, so I always end up getting a more or less fair deal.

These guys buy and sell Pesos, Euros, Dollars, Brazilian Reales, gold, silver, and even jewelry gold. They always have market values for all of them. They are also possible contacts as gray/black market dealers.

Gun Dealers: They are pretty similar to the currency brokers in terms of always having fair prices, but these guys are of course law-abiding businessmen that sell legal firearms.

I have a couple gun dealers with whom I deal most often. I buy from the one that gives me the best deal, but I try to distribute the shopping as well as I can, to keep the "friendships" up, so I'll know of any hot deals either of them has to offer. The kinds of deals that only "good customers" get to know of. I've found some pretty cool stuff thanks to that.

Artisan/Craftsman: To help you on various projects. Hopefully it will be someone that works well with steel, leather, Cordura nylon, and plastic. He can fix gear for you, or make equipment up that you might have thought of or designed yourself.

Debt Collector: Sometimes you need a bit of extra leverage, and it's work you won't want to do yourself. Believe me, it's pretty hard to collect from people that owe money when almost half of the country is broke. So this isn't just a Hollywood thing. You'll need a good debt collector for doing business, especially for collecting rent.

Don't go for the aggressive maniac. You'll need someone that is persuasive, who gets your money, but who won't hurt the person in the process or have you locked up in jail. Besides, you need your client to be healthy, so he can keep paying off his debt. Get a professional debt collector, not just a thug.

Machinist: A bit similar to the Craftsman, but the machinist specializes on precise metal work (lathe, Computed Numerically Controlled (CNC) machines).

You'll need him for gun accessories, help with projects, etc. Things like custom scope mounts, or other items you might want to discuss in private.

Farmer/Rancher: Someone that can get you fresh food if it starts getting scarce, or find you good deals on foodstuffs during the hard times.

Someone in the Local Government Office: Yes, it's like sleeping with the enemy, but someone that knows the ways of the "Dark Side" can save you from a lot of trouble.

A friend "inside" can save you from what otherwise may be month or year long waiting periods, just to mention one benefit. They can "walk your paperwork" through the system, and ensure a positive outcome.

Bank Manager: A guy that is inside a bank and has some rank will know about trouble on the horizon before most other people. Back in 2001, if you had had a buddy in a big bank in Argentina, he would have told you about banks freezing accounts and people emptying their accounts.

As the economy starts to shake, talk often to this guy and ask him, "How are things going on?" and if people are closing out their accounts more than usual. You'll need someone that trusts you enough to tell you these things.

Successful Businessman: What's the advantage here? Well, a person that knows how to do business well will already have many of the contacts listed above. He is a connection to other connections.

He can also give you advice, or help you find a job for yourself or some family member that needs one.

Having a friend or family member with his own successful business is the most common way middle class people find new jobs after the crisis. Poor paying jobs are plentiful, but good ones don't even make it to the papers. They go to friends or family members most of the time.

HOW DO YOU MAKE NEW FRIENDS AND CONTACTS?

Try being friendly, generally speaking. I'm a naturally quiet person, and I don't like talking much with strangers. I'm just not that kind of person. But I saw that this was a flaw in my behavior and I've been working hard to change that.

Try to understand that not everyone thinks like you do, especially if you are a "prepper" or a survivalist. So try speaking their language. Bite your tongue whenever you want to say things such as, "That's the most sheepish piece of brainwashed crap I've ever heard." I find myself avoiding saying that many times a day, but it's important to be able to fit in among the less-prepared.

I'm getting pretty good results lately when I offer to take people shooting. Those who are interested appreciate it after you take them. You "converted" someone, and maybe you made a friend or a valuable contact as well.

You can also volunteer for the local volunteer fire department or volunteer ambulance service if your town has these. Not only will you meet a group of well-trained people, you'll also get excellent training for yourself either for free or at the local community college for a reduced rate! You will also be plugged into another network that receives information the average "sheeple" won't hear.

The pattern has repeated itself many times throughout history and Argentina is just another example. After an economic crisis, or an economic collapse like the one we saw, ordinary people are desperate for a savior.

This happened in Germany with the Nazi regime, and it has happened in many other countries including in Latin America and the former Soviet Union countries. Today Hungary, Latvia and Ukraine are going through something similar, and it's no surprise to see many people located in these nations visiting my blog.

Occasionally during an economic crisis, a charismatic leader arises. He comes as a savior who will fix the economy, get your job back, take the trash out and walk your dog. People know that a lot of the promises are bullshit, but they are so desperate they want to believe that *this time* they are true.

It happened here after the 2001 monetary collapse. After five presidents that came and resigned all inside of one week, Eduardo Duhalde managed to keep things together long enough for a new election.

Guess who won that election?

Carlos Menem. The same man who was largely responsible for the crisis in the first place. The man who destroyed the local economy in favor of a currency artificially pegged to the US dollar, who put Argentina into the greatest foreign debt the country had ever seen, and who led us to the economic collapse.

Yet he won the election. You'd say, "People are stupid!"

Yes, they are. Hey, Hitler got elected too, and he won by a wide margin.

So yes, Menem won, but the difference was small enough that we had to go to a runoff election. On the second ballot, the opposition united and Mr. Duhalde (who didn't want to get involved in the mess he saw clearly and who therefore didn't present himself as a candidate), told the people to vote for a guy named Nestor Kirchner instead.

Kirchner came out of nowhere, from a remote province in distant Patagonia called Santa Cruz. I remember clearly that he was about to become president and few people, even reporters, knew how to spell his name well.

He had a reputation for being somewhat "authoritarian" in his leadership style. A year later he would turn his back on Eduardo Duhalde, the man who had originally recommended him and placed him in power.

People, after an economic crisis, be prepared for an authoritarian regime. It is almost unavoidable, but if people don't unite and clearly make them understand that their abuse of power won't be tolerated, you'll suffer under them for decades. The more that the people stay silent, the worse it gets in terms of the loss of individual liberty and freedom.

When people are desperate, they'll believe fairy tales. In our case, the candidate was presented to us as a savior, and even though people knew he wasn't, they voted for him nonetheless. I didn't vote for him. I just placed my envelope with a torn piece of paper in the ballot box. I'll continue to do so until I find an honest candidate.

Many people in Argentina have sort of "surrendered." They'll vote for the candidate they consider to be "less corrupt," or, "corrupt, but at least does something for the people."

When you do this you have no one to blame but yourself when the thief you placed in power steals from you, or does even worse. The charismatic leader is elected, he promises everything you want to hear, and he only asks for one thing: your freedom.

He always demands more power, more "tools to get the job done."

People want to believe in "change" or "hope" and thus grant him that power.

He promises he'll use this power wisely and only for a little while. Like a little boy with a new toy, he promises to give it back soon. But that toy is SO nice, it makes everything easier for him and it feels so good to play with it…

In Argentina that toy was called the "super powers." So-called emergency powers beyond the powers usually granted to a president by our Constitution.

Combine that with rampant corruption and placing puppets in the Senate and the Supreme Court, and governors in a few key provinces. A president in Argentina holds more power than a king of old Spain or England ever did.

And so freedom is lost and things become more "medieval", as in the relationship between the king and the peasants.

"How does that reporter dare to criticize what I do? How dare the weak, whining opposition question my demands?"

Little by little, they get drunker with power and lose their perception of normal political reality until they no longer even bother covering things up. Eventually dictators just exchange power between their own family members, husbands and wives or brothers like in Cuba. Only fools believe this means democracy.

I'll admit that in Argentina things got beyond ridiculous, but this does not mean that your own country can't go down a somewhat similar path.

Maybe not reelecting the respective spouses, but changing the puppet placed in office while the same heads keep running the show is very do-able. Don't believe me? Just look at Russia today.

In Argentina, the official statistics managed by the INDEC are openly modified to fit whatever the president wants. 22% unemployment looks bad to our international investors, so a good patriot is expected to submit figures of 8% instead. That sounds much nicer. Besides, the worst the media can do is say it's a lie. The "official" number is 8%, and some will call that figure bullshit…but it's so much better than everyone having that 22% number in their heads.

Things reach a point where everything is bullshit.

The unemployment numbers are BS. The crime rates are BS, so is the inflation rate, cost of living, and everything else. It's SO much better to spread lies, even if we all know the numbers are BS, than accepting BAD numbers that tells the truth as it is.

The big problem is that without serious, reality-based data, it's impossible to repair the damage. The vicious circle of a crumbling economy and BS numbers that don't reflect actual reality leads to a path of destruction. It's impossible to fix things until personal greed and the thirst for power is put aside, and an honest effort to rebuild the economy is made.

WHAT TO EXPECT FROM THE GOVERNMENT AFTER THE COLLAPSE

After an economic crisis and with a "benevolent" authoritarian figure in charge, you can expect the following:

Expect Corruption: Maybe in their minds, it's not even corruption. The high ranking politicians simply do extra-legal "favors" for one another, and perhaps they even believe their own BS speech, that they are doing them for "the greater good." Or perhaps not. Perhaps they are just greedy, lying crooks from the very start.

Expect Loss of Freedom: Particularly the loss of gun rights. Americans should keep a close watch, and consider gun rights to be the "freedom barometer."

There will be direct attacks on the right to keep and bear arms. Reinterpretation of the Second Amendment. Indirect attempts such as taxing ammunition and firearms out of the reach of the average citizen. A greater number of legal requirements to own firearms.

Some people believe that armed citizens don't stand a chance against a national military force, especially one as powerful as the United States Army. This is the bullshit lie all governments around the world want you to believe, but the reality is very different.

If every block in every city and town in a country has a dozen men with firearms, the one that doesn't stand a chance is the military force. It's the perfect guerilla setup, and a general's worse nightmare.

You can't nuke or level every block. You can't arrest the entire country. The "fighters" are already armed, fed, spread out, integrated and infiltrated into the military and government branches. It's impossible to win. That's why dictators work desperately to disarm the citizenship.

The objective is an unarmed society unable to defend itself. It also reduces the morale regarding the power to actually fight a tyrannical government. Unarmed people may not even question tyrants, because they believe that since they are unarmed they have no power at all.

In Argentina, they passed a "National Gun Emergency" law that clearly states as its objective eliminating firearms from the average population, leaving gun ownership only to the military, police and influential people who can afford to hire armed personnel. This was done, cunningly, right after Alex Blumberg's death. Alex had been kidnapped and shot in the face by his captors during the rescue attempt by the police. A boy had been murdered! Let's ban guns! This is typical because during those times people are exhausted, not sensible, and they go along with any ban proposed assuming it brings more security.

Expect Censorship: We've experienced a growing amount of censorship in many forms. Calls from the Presidential Office directly intimidate reporters and news directors. There are threats of legal action and tax persecution to anyone that dares to question the government.

Talk about how the crime situation is out of control? Call your accountant and lawyer, because you'll be audited by the government hounds tomorrow. This actually happened to a well known TV figure here named Marcelo Tinelli. The next day after saying he was worried about the situation and admitting he goes nowhere without his armored Hummer and two SUVs with guards, he got an official "visit" to his offices.

Phone tapping and e-mail reading are widespread as well.

At the end of 2009, for example, Channel 13's 24 hour news channel TN and radio station Mitre have been suffering interference and scrambling, replaced by a black screen or the signal entirely gone. Channel TN is one of the two most important TV channels in the country. Imagine FOX News being jammed.

The government is openly against this network and threatens its reporters and editors in subtle and sometimes not-so-subtle ways. Among the hundreds of networks in South America that use this same television satellite, "somehow" their signals are the only ones being affected.

Channel TN was running a report about the thousands of cases of "Chagas" disease in the northern province of Chaco. They were showings footage of the people protesting that the governor wasn't prepared to deal with the disease, and showing dehydrated kids in the hospital.

Surprisingly, their signal in Chaco was scrambled and replace by a black screen.

The same happens when certain reports are aired internationally.

The investigation by the company in charge of the satellite concluded:

1) It only affects the signal of this one news group.

2) This has never happened before to their satellite.

3) The scrambling signal interfering with Channel TN is coming from South America.

I'll also note that the Channel TN signal is suddenly affected when negative news regarding the government is being aired. Censorship is serious business and a very bad sign regarding how democratic a government truly is.

Expect an Inefficient Legal System: With growing crime, fewer resources, and possibly significant amounts of corruption getting in the way, the legal system will become slow, inefficient, and in some cases it may not work at all. For example, in Argentina legal resolutions not only take years, these days you can't even expect justice at all.

For some reason I'm not entirely certain of, even murderers and serial rapists are not being incarcered. A disturbing number of them are being sent right from court to "home imprisonment." I suppose it's mostly due to prisons already containing over three times their maximum population capacity, and there being few resources to build more prison space.

It's not as if the government actually cares about the innocent people being murdered every day. In all these years since the start of the crisis, not a single official declaration has been made regarding the crime problem or attempts to solve it.

Before the crisis, "home imprisonment" was reserved for citizens older than seventy, or seriously ill with terminal diseases. The explanation was that they were no longer considered a potential threat to society and so they could do their time at home, not being allowed to leave their house. It was also carefully reviewed one case at a time, and was only granted under special circumstances. Just being older than seventy wasn't enough.

Today, very fit and extremely brutal criminals in their thirties are just being sent home, supposedly guarded by a police officer that rarely shows up, and with an ankle bracelet monitor that either doesn't work or isn't monitored by anyone. A man wearing such an ankle bracelet murdered the entire family of a man that testified against him, killing him and his wife, along with his two little children.

Still, you should know that even today there's always an open cell ready for political prisoners. You'll have a trial eventually … maybe… but the legal system is just so slow… Meanwhile you will rot in jail.

Expect Failing Public Institutions: Hospitals, schools and public transportation companies that receive government tax subsidies have all collapsed and are in awful condition where they do still function.

Some Argentine doctors working in public hospitals do heroic achievements and save lives in spite of the few resources they have available. Some public hospitals (thanks to private donations), manage to carry on and successfully perform highly complex surgery such as pediatric heart transplants. This is of course, an exception. In most public hospitals in Argentina conditions are mediocre to poor. Many times even essential medical supplies are lacking, and relatives are encouraged to bring food, cotton, bandages and help out.

Our public schools are something to be ashamed of when you consider the education levels we had only a few years ago. Strikes by teachers are common, often costing months worth of classes. Resources are scarce and the education level itself is very poor. Each year we drop a few places in our educational level compared to other countries. Most public schools are simply falling apart, sometimes even injuring students due to lack of maintenance. Very few or no books, even less computers. Public education in Argentina has never been this bad and the dropout rate is alarming.

Expect Crumbling Infrastructure: The roads, bridges and public infrastructure will get worse as time goes by. Most people don't realize it, but without proper maintenance the streets will become full of cracks, potholes and sometimes even craters. This will eventually affect the type of car you choose to drive, as long as you can select them. You'll find out that you'd rather exchange your low riding sedan or sport car for something more rugged with better ground clearance and a tougher suspension. An SUV will be more suitable than a sedan after the SHTF.

Expect a Cultural Change (for the worse): I've seen bookstores, coffee shops and theaters closing, to be replaced by casinos, pastoral churches that are as bad as casinos (they steal people's money promising salvation), bingo halls, drugstores where they mostly sell booze, porno shops and internet booths, gloomy stores where people that mostly look like perverts get online.

Many of the small "mom and pop" businesses that managed to survive the era of large supermarket mega stores will eventually close. People have little money and they will go shopping in the big stores instead, and inflation makes this trend even worse. Combined with the new higher taxes many of the small stores just can't survive.

Many simply end up closing their doors because the frequent armed robberies are just too much to deal with. It isn't worth them risking their lives, given the losses they are taking anyway.

Also, there are a large amount of women (and some men) that will consider selling their bodies. Either working as strippers or going straight to prostitution, it's something a lot of people end up doing given the overall poverty and lack of legitimate job opportunities after an economic crisis sinks in.

Expect More Extreme Poverty and Shanty Towns: No big secret here either. It happened in the USA during the Great Depression and it happened here in Argentina after 2001 as well. Even now, the "villas" (shanty towns and tent or cardboard shack cities) are growing like a fungus all around Buenos Aires. People also take over abandoned factories and hundreds of families live there. Usually a local thug takes over and rents or sells the space.

I remember seeing this once when driving through the Camino Negro. (Its unofficial name is the Dark Road, because there's very poor lighting on it.) Apparently someone got tipped off about land being available, and the political decision was taken to let them take over.

Overnight, THOUSANDS of shacks and tents appeared, and burning barrels and camp fires dotted the settlement at night. This new shanty town extended as far as the eye could see. It was the most depressing sight I had seen in a long time. It made me want to cry for my country.

The new poverty also means more skinny kids begging on the streets. Some are so small that you can't even see them running among the cars trying to clean their headlights and begging for a coin. It gets very depressing.

Expect a Smaller Police Force: And expect the police to concentrate mostly on the capital and major cities, in the downtown business areas and the nicer looking more affluent neighborhoods, usually in that order of preference.

The government behaves very much like a living cellular organism. When resources are scarce, the police mostly concentrate in the center, capital cities and places where high ranking officials live, while leaving the suburbs and smaller towns to fend for themselves.

Keep the brain alive and sacrifice a limb if you have to. At least that way it's easier to maintain a false image of prosperity, especially when the media will only show images of the "prosperous and orderly" well-guarded tourist and business areas of the big cities.

I remember one particular day. I had to go from where I live in Lomas de Zamora to Recoleta for business. Recoleta is a high-end neighborhood in the capital district. The trip takes about an hour if there's little traffic.

I vividly remember the difference when comparing one place to the other, and how different Recoleta and places like that are, compared to what 90% of the citizens of Argentina live through every day. Parts of Lomas de Zamora I had to drive through that day looked like Iraq. Forget Iraq, it looks worse. I've seen photos of Iraq that looked nice compared to Camino Negro in Lomas de Zamora. And the Iraq photos were taken after bombs went off.

It's so different. In places like Camino Negro, Dock Sud, Fuerte Apache (Fort Apache) and many of the poor (or one time middle class) parts in the Southern and Western suburbs, people just look dirty, with worn out clothes and needing haircuts. The streets and buildings look very dirty too. You rarely see a policeman posted on a corner or a patrol car driving around. The cars you see people driving are generally old and some are just rust buckets on wheels.

Then you go to Recoleta or Palermo where the rich folks live and tourists stay when visiting. People look great and they carry themselves differently. Stores look nice and you see much better cars. There are two or three cops per block, and you can tell why people there aren't as afraid as in the rest of the country.

You appreciate that wonderful mixture of European looks and architecture combined with a cosmopolitan American feeling with a sprinkle of Latin in it that tourists from all over the world find so attractive. But then you leave that place and see how the majority of the Argentines live. It's very different.

This cell-like behavior is something that typically occurs after a crisis. This economic division will happen in any first-world cities after a severe economic crisis. Don't be fooled by international media images of the best parts of Buenos Aires. They are a mask or a façade, and even in those places, you can get shot for what's in your pockets, the murderer never to be caught.

Expect "Commando" Criminals: This is how we refer to criminals that have certain "professional" backgrounds. Usually they are ex-cops (or even active duty cops) or ex-military. They are well armed, well organized, know how to use modern communications and they do intelligence work before a "mission."

These are dangerous people and have the skills to do serious bank robberies, kidnap rich people in spite of their security guards, or assault guarded gated neighborhoods. The "Zetas" in Mexico are a good example of a "commando" criminal gang, but most groups are not as large. The point is that a squad of armed men who employ military special operations tactics are much more dangerous than a few disorganized thugs.

And Expect Even More Corruption: One thing we know about in Argentina is corruption. It's everywhere and it has kind of become almost a national sport. What we learned is that you can't expect honest government employees, when the leaders themselves are making very questionable decisions. This grows like a cancer in a democracy and eventually it's impossible to eradicate it. "If my boss is corrupt, then it's okay for me to be corrupt too," and so on. Eventually everyone is doing whatever they want and it gets to the point where not paying a cop or a government inspector a "tip" can get you in serious trouble.

I'm not saying it's happening in your own country. I'm saying it's a possibility and a very dangerous one, after an economic crisis.

Regarding how governments act when the SHTF, this book is arriving a bit too late in some regards for Americans. Some of the things I talk about are already happening and will have a serious impact in the immediate future. There will be consequences that will last for years, maybe even for decades.

Major corporations and politicians doing "favors" for each other and covering each other's backs has started already. Do people seriously believe that a 700 billion dollar bailout is handed out just like candy, forcing generations of ordinary Americans to pay for something that, if you did it yourself, would be considered major fraud and land you in jail? If you believe that I have other cool stories you might believe too. One about a wooden puppet that wanted to be a real boy, and another one about a gorgeous chick that lived with seven dwarfs.

A couple years ago even the more worried survivalists would have laughed at the idea of nationalized banks in the USA. Now it's a reality.

The reality surpasses fiction; it's just that the reality isn't much fun to watch.

A NEW MENTALITY

There are certain things in life that change you forever. You simply never forget them and you can tell exactly what caused such a profound change in you.

I've been through some bad situations in my life. Some of them were pretty unusual things most people will never suffer. Others are much more common and just as bad or even worse.

One of the worst things was seeing my son extremely sick. We had to hospitalize him three times before he was six. The first time was when he was six months old. He almost died that time.

"Why is this happening to my little boy?" is something any parent with a sick son asks the Big Guy above.

Trying to find the correct diagnosis, we visited a number of hospitals and different doctors. One test was performed in the Italian Hospital. My son had to blow through a tube several times, while drinking milk in between blows to see if he was lactose intolerant.

It turned out my son only had a slight intolerance to lactose, which is worse than normal lactose intolerance, because the kid could still drink milk without vomiting it up immediately. Instead, it slowly and progressively irritates the stomach.

He got sick all the time, and since he drank regular milk without vomiting, doctors didn't think it was lactose intolerance, so the real cause went unnoticed.

While we did this test and waited for the results, I saw another father like myself walking with his son. The boy must have been the same age mine was at that time, about five years old. We were waiting right next to the pediatric chemotherapy room, and this guy's son obviously had cancer, since he was bald and could barely walk.

A nurse that was assisting us told me the rest of the story. The boy had brain cancer, and the tumor had left him blind and had spread to his other internal organs. The kid didn't have much time left.

Then I thought about myself, bitching about my son having chronic gastritis for some unknown reason at that time. I compared my own situation to this other father, with a son that was as old as mine, but torn to pieces by cancer. Left blind, and barely able to walk in the last few days he had to live.

After that day, whenever I think about complaining, I remember that man and his son. How the father talked to the boy and smiled in spite of their terrible destiny.

Surviving anything, living through an economical collapse or just living life to its fullest is mostly about learning to cope with the problems life throws your way.

If you compare it to real problems like the one this guy and his kid had, you view things from a new perspective and instead of complaining you thank God for being so blessed.

It's about manning up and learning to deal with the problems you have.

When it comes to the new attitude necessary to live after an economic collapse, that survival nature just kicks in and people simply adapt and overcome. People become more careful about money and spend less. They become more aware regarding their security as well.

Other changes in the society are evident as time goes by.

You soon notice an increase in the number of women "working" the streets. Fashion models and well-educated bilingual secretaries, people who never thought they would do that, end up offering sex services just to survive.

Architects or lawyers happily drive around in improvised taxis called Remises. People do whatever job they can find to survive, regardless of their education, training or social status.

What you once considered major problems are just silly inconveniences, compared to the real problems you have now. I suppose that most people end up becoming tougher after SHTF as time goes by.

BRIBERY

"Son, do you have the latest Technical Revision of your vehicle?"

The technical revision is a state issued paper that says that your vehicle is in proper working condition. You can lose all day to get that paper, after bribing an employee that will always find something wrong with the car. Either that or you can bribe the guys standing outside the building that sells you the authorization directly.

"No officer, I didn't do it yet this year."

The cop was visibly glad I didn't. That was just what he was expecting. This happened many years ago, when I was a bit "greener." Today, I wouldn't get fooled so easily at these control posts and checkpoints.

Most of the time I get close to the car in front of me, try to hide behind it, and speed up a bit as I get close to the post, looking the other way to avoid eye contact. That way I avoid these unpleasant encounters.

The cop said, "Sorry, I'll have to take your car then."

I knew what he wanted but I wanted to at least make him say it, so I said, "Sure officer, you do what you have to do."

"I'm not kidding, I'll take the vehicle and you'll have to go get it at the station." The cop didn't expect my reply.

"That's too bad, sir, but if that's the law then that's what you have to do I guess."

The cop had had enough "Son, those plans and blueprints you have in the back of the vehicle? What are they?"

I told him, "Architectural plans."

"Okay…do you need me to 'draw' what's happening here?" said the nice police officer with a menacing tone of voice.

"No, officer," I said, and handed him my driver's license yet again, but this time with twenty bucks folded under it. The officer grabbed the money, gave me back my license, and I left. Given his threat, it was more of a robbery than a bribe.

This time it happened on the General Paz Highway, but it had already happened to me a dozen times and it happens all day long all over the country.

Another time when I was eighteen years old, I was just back from a trip to the USA. As most Argentines did in those days, I was coming back with a lot of stuff I had bought, since America was so cheap compared to Argentina.

I remember that I had spent nearly all my money, and on the last day of the visit I bought a big trunk to carry everything in. When the woman from the customs office saw me, she immediately set me aside for a closer look. My luggage of choice, a huge black trunk with brass reinforcements, caught a bit of attention.

"What the heck are you carrying in there?" she asked. I always have better luck with women than with guys in these situations. I was eighteen, and the woman must have been in her thirties, so she was a bit friendlier to me.

I opened the trunk: a big Mickey Mouse for my sister, clothes, a stun gun, several knives (including a very nice Spyderco Police with a stainless handle), a laser aiming device, pistol grips, and a number of other gun accessories.

It was during the pre-9-11 era…

The woman opened her eyes wide and said, "What's all this, are you nuts? You'll have to pay import taxes…"

I got closer to her and smiled "Ma'am, I spent every single buck. I just have a twenty left for a cab back home."

"You're kidding me!"

"No, I'm not," I replied calmly.

She looked at me, smiled, closed the trunk as she looked around to see if anyone else had noticed the contents, and said in a low voice "Okay, just go you rascal, you…"

Oh, yes, I was lucky. If I had found a guy that didn't feel such sympathy towards me, I would have lost most of my stuff.

But sometimes this happens, and being nice can get you off the hook. It's not likely, but it happens. Most of the time, it requires cash.

This, of course, doesn't occur in the USA. This is Argentina, and these things are already part of our culture. For example, slipping a 100 USD bill into your passport was how people normally dealt with custom officers, when they came back with a big screen TV or some other major appliance.

For more innocent favors, such as someone speeding up paperwork for you, or helping you to get your passport faster, giving "gifts" is more typical. These are generally women's makeup, perfume, booze or a carton of cigarettes.

People also like tech gadgets such as MP3 players and radios, or some other little gadget that isn't that expensive but people generally enjoy.

Several small 2.99 USD FM radios were neat little gifts many years ago. Today a few cheap MP3 players can achieve the same.

Take a look at the person's cell phone. Maybe he/she will appreciate a new one if the favor requires such a gift. Most people like new shiny cell phones. It's the equivalent of the mirrors the Conquistadors brought from Spain to hand out as gifts to the wives of the Indian chiefs.

RIOTS AND LOOTING

This is one of the things that scares people the most: the idea of looters destroying everything and burning the cities to the ground. People remember incidents such as the L.A. riots, and they imagine how a widespread, continuing situation could completely destroy a city.

I remember the first time I heard looters. That right, heard.

One morning during December 2001, I heard drums. Like what you used to hear in those old Westerns when the Indians were getting close.

Well, these weren't "Indians," these were looters. I looked through the first-floor window of my house and saw a mass of people completely covering the street and the sidewalk, for as far as I could see. This huge wave of people never seemed to end. It was a vast mob coming from the poorest parts of the Buenos Aires suburbs. I had my gun ready, and for a second I imagined what would happen if they started looting the houses. I had lots of ammunition and a very defendable position with an iron fence out front. I doubted they would willingly try to get over it with someone shooting from the inside.

But still, that mass of angry looters passing just fifteen or so yards away from my house was unnerving.

It turned out that they mostly went for supermarkets and shops, and apparently yes, some homes were looted. Does this mean cities will be utterly destroyed by looters? No.

`Tip:` looters don't run towards a building when someone is shooting from the inside of an easily-defendable position. It just doesn't happen, except in the movies.

The houses and shops that were sporadically looted across Argentina during those days were either already empty, or the occupants just surrendered their belongings to the mobs without resistance.

And a few years later, social unrest, riots and roadblocks have just become something we live with. That's what happens, guys. People get mad, they break everything, and some take advantage of the situation and rob shops.

Road blockers try to attract attention by pissing everyone off. They are usually civilians looking for a raise of government welfare payments, sometimes people doing strikes or protesting against taxes or official measures. Sometimes road blockers are government thugs on the payroll, simply demonstrating the power the government has on the streets. Seems that any excuse is good enough to burn a few tires on the middle of a main road and ruin your day.

In Argentina, many of the looters in the mobs eventually sided with the government and became foot soldiers for them, beating people up during citizen or opposing party protests. This would be like union thugs beating up "tea party" protestors in the USA, while the police looked the other way.

I remember last year, during 2008, I was watching some rioting while eating a burger in McDonald's with some friends from work. I told one of the guys: "Dude, you better finish your burger. They usually trash 'capitalist' joints like this McDonald's when they get pissed off." You become used to it. We just hurried up a bit and went back to the office to keep working while the rioting went on.

The important part is these riots can last for a while. Maybe they last for a few days but eventually people get tired, or they've looted what they wanted during the confusion, and everyone goes home. Worst case scenario: after a couple of days the authorities give the order, and the police start shooting rioters and looters.

I'll bet you one of my kidneys my friend: after a few looters go down under a small cloud of pink mist, everyone suddenly behaves like English royalty and calms down and goes home. People, especially looters and rioters, don't want to get shot, and they go home as soon as they see people getting killed.

Looters and rioters are mostly fueled by the notion of anonymity and a sudden lack of law enforcement. They think they'll get away with it. As soon as they see there's a chance to catch a bullet, they quit.

Tip: Though looters will mostly take electronics such as TVs, DVD players and other expensive junk, plus booze and finally food, when looters go wild, the mob just steals everything. We saw them steal a convenience store's Christmas tree during the December 2001 lootings.

As a civilian just wanting to avoid problems, just do that: Walk away from the mob, or run away if necessary. Don't be a rubbernecking "tourist" during a riot!

When in a car, I just try to avoid the road blockers as much as possible. I turn around and find another route, and so should you, unless you see a clear opening where you can get through fast, before the road blockers cover any possible gap.

Tip: If you are surrounded by a mob and you simply can't avoid it, just keep driving, slowly, until you get out of the mass of people. Do NOT get out of your vehicle! Lock the doors and keep moving slowly until you get out of there. A mob is a very lethal threat, since all of them think that due to anonymity they'll be able to beat you to death unpunished.

If someone goes under you'll go to trial and explain that your life was in danger. Hopefully they'll see that the mob was indeed a lethal threat. Getting out of your car in the middle of an angry mob is just a death sentence. You have a better chance in front of the judge or jury.

Squatters are also a big threat. Right until today, people are reluctant in many neighborhoods to leave their homes unoccupied for long periods of time. Of course there's the threat of getting the house picked clean by thieves. It happens a lot. But even worse is coming back after a few weeks out of the city to find not only your house picked clean, but also an entire family living in it as well!

You go nuts. You just want to go in there and shoot everyone. Oh, but no you can't! That's not self defense, since your life is not in immediate danger. You have to call the cops. So the cops eventually come and find a new family well installed, probably with lots of kids.

You say they are squatters. They say you rented the place to them!

Contract? They'll say they are just trusting, simple people and didn't sign any contract, but that they just trusted your "word", or they will produce some bogus scrap of paper they claim is a contract or lease.

The police won't do anything unless you have good connections with the local power structure. A judge will have to rule on who's the rightful owner, and in Argentina that could take years. Meanwhile the squatters will stay in your house!

This situation has happened to a lot of people here, believe it or not. Expect it to happen in your country after an economic crisis.

RELOCATING

During the Spanish Civil War and the Franco dictatorship, you could say that the shit had definitely hit the fan. Food was being rationed and even my grandparents who lived up in the mountains and had a farm were going through very hard times.

The few weapons they had, they'd buried, and my grandfather only kept an Astra 400 pistol in 9mm Largo for self defense. (How much I would love to have that pistol today!)

He said he kept it for self defense against people, but also against the wolves that still populated the region. He had to walk a lot through the woods and mountain trails to reach my grandmother's house, so he always had his pistol in case a wolf attacked. Until 1970, wolves were considered a "pest" in Spain, and it's one of the few places in Europe where even today the European wolf can be found in certain places.

Grandpa didn't have much gun safety training, and he once accidentally shot himself in the hand. Luckily it didn't hit the bone and he didn't have much of a scar.

An Astra 400 pistol in 9mm Largo...it seems that an exquisite taste for handguns runs in the blood. The Astra 400 was one of the best pistols of its time. Not only was it powerful and reliable, but when ammo was scarce it could fire 9mm Luger, 9mm Steyr, and 9mm Browning Long as well.

The military forces would come by and confiscate all the food, barely leaving them enough to get by. It was clear to them that even if the situation eventually got better, it would take decades for things to really change, so they decided to get on a boat and start over again in Argentina.

It sure wasn't easy. I can barely imagine how hard it must have been to move to a completely new land they've never set foot on before. But my grandparents survived like millions of other European immigrants did in Argentina.

My own parents were poor, but they had happy childhood memories, and eventually both of them went to college in Argentina and forged their own futures. Then they eventually decided to leave Argentina, the country where they had raised a family, ironically going back to Spain in 2001. Starting over in a new country when you are over fifty years old isn't easy, but they did it because the situation in this country was out of control.

And this is the most valuable lesson people should learn: When the conditions are no longer sustainable, you don't just "bug-in" inside some bunker and mow down zombies on your front lawn for the next decade or two after the SHTF.

Your homestead won't be protected by some magical force shield. That doesn't happen. If crime is out of control, if there's a real risk of anarchy, it's smarter to just leave the country. Throughout history, people have moved around, and emigrated from one country to another for a number of reasons. War, famine, natural or man made disasters and political or religious persecution.

On the other hand, there are millions of people throughout history who would always regret not bugging out of their home country when they had the chance. They stayed, and they died. History is full of examples. Emigration is the last resort you end up using, when you see that things won't be getting better in your country for a long time.

As sad as leaving your home country may be, it's always easier to do when you prepare for it ahead of time.

THREE COUNTRIES: PLANS A, B, AND C

I am once again applying the "three is two, two is one, and one is none" philosophy. From small examples like the tools in your pocket, up to choosing countries to live in, redundancy is an important survival concept.

Ideally you'll work towards knowing people that could eventually help you out in three countries. In my case, this turned out to be a bit easier. I already have my parents and brothers living in Spain. Most of my relatives never left Spain in the first place.

I also have European citizenship, so my family and I can all become legal residents in any EU country if we need to take that step.

This is a TERRIFIC advantage. When the SHTF in 2001 and 2002, people formed lines that went on for blocks, trying to get visas and passports or citizenship through a relative in order to move out of Argentina. They left by the thousands, at least those that had the chance.

I lived in the USA when I was little. I know the country well and we still have friends living there that would gladly help us. My plan is to move to the USA as soon as possible and live there permanently. That would leave me with Spain as Plan B, and Argentina as plan C.

The rationale behind the selection of these three countries is of course, the opportunity I already have because of family or friends living there, but also something else.

If I'm living in the USA and some event such as war, large scale natural disaster or some other SHTF that affects mostly the USA alone, I still have my plan B, Spain. Spain, and other neighboring countries are first-world countries with a high standard of living. I also have family there which is a great benefit, and my citizenship would make things like finding a job, opening accounts and renting or buying a home much easier.

The not-so-great part is that the USA and Europe are closely connected by both economics and politics. They are usually allies and what happens in one place may affect the other. Just look at the terrorist attacks in the USA and Spain (the Atocha train station bombers), or the current economic crisis.

In this regard, something like Australia (not perfect but still an option) or New Zealand would be better. Preferably countries which are more neutral, and not so tightly connected to your country of origin. The goal is to have a refuge that is not, economically speaking, going down on the same ship while your home country sinks.

My Plan C would be to come back to Argentina. The disadvantages are Argentina's volatile economy and delicate social situation. The advantages would become more obvious in a serious worldwide event such as another world war with NBC weapons being used, or some other serious global SHTF situation. During WWII, for example, Argentina was mostly unaffected and was in fact going through a rather prosperous era.

Argentina is small, with a low population. Yet it produces enough food to feed ten times its own population, and that is a huge advantage during a global crisis.

In a worst-case scenario, if I have to move back to Argentina when I'm older, the currency difference could allow me to have a good standard of living at a modest cost. This is usually true of poorer countries like most South American nations or places like Costa Rica, where many Americans choose to go when they retire.

The cultural level in Argentina is still better than in most neighboring countries in South America, and the population is mostly European and of the same religion. That's an advantage if racial tensions become much greater, and people around the world start attacking each other for no good reason, but only because of religious differences and skin color.

For a black guy, a Plan C country would be one with significant black population, maybe a place like Brazil or a Caribbean island nation. The idea is to go as unnoticed as possible.

Plan A and B countries are most first-world countries. One would probably be the nation you already live in. The other one would be for example the USA, Canada, the European countries, Australia, New Zealand and Japan. I'm just throwing out ideas here for people to consider.

Remember, you'll need good friends or family already there. You've traveled there a few times and you know how to handle yourself. You can move around like a native, and not like either a tourist or an illegal alien who stands out.

You must speak the language, and if you already have IDs such as driver's licenses for that country, that would be great. Having passports for each country is the ultimate goal.

Plan C countries would be more "third-worldly" nations. Again, no offense is intended to anyone, I'm just trying to be objective. You want to choose a country that isn't too violent or known for its social outbursts, and has a convenient currency relationship to your income and investments.

In South America, my first choice because of my personal situation would be Argentina, but other people would do well to take a good look at Uruguay, which is something of a South American safe haven, a Latin Switzerland. I'd also consider Chile and with a few reservations due to its high crime, Brazil.

Again, you need to speak the language. If not fluently, at least well enough to be able to get around. Travel to the country often and build relationships if you simply don't have friends or family from your own nation already there.

From a strictly utilitarian perspective, it might be worth pointing out that Spanish is the first language in over twenty nations, and it's the second language in many more. It's also one of the easier languages to learn, and when you learn Spanish, the other Romance languages can be quickly mastered, opening up many more countries to you.

Other countries to consider could be Costa Rica, Panama, the Philippines, Thailand and some other small Asian countries. What is important is that they have a relatively peaceful history, produce their own food, have a convenient currency exchange rate, and hopefully a basic amount of modern technology and adequate medical facilities.

Foreign Banks: You should open a couple of bank accounts in each of the countries under your consideration for emigration. Some banks will close during an economic crisis, so make sure it's a big reputable bank, or open accounts in two different banks. This makes transferring your money and handling your investments much easier. Don't keep all of your eggs in one basket, in case that basket is suddenly unavailable to you. Ask any Argentine about the importance of this!

Make sure the countries you choose are compatible with each other regarding bank transfers. You don't need to deposit a fortune; you just need the bank accounts to already be available. Don't wait until an economic crisis in your home country to look into opening accounts in foreign banks. It may be too late by then.

One thing I'd look into is getting a small condo or house (a condo is usually safer and cheaper), in my Plan B country. Another one in Plan C would be great, but that can turn out to be more than your budget can handle.

For 40,000 USD or so, in 2010, you can buy a small (one bed room or two small ones) condominium apartment in downtown Buenos Aires, Argentina. You can put it up for rent to tourists on a weekly or monthly basis, with a local broker or real estate agent to take care of things.

This allows you to use your place on relatively short notice in case you need it, and it also works as an investment when you don't, generating profit for you, or at least paying for itself.

Don't try to pull off something like this over the internet; you'll just fall for some scam. You need to visit the country, get to know at least its capital city and makes friends. Only then should you find low-priced real estate in neighborhoods you know for sure are safe, where tourists or travelers would be interested in renting.

You can do basic research using the internet, but you need to travel there yourself to make it actually happen with a minimum amount of financial risk.

The apartment you rent to travelers and tourists can have a hidden safe where you keep a small cache of critical items, in case you arrive in the country with only the clothes on your back. Some extra precious metal, a notebook or USB thumb drive with important information, a pistol and ammo, a passport, a small survival kit, some food and a couple bottles of water.

The apartment can have a safe for the people that rent, and a second safe hidden behind a wall or under the floorboards for your cache.

This may sound a bit "far fetched," shall we say. But going on vacations and buying real estate in other countries as a form of investing and "keeping your eggs in several baskets" is something ordinary people can do. There is no reason why you shouldn't make it a part of your own survival and preparedness plan as well.

"INTERNAL EMIGRATION" WITHIN THE UNITED STATES

Another option that might be viable for Americans is "internal emigration." Not all of the fifty states of the USA might be affected in the same way after an American economic crisis, major natural disaster, or social disorder. Some states might be very badly damaged, while other states might do much better, relatively speaking. In an extreme situation, the United States might even break up into separate regions, without effective central control from Washington D.C.

For example: New England, the Rust Belt states or California might become total wrecks, while Texas or some other states might pull through the crisis intact. I leave it to Americans with better knowledge of these things to ponder the possible advantages of planning for "internal emigration" within the USA.

MY WIFE'S ADVICE

My wife never fired a gun until she met me. She's not into survival and preparedness. At least, she wasn't before our crisis.

She's a lawyer, petite, very pretty and she dresses well. Maybe because of this she's been a crime victim a number of times. She was held hostage at her family's business office during a robbery. She was also robbed in her home when she was very young, and she was robbed by a bunch of kids who were no older than ten years old with a gun last year, just to mention a few cases.

Her theory is that since she's so slim compared to her parents and brothers, that bad guys feel it's more practical to grab her and carry her around as a human shield with a gun to her head during robberies. She takes these things with much more humor than I do.

In spite of not begin "into" survival the way I am, she's adapted and learned out of necessity and has avoided a number of other complicated situations as well.

Meanwhile, I have to make an effort on occasions not to look like a psycho and scare people. Of course, I'm not exactly the type of person a criminal would consider an easy target.

As I explained, bad guys are very good at profiling and choosing their victims.

So since she's not "into" all of this, I asked her to write down some tips and advice, from a female non-survivalist's point of view. I asked her what she would advise people who were about to go through the kinds of things we experienced in 2001 and thereafter. So far, she has only helped on the book when I asked her for legal advice. She hasn't read a single page of this book, at least not yet.

I gave her a pen and this is what she wrote:

> * *I don't think banks are the best way to keep your savings safe. Try not to leave much money in your account.*
>
> * *Buy food and store it for emergencies. Powdered milk, canned food, tuna, water, cookies, rice, dehydrated mashed potatoes, etc.*
>
> * *Take a defensive driving class.*
>
> * *Take First Aid lessons.*
>
> * *If you own a business or a company, try diversifying and finding alternative products to offer at a lower cost.*
>
> * *Expand to other markets taking advantage of your existing work force, capital and machinery.*

Take every possible security measure for your home: alarms, cameras, security bars, reinforced glass for the windows and emergency lights.

Buy a generator.

Buy and store fuel in fuel cans for the generator.

Buy perfume and makeup, since their prices have increased a lot.

Some of the things she wrote surprised me quite a bit, especially the defensive driving class advice.

Some of the things guys don't consider very important mean a lot to women. Things like her favorite shampoos, makeup and other girl stuff. It's not that expensive, it stores well for a long time, and if you have a year's worth of it she'll be very pleased you stored some ahead of the crisis. If nothing else, it helps keep morale up, and that's well worth the price difference compared to the cheaper products you might have to use after the SHTF.

EPILOGUE

So, my dear friend, we've reached the end of this little journey.

Hopefully, you learned a few things required to live in a world that, even though similar to the one you already know, is a bit more dangerous and much less forgiving of mistakes or even bad luck.

The emphasis on fighting and the constant reminder of how important it is to be more than willing to kick ass if necessary has two objectives, and that's why a large percentage of the book is dedicated to it.

It's about the self defense skills you'll need, but also about the mental attitude you'll need to deal with life's problems in general, once those everyday problems become much more complicated than what you are used to.

I firmly believe that you can be a tougher person and still be a loving father or mother. In spite of everything you've read, one of the things I enjoy the most is painting. I've painted all of my life and I have even won a few prizes. Until not so long ago, I painted with oils on canvas.

It's incredible, the twists and turns that life takes.

If you had asked any of my school teachers about what kind of book that quiet boy who spent all day drawing would have written in the future, no doubt they would have said something related to art.

And yet here we are. I suppose modern survival is also an art ... an art of a very different type.

Getting a bit philosophical, I'd say that our surroundings and life experiences mold us in spite of who we were at the start. I guess I'm a good example of that.

I hope I had a measure of success achieving what I intended with this book. I hope I created in you a need for greater independence and self reliance. Not running to the hills and having a cabin roofed with solar panels, but the realistic self reliance a free spirited person can achieve. Not escaping from society, but understanding how society works during troubled times.

I hope you'll prepare better, distrust bankers a bit more, and if you ever have to, strike a bit harder.

I strongly urge you to take the training I wrote about. Not because of ridiculous notions of the world ending, but because they will not only be useful during complicated situations, but also because you'll have a good time and live a more enjoyable life.

Shooting guns with my father is a cherished memory, and so is the time I spend shooting with my own son. My grandfather and his father were shooters before us, and I intend to pass down this tradition for many generations to come. Free men are shooters if they choose to be, but slaves are always disarmed by tyrannical governments.

Working out is something everyone recommends and it certainly makes you feel better. Self defense is just taking it a bit further and burning those calories while you learn something useful, and realizing what you are capable of.

The world is not going to end. It will just change for a while, going through social upheavals and economical cycles as it always has done through the ages.

I just turned thirty, but I feel a million year old sometimes. As of today, all I want is to live in a safe place where my wife and I can enjoy our beautiful children in peace. We've been blessed with so much, and sometimes I fear a piece of crap disguised as a human being will take that away from us.

But you know something? It's only when you live this way, with the danger of actually losing what you love the most, that you really appreciate what you have. Maybe that's why people in much safer and wealthier countries like Japan or Finland have such high suicide rates. They don't appreciate what they have.

Instead, here, knowing you can lose your loved ones any day makes you appreciate life more and love with deeper passion. You kiss your wife more sweetly and hug your kids more tightly.

I'll make sure my sons never forget where they came from, because I know that if they remember that, they'll appreciate everything more. Things other people take for granted.

I know we'll appreciate it once we move to a safer place. Hopefully, a place where we will find like-minded people.

I've got to go. My son is calling me for dinner. My wife made tuna and vegetables pie.

We've reached the end of this little journey, my friend.

I believe we are both better persons because of it.

Fernando "FerFAL" Aguirre

NOTES: